NEGOTIATING THE EURO-MEDITERRANEAN PARTNERSHIP

# Negotiating the Euro-Mediterranean Partnership

Strategic Action in EU Foreign Policy?

RICARDO GOMEZ
*School for Social Policy Studies,*
*University of Bristol*

LONDON AND NEW YORK

First published 2003 by Ashgate Publishing

Reissued 2018 by Routledge
2 Park Square, Milton Park, Abingdon, Oxon OX14 4RN
711 Third Avenue, New York, NY 10017, USA

*Routledge is an imprint of the Taylor & Francis Group, an informa business*

Copyright © Ricardo Gomez 2003

The author has asserted his moral right under the Copyright, Designs and Patents Act, 1988, to be identified as the author of this work.

All rights reserved. No part of this book may be reprinted or reproduced or utilised in any form or by any electronic, mechanical, or other means, now known or hereafter invented, including photocopying and recording, or in any information storage or retrieval system, without permission in writing from the publishers.

Notice:
Product or corporate names may be trademarks or registered trademarks, and are used only for identification and explanation without intent to infringe.

Publisher's Note
The publisher has gone to great lengths to ensure the quality of this reprint but points out that some imperfections in the original copies may be apparent.

Disclaimer
The publisher has made every effort to trace copyright holders and welcomes correspondence from those they have been unable to contact.

A Library of Congress record exists under LC control number: 2003052113

ISBN 13: 978-1-138-71152-5 (hbk)
ISBN 13: 978-1-138-71149-5 (pbk)
ISBN 13: 978-1-315-19977-l (ebk)

# Contents

| | | |
|---|---|---|
| *List of Tables and Figures* | | *vi* |
| *Acknowledgements* | | *vii* |
| *List of Abbreviations* | | *viii* |
| 1 | European Union Foreign Policy and the Concept of Strategic Action | 1 |
| 2 | A Brief History of EU Mediterranean Policy | 25 |
| 3 | Old Wine in New Bottles? The Renovated Mediterranean Policy and the Euro-Mediterranean Agreements | 43 |
| 4 | The Barcelona Process | 69 |
| 5 | The Politics of the Euro-Mediterranean Partnership Theory and Practice | 95 |
| 6 | Influence Without Power? The EU and the Middle East Peace Process | 123 |
| 7 | The EU and the Algeria Crisis | 147 |
| 8 | Conclusions | 169 |
| *Bibliography* | | 183 |
| *Index* | | 203 |

# List of Tables and Figures

| | | |
|---|---|---|
| Table 2.1 | The Mediterranean Network After the Global Mediterranean Policy | 34 |
| Table 3.1 | Debt Statistics for the Mediterranean Associates | 45 |
| Table 3.2 | Trade with the EU (Million ECUs) (1980-1989) | 46 |
| Table 3.3 | Status of Negotiations with Partner Countries, March 2001 | 60 |
| Table 6.1 | Donor Pledges - October 1993, November 1996 (Million ECUs) | 127 |
| Table 7.1 | Trade between the EC and Algeria (Millions ECUs) | 150 |
| Table 7.2 | EC-Algeria Financial Protocols (Million ECUs) | 154 |
| Figure 2.1 | Main Commitments of the Global Mediterranean Policy | 33 |
| Figure 3.1 | Main Commitments of the Renewed Mediterranean Policy | 50 |
| Figure 3.2 | Common Provisions of the Euro-Mediterranean Agreements | 55 |
| Figure 4.1 | Draft Programme for the Barcelona Conference | 74 |
| Figure 4.2 | Programme for the First Chapter of the Barcelona Process | 80 |
| Figure 6.1 | EU Member States' Roles in the Regional Economic Development Working Group | 124 |
| Figure 6.2 | Proposed EU Initiatives in the Peace Process | 127 |
| Figure 6.3 | EU Special Envoy's Mandate | 130 |

# Acknowledgements

This book originated in doctoral research carried out at the University of Glasgow between 1995 and 1999. My work there was supported by an ESRC Scholarship (R00429534376). My thanks must first of all go to the 102 officials, politicians and academics who gave up their valuable time to meet me during the course of my research. Their assistance was absolutely critical to understanding the diplomacy behind the Euro-Mediterranean Partnership. Though several agreed to speak 'on the record', all their identities are protected in the book. For the most part, references to interviews give only dates and locations.

The Department of Politics at the University of Glasgow gave me a great deal of academic and financial support. Special thanks must be reserved for my supervisor, John Peterson, whose patience and encouragement were invaluable. Stephen White and Chris Berry offered generous support from the Department at all times. Glasgow may not be the Mediterranean, but I spent a hugely enjoyable period there.

The period I spent as a *stagiaire* at the European Parliament opened my eyes to a fascinating institution. The civil servant to whom I was assigned in DGIV – Frank Schuermans – must be thanked for the patience he showed as I came to terms with the finer points of macro-economics. Thanks also to Margaret François, who accepted my French with good grace. To the many *stagiaires*, especially Elpida Papahatzi and Nerea San Juan Rodriguez, who assisted me as I found my feet in Brussels and provided me with such a stimulating work environment, I am extremely grateful.

I owe an additional debt of gratitude to colleagues and other academics who provided me with advice and guidance in preparing the book. William Wallace and Helene Sjursen offered very useful comments on draft chapters. Esther Barbé, Stephen Calleya, Stelios Stavridis and Bichara Khader all offered their wisdom about the Euro-Mediterranean Partnership. George Christou, Pat Mackinnon, Rebecca Steffenson, Andrew Smith and Des Compston also provided helpful input. Elisa Roller's kind assistance was far beyond the call of duty. Vicki Craven put in an enormous amount of work to help prepare the final manuscript and was always there for me.

Finally, my family were incredibly supportive during my protracted life in full-time education. It is to them that this book is dedicated. My grandparents and late Aunty and Uncle provided unwavering financial and moral support. My parents continued to back me throughout my education, a huge sacrifice for which I cannot thank them enough.

# List of Abbreviations

| | |
|---|---|
| ACRS | Arms Control and Regional Security working group |
| AHLC | Ad Hoc Liaison Committee |
| AMU | Arab Maghreb Union |
| CAP | Common Agricultural Policy |
| CBMs | Confidence Building Measures |
| CEECs | Central and Eastern European Countries |
| CFSP | Common Foreign and Security Policy |
| COREPER | Committee of Permanent Representatives |
| CSBMs | Confidence and Security Building Measures |
| CSCE | Conference on Security and Cooperation in Europe |
| CSCM | Conference on Security and Cooperation in the Mediterranean |
| DG | Directorate General (European Commission) |
| EC | European Community |
| ECU | European Currency Unit |
| EDF | European Development Fund |
| EEC | European Economic Community |
| EIB | European Investment Bank |
| EMP | Euro-Mediterranean Partnership |
| EP | European Parliament |
| EPC | European Political Cooperation |
| ESC | Economic and Social Committee (EU) |
| EU | European Union |
| FIS | Front Islamique du Salut |
| FLN | Front de Libération Nationale |
| FTA | Free Trade Area |
| G7 | Group of seven industrialised nations |
| G77 | Group of 77 non-aligned countries |
| GATT | General Agreement on Tariffs and Trade |
| GIA | Groupe Islamique Armé |
| GMP | Global Mediterranean Policy |
| GNP | Gross National Product |
| HCE | Haut Comité d'Etat |
| IMF | International Monetary Fund |
| MEDA | Mesures d'Accompagnement |
| MENA | Middle East and North Africa |
| NATO | North Atlantic Treaty Organisation |
| NGO | Non-governmental Organisation |
| OECD | Organisation for Economic Cooperation and Development |
| OPEC | Organisation of Petroleum Exporting Countries |

| | |
|---|---|
| OSCE | Organisation for Security and Cooperation in Europe |
| PA | Palestinian Authority |
| PHARE | Poland and Hungary Aid for the Reconstruction of Economies |
| PLO | Palestine Liberation Organisation |
| PPEWU | Policy Planning and Early Warning Unit |
| REDWG | Regional Economic Development Working Group |
| RMP | Redirected Mediterranean Policy |
| SME | Small and Medium Sized Enterprise |
| UGTA | Union Générale de Travailleurs Algériens |
| UN | United Nations |
| UNESCO | United Nations Educational, Scientific and Cultural Organisation |
| UNRWA | United Nations Relief and Works Agency |
| WEU | Western European Union |

Chapter 1

# European Union Foreign Policy and the Concept of Strategic Action

**Introduction**

This book presents a case study of the European Union's external Mediterranean policy. The 1990s saw the EU's relations with the majority of non-member states of the Mediterranean littoral absorbed into the 'Euro-Mediterranean Partnership' (EMP). The initiative was based on the negotiation of Euro-Mediterranean Association Agreements, a modified form of existing bilateral agreements, a new financial aid package (MEDA) and an ambitious multilateral political declaration and work programme. Over the same period, Mediterranean security became an issue of increased salience for the Union, testing its crisis management capabilities and calling into question the long-term durability of its approach towards North Africa and the Middle East. As Javier Solana, the EU's High Representative for CFSP, has put it, 'if these regions are unstable, Europe will not be able to live in security'.[1]

The central argument of the book is that the Euro-Mediterranean Partnership demonstrates the EU's capacity to embark upon strategic foreign policy behaviour but that the ability to consistently translate strategic objectives into effective action is not yet in evidence. This capacity to design and pursue strategic actions is primarily generated by the EU's pillar I (the European Community), the principal source of the organisation's 'foreign economic policy'.[2] Active, as opposed to merely reactive, foreign policy emanates from the European Community acting as the 'agent' of the European Union.[3] While the Union spent much of the 1990s attempting to develop a stronger common foreign and security policy-making mechanism (pillar II), it is the Union's foreign economic policy that has exerted the greatest, if not always the most highly visible, impact on the outside world.[4] The book's starting point is consequently the assumption that an inclusive and expansive view of EU foreign policy should be adopted. Distinguishing external economic relations from traditional 'politico-security' foreign policy has become anachronistic in an international system in which trade and finance have become 'high politics'.[5]

These core arguments have a number of implications. First, we should expect the EU's strategic action to focus on so-called 'soft security' and 'soft power', meaning the eschewal of traditional politico-military concerns in favour of the economic, societal and environmental aspects of security.[6] That is not to suggest that politico-military security is irrelevant for the EU. As the recent steps forward in the development of a Common European Security and Defence Policy show, the ability to project a credible, collective military capability remains high on the Union's foreign policy agenda. The brutal wars in the former Yugoslavia, the fragility of security in the Balkans and the challenge of modern terrorism have all exposed the EU's deficiencies in this regard. But what matters more may be the EU's qualities as a 'civilian power', deploying resources that derive from its status as the dominant economic force in the region to influence Mediterranean security.[7]

Second, the notion that foreign economic policy instruments provide the foundations for strategic action suggests that we should expect to find greater 'consistency' between pillars I and II.[8] In other words, we might anticipate that the various forms of Association Agreements, financial aid programmes and other mechanisms for 'cooperation' between the EU and non-member countries are being mobilized effectively and systematically in pursuit of political objectives agreed in the context of the CFSP.

Third, the emphasis on foreign economic policy as the platform for strategic action directs our attention to the methodology for formulating strategies. The delegation of policy competence from the member states to the Community in this area is one of the longest established and most highly developed features of the European integration process.[9] Trade diplomacy, the bilateral association system and the negotiation of agreements with other international organisations have been particularly productive areas of activity for the European Commission, which plays an important role in propagating policy ideas and negotiating with 'outsiders' on the Union's behalf. We should therefore expect to find evidence of 'supranational autonomy', exercised by the Commission, in the policy-making process.[10]

This introductory chapter examines the conceptual problems associated with the development of EU foreign policy, assesses the theoretical state of the art in EU foreign policy studies and sets out to define strategic action. Section 1 explores the complex nature of EU foreign policy and gives a brief overview of the Union's competencies in that area. In section 2, the theoretical problems associated with the study of EU foreign policy are examined from a variety of analytical perspectives. Section 3 offers a framework for the analysis of EU strategic action and outlines the contents of the chapters which follow.

**The Elusive Pursuit of EU Foreign Policy**

Making sense of EU foreign policy is still far from straightforward. As Christopher Hill argues;

> apart from a very small group of diplomatic practitioners and specialist commentators, few Europeans (let alone those on the outside looking in) have a clear conception of the multiple layers and contradictions that make up what is often called 'European foreign policy'.[11]

A first problem is the complex multi-institutional, multi-procedural nature of the EU foreign policy-making process. A bewildering array of treaty articles,

European Court of Justice judgements and informal agreements among the institutions and member governments have shaped the EU's *acquis politique*, the totality of the Union's competencies and output in the foreign policy domain. Institutional competencies for policy-making and external diplomatic activity vary with the issue in question and the treaty articles associated with it. In many cases, of which EU Mediterranean policy is a prime example, foreign policy strategies are composites of measures that emanate from several sources and are thus subject to a wide range of decision-making rules and procedures. This complexity affects all phases of the policy process, from the design of strategies to their implementation.

The diffuse nature of authority in EU external policy-making has increased in line with the transfer of policy-making powers from member state to Community level. Since the acceleration of the European integration process sparked by the single market initiative, the externalisation of Community policies has given most policy sectors an international dimension.[12] Trade negotiations, for instance, routinely involve several Commission Directorates General as well as a multitude of national ministries and non-governmental interests. The external impact of the single market, the growing prosperity of the enlarged Union and the dominant position of 'western' capital and markets have all generated demands from outsiders for membership, Association Agreements, trade agreements and other forms of formal relationships with the Union.[13] To illustrate the point, the EU negotiated around 25 different free trade agreements (FTAs) in the 1990s with a range of partners including, for example, Russia and *Mercosur*.[14]

The lack of clarity over the legal bases for external action and the thorny issue of representation continue to handicap the Union's attempts to 'speak with one voice', exemplified by its uncertain status in international negotiations and the difficulties that have arisen in delineating the responsibilities of External Relations Commissioner Chris Patten and CFSP 'High Representative' Javier Solana. On numerous occasions, third countries, and even the member states themselves, have been forced to seek legal clarification of the Union's powers.[15] The EU's attempts to project a unified position during the Uruguay Round of the GATT in 1992 and 1993 were regularly undermined by disputes between member states and the Commission over negotiating authority. More recently, the EU had, 'no clear policy on FTAs: they were mostly negotiated by Commissioners between whom the world was divided into regional responsibilities...[and were] defended as a means to strengthen the Union's hand in their "patch" of the globe'.[16]

However, EU foreign policy – in both its economic and politico-security guises – has proved adaptable enough to overcome the absence of a 'coherent, rational body of law under a single institutional framework'.[17] Rules have incrementally emerged, often a product of practical compromises between those involved in the policy process. A sense of procedural order is gradually being brought to external policy-making that does not necessarily rely on treaties, the adoption of formal, legal bases or the definitive distribution of institutional competencies.

A second, related problem arises from the existence of multiple 'levels' of European foreign policy activity that are enmeshed with, and difficult to separate from, the Union's own foreign policy activities. The most significant of these remains the national level, expressed in the foreign policies of the member states. Indeed, EU external policies – financial aid programmes, for instance – are often specifically designed to complement, or be complemented by, national policies. Work on concepts such as 'Europeanization' suggests that the parameters of national foreign policies are being fundamentally transformed by the practice of European foreign policy-making.[18] Membership of the European Union has fostered a new identity and added a collective dimension to the definition of external interests and the setting of policy objectives. New norms and expectations have been internalized by those involved in European foreign policy-making.

Here, the differences between foreign economic policy and politico-security policy are significant. Although the Community has acquired exclusive competence over most key areas of external economic relations the member states have stubbornly resisted the transfer of authority to the EU level over military, defence and security policy. Europeanization has taken a far stronger hold over the former than the latter. There remains much scope for national foreign policies and divergent national interests to act as a disintegrative force on the European foreign policy process.

At another level, the EU has become increasingly dependent on outside organisations in both the design and implementation of its external policies. Although the memberships of the EU and such organisations may overlap, they are rarely identical.[19] The dependence of the EU on other organisations is almost total in the cases of defence and security policy. NATO continues to dominate European defence and has arguably become an increasingly significant player since it acquired the ability to act 'out-of-area'.[20] The Balkan crises of the 1990s vividly demonstrated Europe's reliance on US military hardware. The eastern enlargement strategy of the EU, and NATO's own strategy for expansion, were inextricably linked and it was virtually unthinkable that one would proceed without the other.[21] Furthermore, the use of NGOs to implement EU funded projects ranging from support for democratisation to assistance for small businesses, has become standard practice. The point here is that policy might originate in the EU, but the implementation of it may be beyond the organisation's direct control. The exposure in 1999 of the maladministration of EU funds, including aid programmes in the Mediterranean, were indicative of this control problem in external policy.[22]

The classification and analysis of the EU's external activities has tended to proceed along two (supposedly) distinct lines, reflecting the distribution of powers laid down in the treaties.[23] External economic relations form the first branch. Its bases in the founding treaties were the Common Commercial Policy (Articles 131-4), relationships with the overseas territories of the member states (Articles 299), the potential to accept new members (Article 237 EEC Treaty) and the power to conclude agreements with other international organisations (Article 300-310).[24] It is primarily these articles that equipped the Union with its toolbox of external policy instruments. Many of the decisions on these instruments are taken according to the 'Community method', implying strongly 'supranational' characteristics.[25]

Much of the literature on external economic relations has tended to treat them as 'low politics', focusing either on the economic implications of agreements for relationships with third countries, or on the effect the agreements have on the EU's status as an international actor.[26] As Lodge argues, however, 'the Common Commercial Policy's scope is so wide that all manner of other issues fall into the supposedly "low political" competence of the EC'.[27] The increased politicisation of trade, capital movements and money during the 1990s has made the term increasingly irrelevant.

European Political Cooperation, superseded by the Common Foreign and Security Policy (CFSP), forms the second branch. Two decades of little more than cautiously worded diplomatic declarations revealed the inherent limitations of EPC as a means to influence international affairs, but many scholars continued to regard it as the closest thing to real foreign policy machinery in the EU, even if what it produced could hardly be described as real foreign policy.[28] The creation of the Common Foreign and Security Policy – the second of Maastricht's three pillars – enshrined the foreign policy-external relations dichotomy in the treaties. Although the TEU (Article C) stressed the need for the Commission and Council to ensure 'horizontal' consistency between the EU's 'external relations, security, economic and development policies', the Treaty paid scant regard to how bridging the divide between the two pillars would actually be achieved. Nor did it address the issue of 'vertical' consistency between EU foreign policy and the foreign policies of the individual member states.[29] A declaration appended to the TEU promised a review of the procedures for consistency, but left the actual arrangements largely open ended. The possibility prior to the IGCs that the two branches might be integrated in a single institutional framework had been excluded by the sensitivity of some of the member states about ceding control over one of the key attributes of the sovereign state, and by a Commission which was wary of pushing the supranational cause too hard. The final package amounted to a codified version of EPC with a modest communitarization of certain procedures, but was initially talked up both by EU policy-makers and the European media as heralding the dawn of a new age in European foreign policy.[30]

The new Title V (Article J.4) broached the taboo subject of EU defence policy for the first time, tentatively setting up the WEU as the Union's defence arm. New decision-making procedures – common positions and joint actions (Article J.2) – were created that potentially paved the way for the Union to take collective 'action' in addition to issuing political declarations. However, the CFSP did not arm the Union with a new set of foreign policy instruments, while decisions about financing actions and the use of pillar 1 external policy instruments were to be made on a case-specific basis rather than through any set formula. In this sense, the new mechanism singularly failed even to clarify the institutional division of labour in EU foreign policy.[31] What has been termed 'ad hocery' remained the standard practice and serious critical reservations quickly began to be expressed about its likely effectiveness.[32]

One of the key tasks mandated to the IGCs that produced the 1997 Amsterdam Treaty was to 'endow the Union with a greater capacity for external action'.[33] Given the ineffectiveness of the CFSP in fostering agreement among the member states, and with eastern enlargement looming, procedural adaptation headed the wish list.[34] But a leap forward in the communitarization of CFSP decision-making was never a realistic prospect. As Bobby McDonagh, an Irish diplomat involved in the IGC negotiations put it:

> the simple fact is that, at the present stage of the Union's development, there is a limit to the extent to which any Member State is prepared to submerge a perceived important foreign policy interest within a single European position.[35]

Rather than wholesale reform, the 1997 Amsterdam Treaty made only incremental changes to the CFSP and preserved intergovernmental dominance of the CFSP.[36] The stubborn adherence to unanimity as the basis for decision-making was mitigated by provision for the 'constructive abstention' of up to a third of the member states and a limited extension of QMV (Article 23). Member states retained the right to block decisions 'for important and stated reasons of national policy', thus preserving a *de facto* veto (Article 23.2). The introduction of an explicit role for the European Council (Article 13) in setting the guidelines for the CFSP and for adopting Common Strategies was intended to ensure stronger political direction to EU foreign policy. To complement this enhanced directional power, the creation of a Policy Planning and Early Warning Unit (PPEWU) housed in the Council Secretariat gave the Union a capacity for the independent (of the member states) analysis of foreign policy situations. The profile of the Union abroad was to be strengthened by the appointment of the Council's Secretary General as 'High Representative' of the CFSP. Although these developments promoted further 'Brusselisation' of the CFSP, the Council was the principal beneficiary of change, a situation which left the member governments in control of the CFSP.[37]

The most striking developments in EU foreign policy originated outside the Treaties. Decisions taken at the 1999 Cologne European Council to press forward with European Security and Defence Policy (ESDP) were followed by agreement at the Helsinki summit to create a Rapid Reaction Force of 50-60,000 troops by 2003.[38] The main purpose of these decisions was to strengthen the EU's capacity to act in crisis situations. Changes to the institutional machinery to serve the ESDP were subsequently agreed in the Treaty of Nice. The long-established Political Committee was renamed the Political and Security Committee and given a permanent presence in Brussels. The Treaty also led to the creation of a Military Committee and the assignment of military personnel from the member states to the Council Secretariat where they were to become the 'Military Staff of the European Union'. However, the retention of unanimity as the basis for decisions left the 'new' ESDP open to the use of the veto, undermining any prospects that it would markedly improve the Union's ability to take swift and unified foreign policy decisions.

On paper, the launch and revision of the CFSP told of slow but visible progress in this most sensitive area of European integration. But its actual record spoke of its limitations.[39] The Union could point to only a handful of successful, high profile joint actions, among them support for the Middle East Peace Process and the Palestinian elections.[40] On issues that ought to have elicited a strong collective political position from the Union, such as the crises in Algeria and the Balkans in the 1990s, a strong Union position was conspicuous by its absence. Like that of its predecessor, the CFSP's output was dominated by statements rather than concrete action. Any bridging between pillars I and II was driven by the imperative of the issue, political expediency and diplomatic creativity rather than by procedural advances brought by the TEU or the changes brought about by the Amsterdam Treaty.

Much of the literature on EU foreign policy initially rode the CFSP wave. Here, for the first time, appeared to be the bare bones of a European security and defence identity and a mechanism for common foreign policy-making in something approaching a constitutionalised form. Yet as Peterson and Sjursen argue, practice showed the CFSP to be best conceived of as a process rather than a policy.[41] The disappointing record of the CFSP, which with a few exceptions has produced little more than carefully worded and politically tentative declarations, suggests that finding a position on which the member states can actually agree – the coordination reflex – is a more important function than the policy's 'output'.[42] What the CFSP failed to do was significantly change the way the member states perceived foreign policy. For most, it remained a bastion of sovereignty and any substantive transfer of authority to the EU was to be resisted.[43] Nor could it induce the political conditions under which all the member states would seek and subsequently adhere to common foreign policy positions as a matter of course. Indeed, the early years of the CFSP were notable for a resurgence of national interests.[44] Foreign policy continued to reflect the uneasy tension between national foreign policy priorities and the faltering sense of the European interest.[45]

Faced with this institutional and procedural 'mixity', identifying the key actors and influences involved in the EU's foreign policy process is always problematic, whether at the initiation, decision or implementation stage.[46] However, as Hill argues, 'only by taking an overview of all the elements of what we optimistically call "European foreign policy" can we identify a pattern of behaviour and assess the respective contributions of the various parts – positive and negative'.[47] Recognising the merit of an inclusive definition of EU foreign policy is also an essential step to understanding the Union's overall impact in the international system. As this book shows, whenever the question of deepening the EU's relationships with Mediterranean third countries has arisen, it has been the Union's trade and aid policies, rather than its defence and military capabilities, which have really mattered.

## Theorising EU Foreign Policy

Scholars of the European Union face considerable ontological and epistemological problems when it comes to their subject area. We are still a long way from consensus on what it is that we are studying, let alone how to study it. For those endeavouring to theorize about EU foreign policy, such difficulties are aggravated by the multi-level, multi-institutional characteristics of the EU's foreign policy-making system described above, by the obfuscating and ambiguous terminology in which EU foreign policy is frequently couched, and by the *sui generis* nature of the Union itself.[48]

Not surprisingly perhaps, theoretical work on EU foreign policy has always lagged some way behind the burgeoning theoretical output on other aspects of the European integration process.[49] The theoretical lacuna in European foreign policy studies is compounded by the relatively small number of detailed empirical case studies. Much of the literature on the subject tends to be descriptive or prescriptive, concerned with making sense of the procedural complexity of the Union's foreign policy-making mechanisms or offering corrective recipes for the EU's deficiencies as an international actor. This section argues that the building blocks of theory may be present, but assembling them into a comprehensible theoretical framework is another matter. As Christopher Hill contends, 'the experience of "European foreign policy" over the last 20 years or so has been so unique that the search for one theory to explain its evolution is doomed to fail'.[50]

What, then, do the major theoretical perspectives on international relations and European integration have to say about EU foreign policy? Traditional realists by and large ignore the EU as an international actor.[51] Since it is not a state, it cannot by definition possess a foreign policy. Henry Kissinger's tome on the history of diplomacy, for instance, barely mentions the diplomatic activity of the EU in international politics.[52] For classical realists, the incessant pursuit of power, primarily through military means, by states in an anarchic state system precludes international cooperation other than alliance diplomacy.[53] By extension, European integration seemed a transitory phenomenon, destined to disintegrate in the chaotic post-Cold War world.[54]

Neo-realism (or structural realism), with its emphasis on systemic structure as the major determinant of the behaviour of states, does see the possibility of cooperation between states. States may occasionally choose to cooperate in order to avoid conflict, whether military or economic, but the anarchic nature of the international system, in which self-reliance is essential, weighs against it.[55] In any case, inter-state bargaining always takes place with governments' eyes firmly fixed on the relative gains from cooperation and the likely impact on the distribution of power.[56] Through this lens, the EU is viewed as a governmental forum in which states participate in order to further their own interests and power. In a rare neo-realist interpretation of EPC, Alfred Pijpers argues that 'the major policies and institutions of Europe's would-be foreign policy are the reflection of deliberate national preferences of the participating states'.[57]

Neither realism nor neo-realism are compatible with the inclusive image of EU foreign policy presented above, based as they are on the assumptions that foreign policy is somehow the privileged domain of governmental elites, isolated from domestic influences, and the exclusive preserve of the unitary state. While the predominantly inter-governmental nature of EPC and the CFSP do lend some credibility to the state-centricity of the two approaches, they cannot satisfactorily account for the institutionalisation of foreign policy coordination, however fragile and limited it may be.[58] Nor can they account for the supranationalization of national foreign economic policy in the Union. As Roy Ginsberg argues, neo-realism:

> Ignores the role of supranational institutions in crafting and facilitating compromises and in overseeing and managing daily processes. It also ignores why, how and when national interests converge and to what extent they are shaped by domestic and international politics and the ethos of Community membership.[59]

A more sophisticated version of state-centric analysis – liberal intergovernmentalism – also experiences difficulties coming to terms with an inclusive definition of EU foreign policy. The basic claims of this perspective are that European integration is driven by the rational, calculated choices of governments to pool in or delegate sovereignty to international institutions in response to domestic economic interests and the need to offset the negative effects of interdependence.[60] The decision to cooperate is made with a clear idea of the resultant costs and benefits. The creation of the Union's Common Commercial Policy, for instance, is explained as an essential extension to the member states' preference for the liberalisation of trade amongst themselves.[61]

Cooperation in the realm of traditional foreign and security policy represents a bigger test for liberal intergovernmentalism. Common foreign and security policy is a 'non-socio-economic collective good' whose costs and benefits are diffuse and uncertain. As Andrew Moravcsik, the leading proponent of this approach, argues, 'the reasoning used to justify policies tends to be symbolic and ideological, rather than calculated and concrete'.[62] In other words, geopolitical factors, concerns about sovereignty and the commitment of governments to the European project are apt to be offered as explanations for how the EU's competencies in this field have developed.

Other variants of intergovernmental institutionalism offer similarly rationalist, instrumentalist interpretations of the EU. Robert Keohane and Stanley Hoffmann see the EU as a highly advanced form of regime, created by European governments for the purpose of managing the increasing levels of interdependence between them.[63] New thinking about international security after the end of the Cold War which foresaw an expanded role for the EU in managing trade and dealing with issues such as environmental protection seemed to validate this claim. However, intergovernmental institutionalists too have comparatively little to say about the development of the EU as a foreign policy actor, citing the weakness of its defence and security capability as evidence of both the primacy of national interests and the *sui generis* character of the organisation.[64] Keohane and Hoffmann concede that in foreign economic policy, some power has been transferred to a central, supranational authority distinct from the states, but see no such prospect in the politico-security sphere.[65]

Clearly, the parameters of EU foreign policy are largely determined by the member states. Furthermore, as this book argues, the member governments' defence of domestic economic interests is frequently decisive at key stages of the policy process. However, intergovernmentalist theories suffer from a number of blind spots. First, the primary concern of these intergovernmentalist and institutionalist theories is to explain the major, formative decisions in the history of European integration rather than the regular policy process. They therefore have rather less utility as tools for policy analysis. Second, and relatedly, there is an inherent tendency in these theories to overlook or downplay the role of supranational agency; institutions being principally viewed as servants of the member governments. Third, in downplaying the impact of geopolitics and systemic change on the bargains that states strike, LI in particular excludes important external stimuli that clearly influence the type of external policies that the EU pursues. Perceptions of a security 'threat' from the Mediterranean, for instance, appear to have been a key factor in propelling the region up the EU's agenda and in stimulating the search for a strategy.

More promising variations on the institutionalist theme are to be found in 'historical' or 'new' institutionalist theories, which emphasise the autonomy of supranational institutions.[66] The chief merit of this school of thought is that it distinguishes distinct phases in the policy process. Governments may determine the basis and set the agenda for cooperation, but 'during later phases of the [policy] process, other actors, rules and EC procedures can exert their effects'.[67] External economic relations work from a long-established script in which the supranational agency and entrepreneurship of the Commission play a crucial role in policy 'output'. The history of EU Mediterranean policy is one of continuity, with responsibility for negotiating and re-negotiating agreements with third countries – the central plank of policy – being vested in the Commission and its activities in pillar I.

Most theoretical perspectives thus offer some insight into either the nature or the process of EU foreign policy. Intergovernmentalist approaches undoubtedly have a stronger claim to explaining EPC/CFSP where conflicting foreign policy positions among the member states have frequently prevented unified stances being adopted on key issues. Approaches that recognise the exercise of effective influence by supranational institutions must figure in theoretical explanations of the EU's foreign economic policy, where governmental domination is checked by the 'Community method' of decision-making. However, a macro-theory of EU foreign policy remains a distant prospect. If a general theory is possible, it is likely to be built from a synthesis of theoretical perspectives that take into account the multi-level character of the EU foreign policy-making system, the multiple outputs of EU external policy and the mixture of governmental and supranational decision-making procedures and policy instruments that comprise the Union's *acquis politique*.[68]

Dissatisfaction with what theory has to offer has led a number of EU foreign policy analysts to seek instead to conceptualise the impact on and roles of the EU in the international system. Concepts such as 'actorness', 'presence' and 'influence' describe and explain the functions and status of the Union at the global or regional level, and contextualise its interaction with the outside world.[69] The common denominator running through this work is that the ambiguous status of the EU as a foreign policy actor and the complexity of its foreign policy-making system give it variable presence or actor capability in different 'issue areas'.[70] Its impact is most tangible in global economic affairs, where its capacity for unified action is greatest. Conversely, where it lacks the capacity for unified action, on military and defence issues for example, its impact is marginal.

Perhaps the most influential analysis of the EU's status and performance as an international actor is Christopher Hill's 'capabilities-expectations gap' thesis.[71] Hill takes the argues that the balancing act between the foreign policy 'resources' at the Union's disposal – its economic and financial power, its policy instruments, and its cohesiveness – and the need to fulfil the growing list of external demands made of it determine its effectiveness as an international actor. In EU Mediterranean policy, the manifestation of the capabilities-expectations gap has centred on the issue of resource allocation issues, specifically on the level of financial assistance and market access for third countries. While the Union has increased the level of resources it provides for the Mediterranean, so the Euro-Mediterranean Partnership has raised expectations about how far the Union will go in offering an economic helping hand to its poorer southern neighbours.[72] The 'capabilities-expectations gap' is perhaps most visible in the Union's relations with the United States and Central and Eastern European countries, but it is an important part of the story of EU Mediterranean policy, too.[73] The EU's habit of 'talking up' its foreign policy may be less acute now than during the early 1990s, thus leading to a partial closing of the gap between the EU's capabilities and the outside world's expectations since then.[74] But the gap undoubtedly remains and it is a considerable obstacle to strategic action in EU external policy.

Another 'conceptual category' applied to the EU's international role is the notion of 'civilian power Europe'.[75] Based on the part practical, part normative argument that 'Europe's leverage cannot and should not be exerted along traditional lines', the post-cold war international system saw the concept acquire renewed resonance as the relevance and utility of military power came under scrutiny.[76] Yet the record of conflicts in the 1990s tells us that recourse to military intervention continues to hold powerful, if politically problematic, sway as a means to influence state behaviour. As Stelios Stavridis contends, the use of force at 'one end of a long spectrum' may be the only way to make the civilian power concept credible in the modern international system.[77] The development of a military dimension to European integration – particularly the creation of the Rapid Reaction Force – attests to the EU's perceived need to endow itself with a foreign policy tool of last resort. It may continue to rely predominantly on trade, aid and non-military diplomacy to exercise influence on international affairs, but the exposure of its weaknesses in conflict resolution has seen momentum swing in favour of a strengthened collective security and defence capability.

So does the civilian power concept still have analytic validity? The case for the EU becoming a global military power is a difficult one to sustain, implying in its most far-reaching sense a return to superpower competition for international dominance. Furthermore, the USA has not withdrawn from its role as security 'guarantor' in Europe to the extent that some anticipated at the start of the 1990s. Admittedly, George W. Bush's Administration did pledge to substantially reduce the numbers of US troops in Europe. But there have been no history-making changes in Europe's security architecture of the kind which might have forced the European Security and Defence Identity into maturity. As Jan Zielonka observes, 'opting for a civilian-controlled Europe would make it clear that collective defence on the continent is provided principally by NATO'.[78] Thus the exercise of civilian power ought to be viewed as a legitimate focus for analysis in its own right.

## Conceptualising Strategic Action

Policy-makers and policy analysts may talk about EU foreign policy strategies, but the actual meaning of strategic action is rarely considered. In basic terms, strategy can be defined as 'a plan of action or policy', denoting purposive rather than reactive behaviour.[79] This dynamic quality to the concept is summarised by Keohane and Hoffmann:

> Strategy is essentially forward looking: beginning where history has left them, actors seek to take advantage of future trends. Their expectations shape their policies as much as does their actual situation.[80]

In turn, the notion of purposive, goal directed behaviour implies a decision to pursue more or less specified objectives, themselves a result of the identification, prioritisation and articulation of interests.[81]

At first sight, the application of this definition to the EU's external activities appears to be relatively straightforward. The Union has gradually built up a hierarchy of strategies towards individual third countries and regional organisations, and developed distinct 'lines' on a wide range of external issues. The Yaoundé and Lomé conventions, and the so-called 'Global Mediterranean Policy', were among the first examples of 'self-styled' external strategies, designed to establish 'frameworks' for relations with groups of third countries.[82] More recent high profile examples include the Union's position in the Uruguay round of the GATT, its Agenda 2000 eastern accession strategy and the 'New Transatlantic Agenda'.

However, unpacking the concept of strategic action in EU foreign policy reveals four significant, related problems. First, foreign policy analysis (FPA) as an academic discipline is held to be inextricably bound up with the state and with the interest-driven behaviour of governments.[83] Besides the obvious fact that the EU is not a state, the lack of a central government and the prominence of the member governments in the policy-making process militates against using the standard box of analytical tools. However, FPA has responded and adapted to changes in the international system. As Brian White argues, 'the focus on policy at the international level is what is important to the foreign policy analyst rather than whether the actor is a conventional government or not'.[84] The point here is that the nature of the EU as an actor need not prevent us from posing the germane questions about foreign policy processes, agendas, instruments, and outcomes.[85]

A second problem concerns the multi-actor, multi-level nature of EU foreign policy. How, for instance, should the analyst factor in the constant interplay between institutions, states and interests that determines EU policy? Where does the formulation and execution of EU foreign policy strategies begin and end? One way around this problem is to view EU foreign policy as a system of external relations.[86] The system clearly has institutionalized procedures, what Ben Soetendorp describes as 'decision regimes', for defining objectives and designing actions to achieve them.[87] The creation of the Policy Planning and Early Warning Unit by the Amsterdam Treaty was intended to improve the Union's capabilities in this area. In the case of the Euro-Med initiative, the Commission, individual member states and, to a lesser extent, the non-EU participants brought with them a diverse range of strategic priorities for the region. Taking the system metaphor a step further, the system responds to 'inputs' both from within the Union (domestic economic and political interests, externalisation) and from its external environment (geo-political changes, specific demands from third countries). The outputs of EU foreign policy feed back into the system from the results of actions, a mechanism which encourages adaptations. While EU foreign policy-making is certainly not as structured and tidy as the systems approach implies, it nevertheless provides a useful canvas on which to paint a picture of how strategies develop.

The third problem centres on the absence of common European interests and some overarching strategic vision as the rationale for action. For former Commission President Jacques Delors, an EU 'vision' for the world and the elaboration of specific common interests were essential pieces of the integration jigsaw.[88] For François Heisbourg, the EU's 'constructive ambiguity' about principles and the 'eventual destination' of its security and defence policy are becoming untenable.[89] But the heterogeneity of the EU's membership means that the opportunities for unity of approach, or even a strong convergence of interests, may be few and far between, particularly when it comes to defence and military matters. When policies are couched in terms of European interests, internal differences are rarely far from the surface. Moreover, claims of a European interest are, to a significant extent, subjective, based on the perceptions, understandings and also interests of those making the claim. If the EU is to be used to further the interests of a member state or institution, then an appeal to the general interest can be an effective tactic.

Again, however, this problem is rather less challenging than it first appears to be. A modern state's foreign policy interests can rarely, if ever, be described as unified. The realist image of the unitary state has long since given way to pluralist images that stress the disaggregated nature of government and the importance of competing interests in policy-making. In a sense, the EU's external policy-making system is just a far more complex manifestation of the same phenomenon. Competition over interests may be fiercer and more protracted than is the case at national level, but the 'bargaining style' of EU decision-making allows for mediation between these interests.[90] Prior agreement over what constitutes the EU's interest on particular issues is clearly desirable, but not essential, and disagreement over interests need not be an insurmountable barrier to devising strategy.

In practical terms, the EU itself has gone some way to narrowing down the loosely defined external interests set out in the treaties.[91] The 1990s saw gradual moves towards more specific statements of what were considered to be the Union's fundamental interests. After the creation of the CFSP, the 1992 Lisbon European Council designated a number of geographical interest areas, among them the Middle East and Maghreb. One effect of the procedures for Common Strategies in the Amsterdam Treaty was to 'clarify the "common interests" of EU member states'.[92] The same Treaty also included a reference to the Western European Union's (WEU) Petersberg tasks (Article 17), listing humanitarian and rescue operations, peacekeeping/peacemaking and crisis management as basic interests of the Union in the security and defence spheres. Those interests were subsequently tied in to the development of ESDP.

In sum, two of the prerequisites for strategic action – the institutional capacity to formulate strategic objectives and the possession of a set of interests – are present in the Union's external policy system. As the Union has increased in size and scope, so its range of interests has greatly expanded. That has lent greater urgency to the development of mechanisms for mediating between different interests and arriving at the expression of collective positions. In the foreign economic policy sphere, political pragmatism has often been preferred to strict adherence to the treaty framework.[93] By contrast, efforts to improve the Union's capacity for collective action in the security and defence spheres have been shaped by the dominance of NATO and by a high level of sensitivity on the part of several member states to making 'concessions' over sovereignty.

The next analytical step is to track the policy-making process from strategy-as-plan to strategy-as-action. It is here that a third, far more serious problem with the concept of strategic action emerges: the gap that appears between the Union's rhetoric and its ability to deliver policies to achieve its strategic objectives. A clear definition of interests, an imperative for action and awareness of the most appropriate form of action do not guarantee that effective action will follow. The often-used cliché 'economic giant but a political pygmy' is testament to the Union's persistent inability to convert its enormous economic weight and potential political power into commensurate influence in global affairs.[94] The constraints on strategic action imposed by the lack of EU military power have been outlined above. But the problem is also present when strategies are based on foreign economic policy. To understand why – a key aim of this book – we must start by returning to the 'system' metaphor and open up the 'black box' that intervenes between inputs and outputs.

The image of EU policy-making employed in this book follows Helen Wallace's lead, who argues that there is:

> No single or uniform Community policy process. The patterns of policy-making and the roles of member governments and Community institutions in the policy process vary considerably from sector to sector depending on the extent of Community involvement.[95]

Thus each policy area has its own logic, a mixture of institutional competencies, decision-making formulae and constellations of actors involved that translate proposals into policy outcomes.[96] The complexity of the EU policy process makes for equally complex logics. In the Euro-Mediterranean Partnership package, the end product – the strategy – comprises a raft of measures, some drawn from the Union's established range of policy instruments (Association Agreements, financial aid, technical assistance), others tailor-made for which no established logics exist (the multilateral dimension of the Euro-Mediterranean Partnership).

Analytically, the implication of multiple logics is that as much attention must be paid to institutional politics as to governmental politics. Where pillar I is the locus for EU strategic action, the Commission exercises leadership in the formulation of strategy, plays a crucial role in negotiating the content of external policy instruments and is responsible for overseeing the implementation of aid programmes and the administration of Association Agreements. The European Parliament, though its involvement in external policy is very limited, performs an important scrutiny function, has budgetary powers in the allocation of financial aid and must give its assent to Association Agreements with third countries. By the same token, the member governments also have considerable agenda setting power and, crucially, a 'final say' over the substantive content of policies. We should therefore anticipate that the behaviour of the member states is a key determinant of effective strategic action.

An additional dimension of policy-making is 'politicisation', the process by which issues become infused with political significance.[97] For Michael Smith, it is the politicisation of economic issues in the modern international system that has made pillar I the core of EU foreign policy.[98] Its consequences are two-fold. First, the degree of politicisation of an issue affects both strategic planning and policy outcomes. Highly politicised issues may be entirely excluded from a strategy if they are deemed to have the potential to hijack the broader objective. Governments are also apt to be less favourable to making concessions on sensitive issues at the decision-making stage, fearing a domestic backlash. Second, the politicisation of issues affects the level at which policy decisions are taken. In pillar I, for instance, many trade issues tend to be treated as 'technical', increasing the Commission's influence over outcomes. If trade issues subsequently become politicised, the final decision tends to shift upwards to ministerial level, placing the onus on governmental preferences in deciding outcomes. The more general point here is that, while politicisation has undoubtedly increased the significance of external economic relations, it is also a powerful constraint on supranational 'agency' and therefore on the EC's effectiveness as the conduit for EU strategic action.

Much of this book focuses on negotiations, the dominant 'mode' of policy-making in EU Mediterranean policy.[99] The terms of Association Agreements, for instance, the EMP's main policy instrument, are largely determined by negotiations between the Union and individual third countries and by negotiations within the Union that decided the level of concessions on import volumes to be offered to each partner. The multilateral dimension of the Mediterranean strategy is also driven by ongoing negotiations between the participating governments. What confronts us resembles an 'inside-outside game', in which negotiations take place at two separate tables.[100] Inside the EU, the member states and institutions engage in negotiations to determine strategic objectives, the policy instruments to be deployed and the Union's subsequent position in the policy process. Simultaneous negotiations take place with third countries to determine the final terms of the policy package. The end result – the Euro-Mediterranean Partnership – arguably represents an attempt to extend a 'negotiated order' to the Mediterranean region.[101]

Mediterranean policy is a particularly good case study of EU strategic action. The Euro-Mediterranean Partnership employs virtually the full range of foreign policy tools available to the Union and spans the divide between external economic relations and traditional politico-security foreign policy. What began as a disparate collection of commercial agreements has grown into a complex policy package embracing a broad range of issues and sectors. The EU's relations with the Mediterranean partner countries provide a crucial test of both its capacity to act as a progressive force in the international order and of its potential to manage security in a region beset by conflicts.

Chapter 2 traces the historical evolution of Euro-Mediterranean relations, identifying the main stages in the development of Mediterranean policy. It shows how the politicisation of agricultural trade, a key policy issue, began in the first round of negotiations between the Union and the Mediterranean third countries during the 1960s. Despite several 'rounds' of renegotiation, and an attempt to create a single framework for relations, the first three decades of Mediterranean policy were notable for the Union's failure to pursue a coherent strategy in the region.

Chapter 3 examines the factors that forced the EU to re-examine its Mediterranean policy at the end of the 1980s. With the end of the Cold War, Mediterranean security suddenly assumed new salience for the Union. Faced with the rising popularity of radical Islam in North Africa, states whose economic weakness and international indebtedness threatened to cause socio-economic breakdown and forecasts of a dramatic rise in illegal immigration into Europe, the

Union was for the first time forced to consider the long-term effects of its Mediterranean policy. The resultant policy changes – the Redirected Mediterranean Policy and the Euro-Mediterranean Partnership – set out a comprehensive plan of action but little genuine reform of Euro-Mediterranean relations.

Chapter 4 explores the multilateral component of the Union's Mediterranean policy – the Barcelona process – from its inception through to the early stages of its implementation. Sold as an innovative multilateral forum that would underpin future international cooperation in the Mediterranean, the Barcelona process quickly became hostage to developments in the Middle East Peace Process, exposing the frailties of the EU as an international political actor.

Chapter 5 presents an analytical synthesis of the theory and practice of Mediterranean policy. By first breaking down the EMP into distinct policy types, it sets up a framework for the analysis of the politics that determined the final outcomes of the policy-making process. The chapter goes on to examine the impact of governmental interests and the EU's institutions upon key decisions in the EMP.

Chapter 6 changes tack, offering the first of two case studies of EU diplomatic activity in the Mediterranean region during the 1990s. It focuses on the role played by the Union in the Middle East Peace Process and considers its attempts to use its economic and political weight to influence the behaviour of the Israelis and Palestinians. Chapter 7 offers a downbeat analysis of the Union's persistent failure to adopt a strong position on the bloody conflict in Algeria. More than a decade has passed since the annulment of the legislative elections by the military sparked a campaign of terror in which both the Islamic 'opposition' and the regime stood accused of crimes against Algerian citizens. In both cases, the Euro-Mediterranean Partnership had little substantive impact.

## Notes

[1] Solana, J. (2001) 'Europe: Security in the twenty-first century', The Olaf Palme Memorial Lecture, *CFSP High Representative Website*, http://ue.eu.int/solana/default.asp?lang=en, 20 June.

[2] The Treaty on European Union (Maastricht Treaty) constructed the EU on three 'pillars'. Pillar one – the European Union – incorporates the majority of the Union's policies and institutional architecture. Pillar two refers to the Union's Common Foreign and Security Policy. Pillar three established the basis for inter-governmental cooperation on Justice and Home Affairs (internal security) matters. For discussion of EU foreign economic policy, see Hocking, B. and Smith, M. (1997) *Beyond Foreign Economic Policy: The United States, the Single European Market and the Changing World Economy*, London: Pinter; Young, A. (1998) *Interpretation and 'Soft Integration' in the Adaptation of the European Community's Foreign Economic Policy*, Sussex European Institute Working Paper No. 29, Brighton: University of Sussex; Young, A. (2000) 'The Adaptation of European Foreign Economic Policy: From Rome to Seattle', *Journal of Common Market Studies*, Vol. 38, No. 1, pp. 93-116.

³ Smith, M. (1998) 'Does the Flag Follow Trade? "Politicisation" and the Emergence of a European Foreign Policy' in J. Peterson and H. Sjursen (eds) *A Common Foreign Policy for Europe: Competing Visions of the CFSP*, London: Routledge, p. 78.
⁴ For a challenging theoretical critique of foreign economic policy, see Tooze, R. (1994) 'Foreign Economic Policy in the New Europe: A Theoretical Audit of a Questionable Category' in W. Carlsnaes and S. Smith (eds) *European Foreign Policy: The EC and Changing Perspectives in Europe*, London: Sage, pp. 61-83.
⁵ Politico-security foreign policy refers to defence, military and so-called 'hard' security policy.
⁶ Nye, J. (1990) *Bound to Lead: The Changing Nature of American Power*, New York: Basic Books, pp. 173-201; Buzan, B (1991) *People, States and Fear: An Agenda for International Security Studies in the Post Cold War Era*, Boulder (CO): Lynne Rienner; Buzan, B. (1994) 'The Interdependence of Security and Economic Issues in the "New World Order"' in R. Stubbs and G.R.D. Underhill (eds) *Political Economy and the Changing Global Order*, London: Macmillan, pp. 96-7; Hill, C. (2001) 'The EU's Capacity for Conflict Prevention', *European Foreign Affairs Review*, Vol. 6, No. 3, pp. 315-33.
⁷ The term was first applied to the Community in Duchêne, F. (1972) 'Europe's Role in World Peace' in R. Mayne (ed.) *Europe Tomorrow: Sixteen Europeans Look Ahead*, London: Fontana, pp. 32-49.
⁸ For an explanation of inter-pillar consistency, see Monar, J. (1993) 'The Foreign Affairs System of the Maastricht Treaty: A Combined Assessment of the CFSP and EC External Relations Elements' in J. Monar, W. Ungerer and W. Wessels (eds) *The Maastricht Treaty on European Union: Legal Complexity and Political Dynamics*, Brussels: European Interuniversity Press, p. 144; Krenzler, H. and Schneider, H.C. (1997) The Question of Consistency' in E. Reglesberger, P. de Schoutheete de Tervarent and W. Wessels (eds) *Foreign Policy of the European Union: From EPC to CFSP and Beyond*, Boulder and London: Lynne Rienner, pp. 120-134; Nuttall, S. (2000) *European Foreign Policy*, Oxford: Oxford University Press, esp. pp. 14-31.
⁹ See Nicolaides, K. and Meunier, S. (1999) 'Who Speaks for Europe? The Delegation of Trade Authority in the European Union', *Journal of Common Market Studies*, Vol. 37, No. 3, pp. 477-501; Meunier, S. and Nicolaides, K. (2000) 'EU Trade Policy: The exclusive versus shared competence debate' in M. Green Cowles and M. Smith (eds) *The State of the European Union: Volume 5*, Oxford: Oxford University Press, pp. 325-46.
¹⁰ There is a substantial literature on the concept of supranational autonomy and leadership in the EU context. See, for example, Sandholtz, W. and Stone Sweet, A. (eds) *European Integration and Supranational Governance*, Oxford: Oxford University Press; Moravcsik, A. (1999) 'A New Statecraft? Supranational Entrepreneurs and International Cooperation', *International Organization*, Vol. 52, No. 3, pp. 267-306. The concept has rarely been applied to EU external policy.
¹¹ Hill, C. (1992) 'The foreign policy of the European Community: Dream or reality?' in R.C. Macridis (ed.) *Foreign Policy in World Politics*, 8th edition, London: Prentice Hall, p. 109.
¹² Devuyst, Y. (1999) 'The Community Method After Amsterdam', *Journal of Common Market Studies*, Vol. 37, No. 1, p. 53.
¹³ Schmitter, P. (1969) 'Three Neo-Functional Hypotheses About International Integration', *International Organization*, Vol. 33, No. 2, pp. 161-66; Ginsberg, R. (1989) *Foreign Policy Actions of the European Community: The Politics of Scale*, London:

Admantine Press, pp. 26-7; Smith, K. (1999) *The Making of EU Foreign Policy: The Case of Eastern Europe*, Basingstoke: Macmillan, p. 123.
[14] Peterson, J. and Bomberg, E. (1999) *Decision-Making in the European Union*, Basingstoke: Macmillan, pp. 104-12.
[15] Groux, J. and Manin, P. (1985) *The European Communities in the International Order*, Luxembourg: Office for Official Publications of the European Communities, p. 45.
[16] Peterson, J. and Bomberg, E. (1999) op. cit., pp. 104-5.
[17] Smith, M. E. (2001) 'Diplomacy by decree: The legalization of EU foreign policy', *Journal of Common Market Studies*, Vol. 39, No. 1, p. 101.
[18] See Tonra, B. (2000) 'Denmark and Ireland' in I. Manners and R. G. Whitman (eds) *The Foreign Policies of European Union Member States*, Manchester: Manchester University Press, p. 229; White, B. (2001) *Understanding European Foreign Policy*, Basingstoke: Palgrave, p. 118-141.
[19] The memberships of NATO and the WEU are cases in point. Austria, Finland, Ireland and Sweden are not members of NATO. Similarly, Austria, Denmark, Finland, Ireland and Sweden have only 'observer' status in the WEU.
[20] Rühle, M. and Williams, N. (1996) 'The Greater Union's New Security Agenda: NATO and the EU' in F. Algieri, J. Janning and D. Rumberg (eds) *Managing Security in Europe: The European Union and the Challenge of Enlargement*, Gütersloh: Bertelsmann Foundation, pp. 89-109; Hill, C. (1998) 'Convergence, Divergence and Dialectics' in J. Zielonka (ed.), op. cit., p. 43.
[21] Croft, S., Redmond, J. Wyn Rees, G. and Webber, M. (1999) *The Enlargement of Europe*, Manchester: Manchester University Press, p. 44.
[22] Committee of Independent Experts (1999) *First Report on Allegations Regarding Fraud, Mismanagement and Nepotism in the European Commission*, Brussels, 15 March, http://www.europarl.eu.int/experts/en/3.htm.
[23] Soetendorp, B. (1999) *Foreign Policy in the European Union: Theory, History and Practice*, London and New York: Longman, p. 68.
[24] Articles referred to in the book use the numbering which appears in the consolidated text of the EU's treaties produced after the Treaty of Amsterdam.
[25] Devuyst, Y. (1999) op. cit.
[26] On the distinction between high and low politics, see Morgan, R. (1973) *High Politics, Low Politics: Towards a Foreign Policy for Western Europe*, London: Sage. For an application of the distinction in the context of European integration, see Hoffmann, S. (1995) *The European Sisyphus: Essays on Europe, 1964-1994*, Boulder and Oxford: Westview Press, pp. 71-106.
[27] Lodge, J. (1989) 'European Political Co-operation: Towards the 1990s' in J. Lodge (ed.) *The European Community and the Challenge of the Future*, London: Pinter, p.226.
[28] Krenzler, H.G. and Schneider, H.C. (1997) op. cit., p. 134.
[29] Ibid.
[30] Peterson, J. and Bomberg, E. (1999), op. cit., p. 229.
[31] Rummel, R. and Wiedemann, J. (1998) 'Identifying institutional paradoxes of CFSP' in J. Zielonka (ed.) *Paradoxes of European Foreign Policy*, The Hague: Kluwer Law International, pp. 53-66.
[32] Lodge, J. (1993) op. cit., p. 230.
[33] European Council and Council of the Union (1995) *Draft Mandate for the 1996 Intergovernmental Conference*, Brussels, 16 January.

[34] McDonagh, B. (1998) *Original Sin in a Brave New World: An Account of the Negotiation of the Treaty of Amsterdam*, Dublin: Institute of European Affairs, p. 114.
[35] Ibid.
[36] See, for example, Wessels, W. (2001) 'The Amsterdam Treaty in Theoretical Perspective: Which Dynamics at Work?' in W. Wessels and J. Monar (eds) *The European Union after the Treaty of Amsterdam*, London and New York: Continuum, pp. 70-86.
[37] Allen, D. (1998) 'Who Speaks for Europe? The Search for an Effective and Coherent External Policy' in J. Peterson and H. Sjursen (eds) op. cit., p. 58; Soetendorp, B. (1999) op. cit., p. 77.
[38] A key precursor to the Cologne decision was the St. Malo Declaration (December 1998) in which the UK and France called for the EU 'to have the capacity for autonomous action, backed up by credible military forces'.
[39] For official and academic critiques of the CFSP, see Reflection Group (1995) *Report for the 1996 IGC*, Brussels: Office for Official Publications of the European Communities, pp. 39-49; Reglesberger, E. and Wessels, W. (1996) 'The CFSP Institutions and Procedures: A Third Way for the Second Pillar', *European Foreign Affairs Review*, Vol. 1, No. 2, pp. 29-54; European Parliament (1996a) *Briefing on the Common Foreign and Security Policy*, JF/bo/103/96, Luxembourg, March; Smith, M.E. (1998a) 'What's Wrong with the CFSP? The Politics of Institutional Reform' in P-H. Laurent and M. Maresceau (eds) *The State of the European Union: Volume 4*, Boulder and London: Lynne Rienner, pp. 149-75.
[40] The severest criticism has been levelled at the Union's performance over the conflict in the former Yugoslavia. See Kintis, A.G. (1997) 'The EU's Foreign Policy and the War in the Former Yugoslavia' in M. Holland (ed.) *Common Foreign and Security Policy: The Record and Reforms*, London and Washington: Pinter, pp. 148-73.
[41] Peterson J. and Sjursen, H. (1998) op. cit., p. 167.
[42] Christopher Hill, for instance, contends that displays of solidarity among the member states have 'instrumental value', demonstrating to prospective candidates and third countries the strength of the *acquis politique*. Hill, C. (1997) 'The Actors Involved: National Perspectives' in E. Regelsberger, P. de Schoutheete de Tervarent and W. Wessels, *Foreign Policy of the European Union: From EPC to CFSP and Beyond*, Boulder: Lynne Rienner, p. 88.
[43] Müller-Brandeck-Bocquet, G. (2002) 'The New CFSP and ESDP Decision-Making System of the European Union', *European Foreign Affairs Review*, Vol. 7, No. 3, p. 262.
[44] Hill, C. (1997), op. cit., p. 86; Stavridis, S. (1997) 'The Common Foreign and Security Policy: Why Institutional Arrangements Are Not Enough' in S. Stavridis, E. Mossialos, R. Morgan and H. Machin (eds) *New Challenges to the European Union: Policies and Policy-Making*, Aldershot: Dartmouth, p. 103.
[45] Allen, D. (1996) 'Conclusions: The European Rescue of National Foreign Policy' in C. Hill (ed.) *The Actors In Europe's Foreign Policy*, London and New York: Routledge, p. 296.
[46] See Hill, C. (1998a) 'Convergence, Divergence and Dialectics' in J. Zielonka (ed.) op. cit, p. 45.
[47] Hill, C. (1998b) 'Closing the Capabilities-Expectations Gap?' in J. Peterson and H. Sjursen (eds) op. cit., p. 18.
[48] On the problems of conceptualising EU foreign policy see Ginsberg, R. (1999) 'Conceptualising the European Union as an International Actor: Narrowing the Theoretical Capabilities-Expectations Gap', *Journal of Common Market Studies*, Vol. 37, No. 2, pp. 439-54. See also Smith, H. (1995) *European Union Foreign Policy and Central America*,

London: Macmillan, p. 17; Hill, C. and Wallace W. (1996) 'Introduction: Actors and actions' in C. Hill (ed.) *The Actors in Europe's Foreign Policy*, London: Routledge, p. 2; Soetendorp, B. (1994) 'The Evolution of the EC/EU as a Single Foreign Policy Actor' in W. Carlsnaes and S. Smith (eds) op. cit., pp. 103-19; Smith, H. (1998) 'The EU in Latin and Central America' in J. Peterson and H. Sjursen (eds) *A Common Foreign Policy for Europe? Competing Visions of the CFSP*, London: Routledge, p. 153; Soetendorp, B. (1999) *Foreign Policy in the European Union: Theory, History and Practice*, London and New York: Longman; Smith, H. (2002) *European Union Foreign Policy: What it is and What it Does*, London: Pluto, esp. pp. 1-29.

[49] Weiler, J.H.H. and Wessels, W. (1988) 'EPC and the Challenge of Theory' in A. Pijpers, E. Regelsberger and W. Wessels (eds) *European Political Cooperation in 1980s: A Common Foreign Policy for Western Europe?*, Dordrecht: Martinus Nijhoff, pp. 229-57; Jorgensen, K.E. (1993) 'EC External Relations as a Theoretical Challenge: Theories, Concepts and Trends' in F.R. Pfetsch (ed.) *International Relations and Pan Europe: Theoretical Approaches and Empirical Findings*, Munster: Campus Verlag, p. 212.

[50] Hill, C. (1993) 'The Capability-Expectations Gap, or Conceptualising Europe's International Role', *Journal of Common Market Studies*, Vol. 31, No. 3, p. 306.

[51] On this point, see Ginsberg, R. (1999), op. cit., p. 24.

[52] Kissinger, H. (1994) *Diplomacy*, New York and London: Simon and Schuster.

[53] Grieco, J. (1988) 'Anarchy and the Limits of Cooperation: A Realist Critique of the Newest Liberal Institutionalism', *International Organization*, Vol. 42, No.3, p. 487.

[54] Mearsheimer, J. (1990) 'Back to the Future: Instability in Europe After the Cold War', *International Security*, Vol. 15, No. 1, pp. 5-56; Waltz, K. (1993) 'The Emerging Structure of International Politics', *International Security*, Vol. 18, No. 2, pp. 44-79.

[55] Waltz, K. (1986) 'Anarchic Orders and Balances of Power' in R.O. Keohane (ed.) *Neorealism and its Critics*, New York: Columbia Press, p. 104.

[56] Baldwin, D.A. (1993) 'Neoliberalism, Neorealism and World Politics' in D.A. Baldwin (ed.) *Neorealism and Neoliberalism: The Contemporary Debate*, New York: Columbia University Press, p. 6. For a sharp critique of the distribution of power argument in the context of contemporary European integration, see Hoffmann, S. (1995) op. cit., pp. 281-300.

[57] Pijpers, A. (1991) 'European Political Cooperation and the Realist Paradigm' in M. Holland (ed.) *The Future of European Political Cooperation: Essays on Theory and Practice*, Basingstoke: Macmillan, p. 21.

[58] On the theoretical implications of EPC's institutionalisation, see Smith, M.E. (1998b) 'Rules, Transgovernmentalism and the Expansion of European Political Cooperation' in W. Sandholtz and A. Stone Sweet (eds) op. cit., pp. 305-333.

[59] Ginsberg, R. (1999), op. cit.

[60] Moravcsik, A. (1998) *The Choice for Europe: Social Purpose and State Power from Messina to Maastricht*, London: UCL Press, p. 18. A more general theory of the relationship between domestic interests and international bargaining is offered by Putnam, R. (1988) 'Diplomacy and Domestic Politics: The Logic of Two-level Games', *International Organization*, Vol. 42, No. 3, pp. 427-460. The two-level game analogy is usefully applied to EPC by Simon Bulmer. See Bulmer, S. (1991) 'Analysing EPC: The Case for Two-tier Analysis' in M. Holland (ed.) op. cit., pp. 70-91. On governmental demand for international institutions, see also the collection of essays in Ruggie, J-G. (1993) (ed.) *Multilateralism Matters: The Theory and Praxis of an Institutional Form*, New York: Columbia University Press.

[61] Moravcsik, A., Ibid., p. 206.

[62] Moravcsik, A. (1993) 'Preferences and Power in the International Community: A Liberal Intergovernmentalist Approach', *Journal of Common Market Studies*, Vol. 31, No. 4, p. 495.

[63] Keohane, R.O. and Hoffmann, S. (1989) 'Institutional Change in Europe in the 1980s' in R.O. Keohane and S. Hoffmann (eds) *The New European Community: Decision-Making and Institutional Change*, Boulder and Oxford: Westview, esp. pp. 10-15. A classic work on regime theory is Krasner, S.D (1983) *International Regimes*, Ithaca (NY): Cornell University Press.

[64] Keohane, R.O and Hoffmann, S. (1989) ibid., p. 28; Keohane, R.O. (1993) 'Institutional Theory and the Realist Challenge After the Cold War' in D.A. Baldwin (ed.) *Neorealism and Neoliberalism: The Contemporary Debate*, New York: Columbia University Press, p. 286; Hoffmann, S. (1995), op. cit., p. 290.

[65] Keohane, R.O. and Hoffmann, S. (1989), Ibid, p. 13.

[66] Bulmer, S. (1994) 'The Governance of the European Union: A New Institutionalist Approach', *Journal of Public Policy*, Vol. 13, No. 4, pp. 351-80; Garrett, G. and Tsebelis, G. (1996) 'An Institutionalist Critique of Intergovernmentalism', *International Organization*, Vol. 50, No. 2, pp. 269-99; Pollack, M. (1997) 'Delegation, Agency and Agenda-Setting in the European Union', *International Organization*, Vol. 51, No.1, pp. 99-134; Armstrong, K. and Bulmer, S. (1998) *The Governance of the Single European Market*, Manchester: Manchester University Press. Much of the institutionalist literature takes inspiration from early theoretical work which sought to explain European integration using 'neo-functionalist' theory. The usefulness of neo-functionalism itself in explaining the evolution of EU external policy seems limited, except insofar as it highlights the relative lack of social demand within Europe for coherent external policy. For example, one treatment with strong neo-functionalist overtones argues that 'though some argue for the political benefits that CFSP would bring, few societal transactors find its absence costly'. See Stone Sweet, A. and Sandholtz, W. (1997) 'European Integration and Supranational Governance', *Journal of European Public Policy*, Vol. 4, No. 3, p. 309.

[67] Smith, M.E. (1998b) op. cit., p. 310.

[68] In this respect, Wolfgang Wessels' 'fusion thesis' of the European integration process might be a useful point of departure in the search for a 'middle range' theory of EU foreign policy. However, Wessels himself is unsure how to approach the CFSP which, although it has 'some kind of binding character and further impact', does not fit the normal criteria of public policy with which his theory is concerned (p. 276). Wessels, W. (1997) 'An Ever Closer Fusion? A Dynamic Macro-political View on Integration Processes', *Journal of Common Market Studies*, Vol. 35, No. 2.

[69] Sjostedt, G. (1977) *The External Role of the European Community*, Farnborough: Saxon House; Allen, D. and Smith, M. (1990) 'Western Europe's Presence in the Contemporary International Arena', *Review of International Studies*, Vol. 16, No. 1, pp. 19-37; Hill, C. (1990) 'European Foreign Policy: Power Bloc, Civilian Model or Flop?' in R. Rummel (ed.), op. cit., pp. 31-55. Smith, M. (1996) 'The EU as an International Actor' in J.J. Richardson (ed.) *European Union: Power and Policy-Making*, London: Routledge, pp. 247-62.

[70] Allen, D. and Smith, M. (1990) Ibid, p. 21.

[71] Hill, C. (1998) 'Closing the capabilities-expectations gap?' in J. Peterson and H. Sjursen (eds) *A Common Foreign Policy for Europe? Competing Visions of the CFSP*, London: Routledge.

72 Ibid., p. 26.
73 See Peterson, J. and Bomberg, E. (1999), op. cit., pp. 238-9; 250-1.
74 Hill, C. (1993) op. cit.; Hill, C. (1998), op. cit.
75 For a variety of perspectives on the idea of civilian power Europe, see Bull, H. (1982) 'Civilian Power Europe: A Contradiction in Terms?', *Journal of Common Market Studies*, Vol. 21, No.1, pp. 149-70; Hill, C. (1990) 'European Foreign Policy: Power Bloc, Civilian Model or Flop?' in R. Rummel (ed.) *The Evolution of an International Actor: Western Europe's New Assertiveness*, Boulder and Oxford: Westview, pp. 31-55; Rummel, R. (1997) 'The CFSP's Conflict Prevention Policy' in M. Holland (ed.) *Common Foreign and Security Policy: The Record and Reforms*, London: Pinter; Zielonka, J. (1998) *Explaining Euro-paralysis: Why Europe is Unable to Act in International Politics*, Basingstoke: Macmillan, esp. pp. 226-9; Whitman, R. (1998) *From Civilian Power to Superpower? The International Identity of the European Union*, Basingstoke: Macmillan.
76 Zielonka, J. (1998), op. cit., p. 227.
77 Stavridis, S. (2001) '"Militarising" the EU: The Concept of Civilian Power Europe Revisited', *The International Spectator*, Vol. 36, No. 4, p. 50.
78 Ibid., p. 229.
79 Northedge, F.S. (ed.) (1969) *The Foreign Policy of the Powers*, London: Faber and Faber, p. 28; White, B. (1989) 'Analysing Foreign Policy: Problems and Approaches' in M. Clarke and B. White (eds) *Understanding Foreign Policy: The Foreign Policy Systems Approach*, Aldershot: Edward Elgar, p. 6. Both the works cited above distinguish policy by design from the daily activities in which foreign ministries are engaged.
80 Keohane, R.O. and Hoffmann, S. (1993) 'Conclusions: Structure, Strategy and International Roles' in R.O. Keohane, J.S. Nye and S. Hoffmann (eds) *After the Cold War: International Institutions and State Strategies in Europe, 1989-1991*, Cambridge (MA): Harvard University Press, p. 393.
81 Allen, D. (1998), op. cit., p. 46.
82 Ginsberg, R. (1989) op. cit., p. 120.
83 White, B. (1989), op. cit, p. 1; Smith, S. (1994) 'Foreign Policy Theory and the New Europe' in W. Carlsnaes and S. Smith (eds) op. cit., pp. 1-20; Allen, D. (1998) op. cit., p. 44.
84 White, B. (2001) op. cit., p. 36.
85 Ibid., p. 40.
86 This section heavily draws on Roy Ginsberg's model of European foreign policy decision making. See Ginsberg, R. (1999) op. cit. The FPA literature is replete with systems analyses of national foreign policy-making systems. Many proceed from the classic and lucid work of David Easton's original framework. See Easton, D. (1965) *A Framework for Political Analysis*, Englewood Cliffs: Prentice-Hall.
87 Soetendorp, B. (1999) op. cit., pp. 11-12.
88 Delors, J. (1990) 'Europe's Ambition', *Foreign Policy*, No. 180, Autumn, pp. 14-27.
89 Heisbourg, F. (2000) 'Europe's strategic ambitions: The limits of ambiguity', *Survival*, Vol. 42, No. 2, p. 5.
90 Scharpf, F. (1988) 'The Joint-Decision Trap: Lessons from German Federalism and European Integration', *Public Administration*, Vol. 66, No. 3, pp. 239-78; Friis, L. (1997) *When Europe Negotiates: From Europe Agreements to Eastern Enlargement*, Copenhagen: Institute of Political Science, p. 82.

[91] The preamble to the Single European Act (1986), for instance, talks about the need to protect Europe's independence, promote democracy, compliance with the law and human rights.
[92] Spencer, C. (2001) 'The EU and Common Strategies: The Revealing Case of the Mediterranean', *European Foreign Affairs Review*, Vol. 6, No. 1, p. 43.
[93] Young, A. (1998) op. cit., p.1.
[94] Wistrich, E. (1992) *After 1992: The United States of Europe*, London: Routledge, p.121.
[95] Wallace, H. (1983) 'Negotiation, Conflict and Compromise: The Elusive Pursuit of Common Policies' in H. Wallace, W. Wallace and C. Webb (eds) *Policy Making in the European Community* (2$^{nd}$ edition), Chichester: John Wiley and Sons, p. 52.
[96] Wallace, H. (1996a) 'Politics and Policy in the EU: The Challenge of Governance' in H. Wallace and W. Wallace (eds) *Policy Making in the European Union*, Oxford: Oxford University Press, p. 30; Friis, L. (1997) *When Europe Negotiates: From Europe Agreements to Eastern Enlargement*, Copenhagen: Institute of Political Science, p. 6; Smith, M. (1998) op. cit, p. 80.
[97] Smith, M. (1998), op. cit., pp. 83-4.
[98] Ibid., p. 84.
[99] Wallace, H. (1996a), op. cit., pp. 32-3.
[100] The 'inside-outside game' metaphor is taken from Likke Friis' excellent study of the negotiation of the Europe Agreements with the Central and Eastern European accession candidates. The term 'game' is something of a misnomer, since it implies a game theoretical approach to negotiation analysis. Friis instead uses the game metaphor as the basis for a model of the policy-making process, but stops short of the quantitative analysis usually associated with that method. Friis, L. (1997) op. cit., p. 65.
[101] Smith, M. (1996) 'The European Union and a Changing Europe: Establishing the Boundaries of Order', *Journal of Common Market Studies*, Vol. 43, No. 1, pp. 5-28; Friis, L. and Murphy, A. (1999) 'The European Union and Central and Eastern Europe: Governance and Boundaries', *Journal of Common Market Studies*, Vol. 37, No. 2, pp. 211-32.

Chapter 2

# A Brief History of EU Mediterranean Policy

**Introduction**

The Euro-Mediterranean Partnership initiative cannot be understood without first considering the historical evolution of the EU's relations with the Mediterranean non-member countries. The Euro-Mediterranean Agreements were essentially repackaged and upgraded versions of agreements negotiated during the early years of EU Mediterranean policy. Issues that were politicised in the first rounds of negotiations, such as agricultural import quotas, have tended to remain politicized, creating a 'shadow of the past' in which contemporary negotiators and policy-makers must operate.[1] When policy change did take place, it occurred mainly through renegotiation and the adaptation of existing policy instruments. The purpose of this chapter is to trace the main patterns of negotiation and associative diplomacy that shaped and re-shaped Mediterranean policy over the course of three decades.

A key measure of the effectiveness of Mediterranean policy is its impact on trade. For the majority of Mediterranean third countries, western Europe has long been the most important source of imports and destination for exports, a legacy of the colonial period. As a result, access to the European market has always been a primary concern, and disputes over the terms offered by the Community became a recurring feature of each round of negotiations. The distributive outcomes of trade concessions usually resulted in immediate, identifiable costs to be borne by domestic producers within the member states, and a quantifiable and comparable 'deal' for each associate. With clear internal and external winners and losers from the agreements, any attempt to build a strategy for the region was invariably subordinated to the defence of domestic interests by individual member states, as well as to the limitations on concessionary diplomacy imposed by the CAP and other Community policies. The history of Mediterranean policy, as this chapter sets out to demonstrate, is one of an absence of effective strategic action on the part of the EU.

Section one outlines the formative phase of the EU's relations with the Mediterranean partners and the main determinants of the Community's choice of policy instruments. Section two evaluates the first major policy development in the 1970s – the Global Mediterranean Policy (GMP) – and discusses the politics behind the Community's first attempt to develop a comprehensive policy framework for the region. Section three assesses how the Community adapted its Mediterranean policy at the time of the accession of Greece, Portugal and Spain during the 1980s. It argues that this third phase of Mediterranean policy was more concerned with managing the impact of accession on EU policies and satisfying the interests of the member states than with making the adjustments needed to offset the negative impact of enlargement on third countries.

**A Slow Start: The Treaty of Rome and the Patchwork of Associates**

The Treaty of Rome (1957) contained no formal foreign policy provisions and offered little stimulus for the definition and pursuit of common external interests and objectives. The Community was equipped with a limited range of explicit powers, scattered throughout the founding treaties, to develop relations with the outside world. Furthermore, there were considerable uncertainties about the distribution of competencies between the institutions and the member states. On the one hand, key features of external policy that were to emerge later – including development policy and cooperation on politico-security matters — remained the responsibility of the member states. On the other hand, the Community had responsibility for the regulation of external trade through the Common Commercial Policy (Article 133) harnessed to a Common External Tariff, the right to conclude treaties, and the power to manage the externalities' of internal policies.[2] It was left to political and economic exigencies, and the judgements of the ECJ, to incrementally define the parameters of Community external policy.

The Community had several motives for seeking to draw the Mediterranean third countries towards it during the 1960s. The first of these was the strategic importance of the Mediterranean region to the Western camp in the context of the Cold War. Indeed, for Habib Ben Yahia, Tunisia's Foreign Minister, 'the north's interest in the southern shore has always been about security.'[3] Attention primarily focused on security in the north east Mediterranean, while the Maghreb was seen more as a problem for France than a military problem for the 'West'.[4] Yet both regions were sufficiently close to the Community to pose serious security problems were they to become hostile.

Commercial ties between the Six and the Mediterranean non-members linked to imperial trading patterns were a second imperative for a Community Mediterranean policy. In 1960, the Mediterranean non-member countries as a group (including Portugal and Spain) absorbed over 15 per cent of Community exports. In turn, over 60 per cent of the exports of Mediterranean third countries went to the Community. South-north trade was dominated by the agricultural and energy sectors.[5] Unprocessed agricultural exports to the Community were a vital source of export revenues for countries such as Morocco and Tunisia. On the EC side, the member states, particularly France and Italy, exported manufactured and capital goods to the Mediterranean countries.

The prime mover on Mediterranean policy was France, which dominated Community trade in the region. In the early 1960s it accounted for 40 per cent of exports to the Maghreb and received around 45 per cent of Maghrebi imports to the Community, as well as benefiting from a strong commercial presence in the region through a mixture of private and public investment. De Gaulle's government sought to protect French economic interests when responsibility for commercial policy shifted to the EEC. Moreover, rapid economic growth in the 1960s meant a growing demand for North African labour in France. Taking these factors together it was clear that, initially at least, Community policy would be driven by Paris.

Lacking the policy instruments to pursue a comprehensive policy strategy for the region, the EEC's relations with Mediterranean third countries instead evolved in what Stanley Henig accurately described as 'a doctrinal vacuum'.[6] Since the Treaty of Rome gave only vague directions as to how relations with the Mediterranean third countries should evolve, it was relatively easy for the Community to avoid making substantive commitments. As governments lined up to establish formal relations with the Community, it responded with a mixture of Association Agreements with Greece, Malta and Turkey, special preferential commercial arrangements for France's former colonies in North Africa, and a series of commercial accords with the remainder of the Mediterranean non-member countries. The result was a 'pyramid' of agreements based on differentiated commercial and political privileges.[7] The choice of one form of agreement over another and the emergence of a hierarchy of more and less favoured third countries reflected the economic and political priorities of the member states and, albeit in a very limited and disparate way, the identification and defence of certain Community interests in the region.

The most comprehensive policy instrument proved to be full association, based on Article 310. The provisions of Article 310 left open the goals, form and content of agreements, stating only that association should involve 'reciprocal rights and obligations, common action and special procedures'. In theory, association was therefore flexible enough to accommodate both the demands of third countries and the numerous limitations imposed by the political and economic situation inside the Community, although finding a mutually acceptable balance was usually difficult.[8] Association Agreements, and variants of them, were to become the instrument of choice in Mediterranean policy.

The precise terms of association were a function of the strategic and commercial importance of the associate to the Community and, arguably, to its cultural proximity to western Europe. As John Redmond puts it, at best, association was a 'stepping stone to full membership; at worst, a poor relation to membership'.[9] Greece and Turkey concluded Association Agreements in 1962 and 1963 respectively as the Community sought to prevent the two countries from falling into the hands of the communist bloc. Both the agreements, of unlimited duration, were to lead to full customs unions over transitional periods of between 12 and 22 years, and both states had their eligibility for membership recognized.[10] But Greece was offered a clear timetable for membership and more generous commercial terms – including higher import quotas – than those offered to Turkey. The Community was also studiously imprecise about the timing and end-state of Turkey-EEC integration. With its self-professed European vocation, small population and relatively small economy, Greek accession was both a more attractive and a less problematic proposition.[11]

The second kind of association, based on articles 182-7 of the Treaty, was designed to safeguard the 'special' relationships of the member states with their dependencies, principally the Francophone African countries. These provisions gave rise to the 1963 Yaoundé Convention which gave duty and quota free access to the Community's markets for a range of exports from former colonies, and financial aid worth 800 Million ECU. However, although the Article 182 provisions were dressed up in the rhetoric of economic development, their main purposes were to protect imports of cheap primary products and maintain the privileged position of colonial imports in home markets.[12] For non-members, preferential trading arrangements partly offset the economic cost of the Community's customs union.[13] The chief advocate of Article 182 was France, which made special arrangements for its overseas territories a condition of its decision to sign the Treaty of Rome.[14] As Gobe argues, 'she [France] developed the idea of Euro-Africa, which allowed her to implement towards the old colonies a policy she could not work out herself.'[15] The multilateralization of colonial economic relations spread the costs of continuing to support the territories by 'Europeanising' reduced tariffs on imports among the six.

The third policy instrument for the Mediterranean, earmarked for the states of the CFA franc zone, was an alternative form of economic association. Although it too was based on Article 310, this form of association did not include financial aid, technical assistance and provisions for the free movement of workers. In effect, it was a half-way house between a simple trade agreement and full association. Having conceded to French pressure to include Article 182 in the Treaty of Rome, the other member states were more circumspect about granting similar status to the Mediterranean non-member states.[16] The message was clear: for various reasons, these states were of secondary importance to the Community and would have to wait to have their status upgraded.

From the outset, the member states were in a strong position to determine the form, content and terms of associations. The decision-making procedure entitled the Council of Ministers to approve the Commission's negotiating mandate, required unanimity in the Council to conclude agreements, and subjected the agreements to ratification by national parliaments.[17] Furthermore, associations usually covered several subjects outside the Community's exclusive remit, requiring 'mixed' agreements in which both the Community and the member states participated as legal parties.[18] Even where the Community possessed exclusive competence to conclude agreements (Article 133), *de facto* use of unanimity to approve the Commission's negotiating mandates and the oversight function of the Council enabled the member states to keep the Commission on a tight rein.[19]

Morocco and Tunisia were the first Mediterranean states to take up the offer of economic association, opening negotiations with the Community in 1965. However, they quickly ran into opposition from Italy, which embarked on a 'three year long filibuster' in defence of its agricultural industry.[20] Southern Italian agriculture, particularly the citrus fruit industry, was in a weak position in the mid

1960s and faced direct competition from Moroccan and Tunisian imports of Mediterranean products. Concessions in this sector were therefore a highly sensitive issue for the Italian government. Crucially, France – the chief ally of the Maghreb states within the Community – chose 1965 to walk out of the Council in the infamous 'Empty Chair' crisis. Much of the Council's business was suspended and Morocco and Tunisia found themselves sidelined during 1965 and 1966. When the talks resumed at the end of 1966, lengthy internal negotiations were required to find a compromise satisfactory to the Italian government. A combination of compensatory measures for Italian farmers and intensive diplomacy by Commission officials and the Maghrebi ambassadors to the Community finally persuaded Italy to accept the agreements.[21]

Underlying the member states' hesitancy over the Association Agreements were more fundamental differences over the Community's approach to economic development policy. In the protectionist camp, France advocated a regionalist approach to EC external relations, favouring privileged treatment for a restricted group of third countries which would in turn safeguard French commercial interests. The Netherlands and West Germany, by contrast, argued for a 'single international cooperative movement in line with the liberalising agenda of the GATT.'[22] The Federal Republic adopted a global view of the Community's development policy, befitting its lack of colonial ties and the relative lack of competition to its own agricultural sector from imports of Mediterranean products.[23] Subsequent enlargements of the Community would accentuate these divergent approaches and make the development of a coherent strategic approach a remote prospect.

On the external front, the conclusion of preferential trading agreements provoked criticism from both non-associates and the USA. Non-associates claimed that preferential terms of trade for associates discriminated against their exporters. The USA had sought the dismantling of imperial preferences since the end of the second world war.[24] But the Community stood firm and sought waivers where the agreements contravened GATT principles.[25]

A major problem for the Community at this juncture in the 1960s was to obtain the approval of Morocco and Tunisia for a deal that fell short of their expectations. Despite having resorted to the lowest-common denominator to win the assent of all the member states to the accords, the Community could not ignore the fact that it had invited the two states to apply for full association. The solution was a clause in the agreements stating that they;

> appear clearly as a first step towards more global accords to be concluded later...do not preclude the maintenance of preferential commercial relations with France...and are able to be rapidly implemented.[26]

It is important, however, not to over-state either the politicisation of key issues in this first round of agreements or the political importance of Mediterranean policy in general. In a detailed study of the Maghreb negotiations, Glenda Rosenthal found 'little solid evidence of the effective exercise of public opinion and interest group pressures in the negotiation of the Maghreb treaties. Primarily, the conclusion of the Maghreb agreements was a strictly EEC-Maghreb affair and involved almost no external pressures'.[27] In the overall scheme of the European integration process, Mediterranean policy was a low priority at this stage.

The end product of the Community's first phase of associative diplomacy in the Mediterranean resembled a 'patchwork' rather than a coherent, purposive network. As Eberhard Rhein argues:

> The Community handled the association relationship as if it were a formal, rather superficial international agreement. It did not really care what was going on behind the scenes, what economic and social policies were being pursued.[28]

Nevertheless, the agreements sparked a 'chain reaction' among other Mediterranean countries which sought to enter into new agreements, or upgrade their existing relationships, with the Community.[29] As the list of *demandeurs* grew, the Community was forced to rethink its approach.

## From Patchwork to Framework: The Global Mediterranean Policy

The 1970s saw the first noteworthy attempt to formulate a strategy for the region. It occurred during a period when the Community was making serious efforts to establish its credentials as an international actor. At the 1969 Hague Summit, EC member governments agreed to improve the coordination of their individual foreign policies, a process which included discussion of the Community's common external interests. In 1970, the launch of European Political Cooperation gave rise to the first inter-governmental meetings at which the member states set out to identify the Community's political interests and prepare the ground for future foreign policy positions. At the 1972 Paris Summit, the member states duly resolved to ensure 'an overall and balanced handling' of the Community's relations with the Mediterranean third countries, and instructed the Commission to look again at the Association Agreements.[30]

The Commission responded by submitting proposals to the Council for a new policy framework – the Global Mediterranean Policy (GMP) – centring on 'Cooperation Agreements' that covered financial, technical and social matters as well as the expansion of the geographical scope of the associative network. The long-term objective was the creation of a Mediterranean free-trade area.[31] To increase competition in the region and boost exports, France proposed that the associates should open up their markets to Community exports. However, the Commission argued that the free-circulation of goods alone would not promote development in the region, and that the GMP should also include provisions on capital movements, technology transfers, technical cooperation, labour, environmental and financial cooperation.[32]

External events appeared to play a much more prominent part in shaping Mediterranean policy during this period than had previously been the case. First, unity among the developing countries, expressed in demands by the G77 for a new and more benevolent international economic order, put the Community's relations with developing countries under the spotlight.[33] For third countries subject to Article 182 of the Treaty, the Community responded with the Lomé convention in 1975. In turn, greater equity was demanded between the level of commercial privileges granted to the African associates and those offered to the Community's other partners.[34]

Second, the 1973 Arab-Israeli war and the subsequent Arab oil embargo compelled the Community to look at the political dimension of its Mediterranean policy. Although these events occurred after the launch of the GMP, the OPEC embargo exposed the vulnerability of the Community's petroleum supplies and demanded rapid diplomatic action from the member states. Their response – the Euro-Arab Dialogue – was the first explicitly political form of association.[35] It established a forum for diplomatic exchanges between the Community and the Arab League at ministerial and civil-servant level on issues ranging from the status of the Palestinian Liberation Organisation and Israeli foreign policy to cultural, social and technological collaboration. Even if the 'Dialogue' proved to be essentially gesture politics, it at least signalled that the Community recognized the increased political salience of good relations with Mediterranean non-member states.

The Arab-Israeli conflict presented the Community with a problem of a different order. The Community's commitment to negotiate agreements with any Mediterranean country that applied or requested one left it facing a delicate political balancing act between its policies towards the Arab states and its relationship with Israel. Condemnation of Israel's occupation of Gaza and the West Bank by the member states through the EPC mechanism sat uneasily alongside the ongoing discussion of a new Cooperation Agreement with the Community. The lack of obvious linkage between the Community's criticism of Israel's policies and its 'routine' external economic relations with Israel exemplified the inconsistency of Community foreign policy-making.

Internally, several factors paved the way for a more comprehensive Mediterranean policy. First, the Commission took a more prominent role in setting the agenda on Mediterranean policy. It attempted to sell to the member states the idea that the economic development of the Mediterranean – the long term goal of the GMP – was 'a natural extension of European integration'.[36] In doing so, the Commission stood to have its own powers as policy initiator and negotiator augmented, since the GMP called for the scope of Community action to be expanded.[37] The pay off for the Community would be improved coordination of policy and, arguably, a clearer sense of purpose in the areas covered by the Cooperation Agreements.

Second, the early 1970s witnessed a subtle but important shift in French foreign policy. De Gaulle's resignation and the legacy of the war in Algeria precipitated the gradual reform of France's relations with its former colonies in North Africa, although it continued to claim special responsibility for the region. As far as Community policy was concerned, France adopted a more favourable attitude to the multilateralization of its own economic and political relations with

Mediterranean third countries while seeking to retain its status as a dominant influence on the policy.[38]

Third, the 1973 enlargement of the Community necessitated adjustments to the existing Association Agreements and, perhaps more importantly, tilted the scales towards the northern liberalizers. Adaptation measures were attached to each agreement in order to extend the Mediterranean preference system to Denmark, Ireland and the UK.[39] Despite being dressed up as 'technical' negotiations by the Commission, a number of Mediterranean associates used the talks to express their dissatisfaction with the terms of their agreements. Community imports of Moroccan oranges, for instance, had fallen by eight per cent between 1970 and 1972, provoking complaints of protectionism from Moroccan diplomats in Brussels.[40] Non-associates argued that the implementation of preferential trade provisions by the new member states would adversely affect their trade with those countries. This problem further strengthened the case for a uniform association system across the region.

The accession of Denmark, the UK and Ireland brought three states into the Community which faced no significant competition from Mediterranean imports and had comparatively fewer direct interests in Mediterranean policy than France and Italy. As Alfred Tovias argues, 'they did not share the Commission's desire to create a sphere of influence there, even questioning at times the need for a Mediterranean policy at all.'[41] Also, West Germany found in the UK a powerful ally for its campaign to open up the Community's markets to Mediterranean imports. The progression of the GMP proposals through the Council was impeded by an increasingly bitter dispute between free-traders and protectionists.[42] By June 1973, the Council had draft negotiating mandates for the Cooperation Agreements. The principal commitments of the GMP are shown in Figure 2.1.

A cursory glance suggests that the GMP fulfilled the Community's promises. The agreements included provisions for cooperation in a variety of fields, including the environment, industry, investment and science. On the particularly sensitive subject of the movement of labour, existing bilateral arrangements on the treatment and status of Maghrebi workers in the Community were supplemented by a new agreement on non-discrimination and the equal treatment of workers.[43] Pension rights were to be made transferable between EC countries, and remittances of pensions and other payments to countries of origin were to be allowed. The creation of Cooperation Councils gave the agreements an institutional structure to facilitate regular political exchanges between the Community and associates and to deal with implementation problems when they arose.

The enhanced scope of the agreements also met some of the Community's key strategic interests, though these were not necessarily expressed in policy documents. Most notably, the provisions for cooperation in the energy sector aimed to 'foster participation by Community firms in programmes for the exploration, production and processing of energy resources and to ensure that long term contracts for the delivery of petroleum products are properly performed'.[44]

> i) Barriers to trade in industrial products, with the exception of textiles and refined petroleum, to be removed by July 1 1977.
> ii) Improved access to the Community for Maghrebi agricultural exports, 'without endangering the legitimate interests of the member states'.[45] Reduction of customs duties by 20-80 per cent according to the product and time of year.
> iii) Development aid – described as financial and technical cooperation – would be attached to each agreement in financial protocols. This bilateral aid would be supplemented by loans and grants from the EC budget and European Investment Bank (EIB).
> iv) Individual Cooperation Councils and Committees for each agreement bringing together representatives from the Commission, member states and individual non-member governments.

**Figure 2.1 Main Commitments of the Global Mediterranean Policy**

For the more economically advanced Mediterranean states, the GMP undoubtedly drew them closer to the Community. To varying degrees, Greece, Portugal and Spain, as well as Malta and Turkey, had their European vocations confirmed.[46]

However, beneath the surface, the deep-rooted asymmetry of Euro-Mediterranean relations was barely addressed. The idea of free-trade foundered in the face of differences among the member states about the balance between preferential treatment and liberalisation. The eventual compromise upheld the principle of reciprocity, but allowed differentiation among the Mediterranean associates on a case-by-case basis, removing suggestions of uniformity in the GMP.

Concessions on agricultural trade again required protracted internal negotiations before an offer could be made to the third countries. The Italian government, for instance, mounted a campaign in the Council for additional protection for its producers before it would accept any new concessions to the Maghreb states. In the absence of progress, the Community had to resort to temporary agreements, since the first generation of accords expired in 1974. A second round of talks was held in October and November 1974, but the Community's revised offer on agricultural trade met with a lukewarm response.[47] Existing arrangements were extended as the talks laboriously progressed through the minutiae of concessions on citrus fruits, olive oil, tomato concentrates and wine. The introduction of the CAP had only served to increase the politicisation of agriculture and the Community had to negotiate from a position even less flexible than had been the case in the 1960s.

Momentum was finally injected into the negotiating process in April 1975 when the Council agreed a series of so-called 'market organisation measures' for the most contentious sectors, which subsequently freed the Commission to re-commence negotiations.[48] The new measures were essentially defensive, installing safeguard measures against imports of the so-called 'sensitive' products.[49] Tariff concessions ranged from 30-100 per cent and covered 86-89 per cent of agricultural exports, an average tariff reduction of 30-40 per cent for Tunisian and

Morocco imports over the 1969 accords.[50] But new quantitative restrictions were also applied to wines, tinned sardines, potatoes, oranges and tomatoes. Taken collectively, these products ranked among the most valuable exports for the Mediterranean non-member countries.

Beyond agricultural trade, quantitative import ceilings were introduced on refined petroleum products above which punitive duties would apply. The Community was anxious to guarantee uninterrupted supplies of oil and gas, but was less keen to encourage the development of potentially competitive indigenous processing industries in the associate countries. Trade in textiles, a sector in which Morocco, Egypt and Tunisia had a clear comparative advantage over Community manufacturers, was totally excluded from the agreements and subject to voluntary export restraints.[51] Effective lobbying by European textile manufacturers and the already stiff competition faced by the industry from external sources ruled out any possibility of preferential treatment for textile imports.

The new agreements were undoubtedly more comprehensive than the earlier trade agreements, but the underlying pattern of the EC's relations with the Mediterranean non-members remained: qualified and limited assistance, with member states insisting on derogations and protective measures when the interests of domestic producers were threatened.[52] From the associates' point of view, the agreements failed to take into account the commercial, cultural and historical specificities of their relationships with the Community. Put simply, the accords merely perpetuated economic dependence.

Roy Ginsberg describes the GMP as 'the first successful attempt by the EC at a self styled foreign policy'.[53] Eberhard Rhein, a former Director General in the Commission's DG1, sees it as the 'first example of a coherent piece of Community foreign policy'.[54] However, while the GMP undoubtedly brought a sense of structure to the Community's relations with the Mediterranean associates, it failed to change either the bilateral basis of the policy or the underlying asymmetry of economic relations. The limited scope of the GMP is thrown into sharp relief even when compared to the 1963 Yaoundé and 1975 Lomé Conventions, which created an elaborate system of market access, a development fund of 1 billion ECUs (Lomé) and an institutional structure that included a consultative assembly and a council of ministers. As the Community contemplated enlarging to the south, the inadequacies of the GMP became increasingly apparent.

**Table 2.1 The Mediterranean Network After the Global Mediterranean Policy**

| Country | Date of Agreement | Type of Agreement |
|---|---|---|
| Algeria | April 1976 | Cooperation |
| Cyprus | December 1972 | Association |
| Egypt | January 1977 | Cooperation |
| Greece | November 1962 | Association |

| Country | Date of Agreement | Type of Agreement |
|---|---|---|
| Israel[55] | May 1975 | Free trade / Cooperation |
| Jordan | January 1977 | Cooperation |
| Lebanon | May 1976 | Cooperation |
| Malta | December 1970 | Association |
| Morocco | April 1976 | Cooperation |
| Syria | January 1977 | Cooperation |
| Tunisia | April 1976 | Cooperation |
| Turkey | September 1963 | Association |
| Yugoslavia | April 1970 | Trade |

**Southern Enlargement: Managing Internal Change**

The accession of Greece (1981), Portugal (1986) and Spain (1986) to the Community marked a distinct phase of Mediterranean policy in its own right. On the economic front, southern enlargement had major implications for the Community's internal market in Mediterranean-type agricultural products. With significant overlap between the production structures of the three new member states and those of the Mediterranean non-members, the potential and actual trade diversion effects of enlargement represented a further challenge to the developmental objectives of the GMP. On the political front, the Community absorbed three states with an extensive range of commercial and political interests in the region. The emergence of a Mediterranean 'group' within the EC promised to even up the balance of power between northern and southern member states

At the start of the 1980s, the economies of many of the Mediterranean associates were in a parlous state. Rapid economic growth in the early to mid 1970s was followed by stagnation and rising external indebtedness as import substitution strategies and indigenous economic development policies faltered. By 1979, the aggregate trade deficit of the Mediterranean third countries with the EC stood at nine billion ECU compared with four billion ECU in 1973.[56] Notwithstanding exogenous factors – the global oil price shocks, commodity price collapses and the global recession, the Cooperation Agreements had manifestly failed to ameliorate economic conditions in the non-member countries.

Even before enlargement, the margin of preference for the Mediterranean associates in relation to those states with no preferential trade deal from the Community had fallen by a third as a result of global tariff reductions in the Kennedy Round of the GATT.[57] Import volumes of tomatoes, Morocco's most important agricultural export, fell every year between 1978 and 1983 provoking protests from the Moroccan delegation in Brussels that subsidised Community production was putting its farmers out of business.[58] Heinz was forced to close a tomato concentrates factory in Morocco as the Community's defensive 'market organisation measures' took effect.[59] Employment opportunities for migrant workers were also hit by the recession, which in turn diminished income from migrant workers' remittances.[60]

The Community entered the 1980s ill prepared for the effect that southern enlargement would have on the GMP. Not until 1979 was a detailed study of its potential impact on the GMP produced.[61] A key finding of the report was that the Community's self-sufficiency ratio in most Mediterranean agricultural products would rise from between 80-90 per cent to a situation of surplus. Spanish accession alone was projected to raise Community vegetable production by 25 per cent, fresh fruit by 48 per cent and olive oil by 59 per cent, threatening to displace Maghrebi imports of these products.[62] Morocco and Tunisia stood to lose the most. The Tunisian agricultural sector, for instance, was heavily dependent on exports of olive oil (50 per cent of its total agricultural exports) but the entry of Greece and Spain threatened to devastate the industry. The report also predicted that Cyprus, Malta, Israel and Turkey would suffer net falls in their trade with the EC.[63]

The associates demanded the renegotiation of certain clauses in the agreements that would increase import quotas in order to offset the trade displacing effects of free access to the Community market for Portuguese and Spanish goods.[64] France, still committed to preserving its special import regime for cheap Moroccan and Tunisian agricultural exports to the Community, offered strong support for revising the agreements so as to offset the trade displacement effects of enlargement.[65]

The Commission tried to deal with the renegotiation as a set of 'technical' issues in order to depoliticise any trade concessions and give itself the maximum possible flexibility to put an acceptable package together. The proposed deal was based on two measures. First, in the event of changes in the volume of agricultural production, the Community undertook to proportionately adjust market access for the associates. Import volumes would therefore rise and fall with trends in internal production. At the same time, the Community pledged Community assistance to reduce the associates' growing dependency on food imports, another consequence of the failure of economic self-reliance strategies. Second, the Community aimed to reduce customs duties and tariffs in a number of particularly sensitive sectors such as processed foodstuffs, petrochemicals and textiles.

Yet again, however, the major battles over the terms of the 'protocols' on agricultural trade were fought in the Council as member states' interests collided. As Crouzatier argues, 'enlargement brought home to the northern partners the specific difficulties of the Mediterranean economy, and accentuated internal discord within the Community over the correct policy to pursue for the region'.[66] The Iberian member states quickly situated themselves in the protectionist camp. Spain, backed by Italy, put pressure on the Council to withhold its approval of the Commission's negotiating mandate until after the entry of the Iberians into the Community. This ad-hoc alliance ensured that the Mediterranean member states as a group would carry extra weight to block additional trade concessions in the post-accession period.

The negotiations resulted in a compromise between the Spanish government and the Commission that restricted future imports of Mediterranean agricultural products to 'traditional exports', thus reducing the associates' scope for product diversification and limiting the potential for competition with European producers.[67] Quotas were calculated on the basis of production levels between 1980 and 1984, a period of severe drought in the Maghreb and therefore an atypical production period. On a more positive note, customs duties were gradually reduced over a transitional period of ten years from 1986 in parallel with the transitional period for Portugal and Spain. Mandates for the Commission to negotiate protocols to the existing Cooperation Agreements were approved by the Council in November 1985.[68] Greek, Portuguese and Spanish tariffs on many products were phased out incrementally, and removed altogether by 1996. The CAP's reference price system for Mediterranean products, a measure which discriminated against lower priced imports, was also to be abolished by 1996. However, the reference price was simply replaced by a countervailing charge on exports above quota limits. This combination of factors prompted an angry reaction from Rabat and Tunis and demands for compensation in the form of financial aid.[69] Extra funds were provided in the fourth financial protocols (1987-1991), but the total increase of 20 per cent for the whole region failed to appease the associates.

The economies of the Mediterranean associates continued to weaken during the 1980s, despite modest growth in trade with the Community. As imports rose, export revenues failed to deliver sufficient coverage rates, trade deficits rose and external debts rapidly grew, leading to increased pressure for unpopular reforms demanded by the IMF.[70] A powerful indication of the growing dissatisfaction of the Mediterranean countries was Morocco's application for Community membership, made in July 1987.[71] The failure of the GMP and the apparent inability of the Community to reform its Mediterranean policy provoked Rabat into what was more a sign of frustration than a serious attempt to join.[72] By the end of the decade, the case for wholesale policy reform was strong.

## Conclusions

What this brief history of Mediterranean policy shows is the centrality of trade in the development of Euro-Mediterranean relations. The foundation for the policy was the management of trade relations with Mediterranean third countries and the preservation of import/export patterns inherited from the colonial period. To the extent that policy objectives existed, they were initially driven by the commercial interests of the member states and, in the cases of Greece and Turkey, by wider Cold War strategic considerations.

When the first set of agreements were absorbed into the GMP, the Union's ambitious rhetoric far exceeded the reality of the deal it offered the Mediterranean non-member countries. It is difficult to avoid the conclusion that the advancement of economic development in the Mediterranean was simply not a priority for the Community, and that economic self-interest dictated that it preserve the overall balance of its trade relations with the non-member states. Association and Cooperation Agreements tended to sustain the 'North-South' character of the relationship and the economic status quo left by colonialism. Furthermore, the first generation of Association Agreements hardly justified the label 'Mediterranean policy', accomplishing little more than the codification of existing terms of trade. The weak bargaining power of the Mediterranean third countries left them with little choice other than to accept the deals that the Community offered.

The reasons for the Community's conservatism lay in the defensive positions adopted by the southern member states and in the protectionist bias of the Common Agricultural Policy. Agriculture was repeatedly the most contentious issue in negotiations, politicized from the outset by the Italian government, and later by France, Portugal and Spain. Recurring arguments about agricultural trade reflected the similarity of the production structures of the southern member states and the non-members. The Community was faced with a conflict between the need to safeguard the interests of European producers and the recognition that market access for non-member countries had to be improved. It was a conflict that it consistently proved incapable of resolving.

## Notes

[1] Friis, L. (1997) *When Europe Negotiates: From Europe Agreements to Eastern Enlargement*, Copenhagen: Institute of Political Science, p. 80.

[2] See Lasok, D. (1994) *Law and Institutions of the European Union*, 6$^{th}$ Edition, London: Butterworth and Co., especially. pp. 57-66.

[3] Ben Yahia, H. (1993) 'Security and Stability in the Mediterranean: Regional and International Changes', *Mediterranean Quarterly*, Vol. 4, No. 1, p. 2.

[4] Joffé, G. (1994) 'The European Union and the Maghreb' in Gillespie, R (ed.), *Mediterranean Politics: Volume 1*, London: Pinter, p. 25.

[5] For detailed statistical analyses of Euro-Mediterranean trade, see Bensidoun, I. and Chevallier, A. (1996) *Europe-Méditerranée: Le pari de l'ouverture*, Paris: Economica; Ayari, C. (1992) *Enjeux Méditerranéens: Pour une coopération euro-arabe*, Paris: CNRS.

[6] Henig, S. (1976) 'Mediterranean Policy in the Context of the External Relations of the European Community, 1958-73' in A. Shlaim and G.E. Yannopoulos (eds) *The EEC and the Mediterranean Countries*, Cambridge: Cambridge University Press, p. 305.

[7] Hugon, P. (1993) 'L'Europe et le tiers monde: entre la mondialisation et la régionalisation', *Revue Tiers Monde*, Vol. 34, No. 136, p. 729.

[8] Feld, W.J. (1965) 'The Association Agreements of the European Communities: A Comparative Analysis', *International Organization*, Vol. 19, p. 228.

[9] Redmond, J. (1994) 'Introduction' in J. Redmond (ed.) *Prospective Europeans: New Members for European Union*, Hemel Hempstead: Harvester Wheatsheaf, p. 7.

[10] For a good account of the diplomacy behind Greece's association agreement, see Siotis, J. (1981) 'The Politics of Greek Accession' in G. Minet, J. Siotis and P. Tsakaloyannis (eds) *The Mediterranean Challenge: VI*, Brighton: Sussex European Research Centre, pp. 85-120.

[11] The costs of the Greek agreement worried several member states, which argued that it should not serve as the model for similar accords with other states. See Coffey, P. (1976) *The External Economic Relations of the EEC*, London: Macmillan, p. 18.

[12] The relevant articles established the procedures for establishing customs unions with the associates. They included provisions on Community investment, rights of establishment and the mutual protection of workers' rights.

[13] Pomfret, R. (1992) 'The European Community's Relations with the Mediterranean Countries' in J. Redmond (ed.) *The External Relations of the European Community*, Basingstoke: Macmillan, p. 79.

[14] Grosser, A. (1963) 'General De Gaulle and the Foreign Policy of the Fifth Republic', *International Affairs*, Vol. 39, No. 2; Babarinde, O. (1998) 'The European Union's Relations with the South: A Commitment to Development?' in C. Rhodes (ed.) *The European Union in the World Community*, Boulder and London: Lynne Rienner, p. 129; Matthews, J.D. (1977) *Association System of the European Community*, New York: Praeger, p. 13.

[15] Gobe, E. (1992) 'The Maghreb in Contemporary French Politics', *Journal of Arab Affairs*, Vol. 11, No. 2, p. 135.

[16] Rosenthal, G.G. (1975) *The Men Behind the Decisions: Cases in European Policy-Making*, Lexington, USA: DC Heath and Company, p. 49.

[17] Until the Single European Act, the Council only had to consult the European Parliament when concluding agreements with third parties. The Single European Act gave the Parliament the power of assent for Article 310 agreements.

[18] For a comprehensive analysis of mixed agreements, see Weiler, J.H.H. (1983) 'The External Legal Relations of Non-unitary Actors: Mixity and the Federal Principle' in D. O'Keefe and H.G.Schermers (eds) *Mixed Agreements*, London: Kluwer, pp. 35-83.

[19] In practice, those elements of association agreements subject to Article 133 procedures were often implemented in advance of ratification of the full agreement (Article 310 procedures) by the national parliaments.

[20] Rosenthal, G.G. (1975), op. cit., p. 55.

[21] The Italian government secured a) Side payments of 18 million ECU from the European Agricultural Fund to improve production of olive oil and citrus fruits, two sectors in which Morocco and Tunisia enjoyed a comparative advantage over Italy. b) A 'price cushion' for citrus products that could not be extended to countries outside the Mediterranean region.

[22] Guazzone, L. (1990) 'The Mediterranean Basin', *The International Spectator*, Vol. 25, No. 4, p. 301. In Italy's case, its demand for across the board negotiations owed more to its fear that product by product deals with each associate would gradually whittle away the market shares of its own producers than any wish to extend the association concept to the whole region or to join the liberalisation camp.

[23] Ibid., p. 301.

[24] Matthews, L. (1977) op. cit., p. 63.

[25] In 1967, for instance, the Community was forced to seek a waiver under Article 25 of the GATT after extending the citrus fruit importing system established in the Maghreb association accords to Israel and Spain. The extension would not directly lead to the creation of a customs union or free-trade area, so conflicted with GATT provisions.

[26] Secrétariat des Conseils des Communautés Européennes (1969) *12ème Aperçu des Activités des Conseils*, Aug 1968-July 1969, p. 137.

[27] Rosenthal, G.G. (1975) op. cit., p. 60.

[28] Rhein, E. (1992) 'The Community's External Reach' in R. Rummel (ed.) *Toward Political Union: Planning a Common Foreign and Security Policy in the EC*, Boulder, USA and Oxford: Westview, p. 32.

[29] Lambert, J. (1971-2) 'The Cheshire cat and the pond: EEC and the Mediterranean area', *Journal of Common Market Studies*, Vol. 10, No. 1, p. 43.

30  Bulletin of the European Communities, EC 10-1972, pp. 20-1.
31  Gobe, E. (1992) op. cit., p. 135.
32  Crouzatier, J. (1988) *Géopolitique de la Méditerranée*, Paris: Publisud, p. 207.
33  The G77 was established by the less-developed countries of Africa, Asia and Latin America to articulate their demands in the international system. One of their main demands was for commercial preferences as opposed to the GATT's rule of equal treatment regardless of the level of economic development.
34  Shlaim, A. (1976) 'The Community and the Mediterranean Basin', in K.J. Twitchett (ed.) *Europe and the World: The External Relations of the Common Market*, London: Europa Publications, p. 82.
35  A comprehensive account of the Euro-Arab dialogue is provided by Bourrinet, J. (1979) *Le Dialogue Euro-Arabe*, Paris: L'Harmattan. For an Arab perspective, see Saleh, A. (1983) *The Euro-Arab Dialogue: A Study in Associative Diplomacy*, London: Pinter.
36  Grilli, E.R. (1993) *The European Community and the Developing Countries*, Cambridge: Cambridge University Press, p. 186.
37  The European Court of Justice's 1971 ERTA ruling, and subsequent ECJ opinions, took an expansive view of the Community's external powers. The Court ruled, *inter alia*, that the Community could enter into formal, contractual relations with non-member countries across all the objectives set out in part one of the EEC Treaty.
38  Gobe, E. (1992), op. cit., p. 135.
39  Bulletin of the European Communities, EC 2-1973, p. 61.
40  'Morocco' (1973) *Africa Contemporary Record*, Volume 5, London: Rex Collings, London and New York: Africana Publishing Corporation, p. B82.
41  Tovias, A. (1996) 'The EU's Mediterranean policies under pressure' in R. Gillespie (ed.) *Mediterranean Politics, Volume 2*, London: Pinter, p. 10.
42  Levi, M. (1972) 'La C.E.E. et les pays de la Méditerranée', *Politique Etrangère*, Vol. 37, No. 6, p. 808.
43  Rosenthal, G.G. (1982) *The Mediterranean Basin: Its Political Economy and Changing International Relations*, London: Butterworth Scientific, p. 26.
44  Bulletin of the European Communities, EC1-1976, p. 15.
45  Bulletin of the European Communties, EC10-1972, p. 21.
46  The democratisation of Greece, Portugal and Spain during the 1970s opened the door to their membership of the Community.
47  Bulletin of the European Communities, EC11-1974, p. 79.
48  Official Journal of the European Communities, OJL198, 29 July 1975.
49  Bulletin of the European Communities, EC 4-1975, p. 75.
50  Bulletin of the European Communities, EC1-1976, pp. 15-16. The concessions were based on the level of self-sufficiency in the Community for each product and were limited to 'off-season' imports.
51  Fridhi, N. and Quatremer, J. (1996) *Le Nouvel Espace Economique Euro-Méditerranéen*, Brussels: Club de Bruxelles, p. 12.
52  A good summary of the GMP is provided by Renier, Y. (1988) 'L'Europe et le sud de la Méditerranée', *Le Courrier*, No. 108, Brussels: Economic and Social Committee of the European Communities, March/April, pp. 53-57.
53  Ginsberg, R.H. (1989) *Foreign Policy Actions of the Community: The Politics of Scale*, Boulder, Colorado: Lynne Rienner Publishers and London: Admantine Press, p. 120.
54  Rhein, E. (1992) op. cit., p. 33.

⁵⁵ Israel's advanced state of economic development compared to the other Mediterranean associates put it on a different footing with the Community. Moves towards a free trade agreement between the two began in 1964, and concluded with the agreement of 1975.
⁵⁶ Minasi, N. (1998) 'The Euro-Mediterranean Free Trade Area and its Impact on the Economies Involved', *Jean Monnet Working Papers in Comparative and International Politics*, JMWP 16.98, Catania: University of Catania, http://www.fscpo.unict.it/vademec/jmwp16.htm, p. 2.
⁵⁷ Pomfret, R. (1992) op. cit., p. 78.
⁵⁸ Sutton, M. (1989) 'Economic aspects of Morocco's relations with Europe' in G. Joffé (ed.) *Morocco and Europe*, Occasional Paper 7, London: School of Oriental and African Studies, p. 29.
⁵⁹ Ibid., p. 29.
⁶⁰ Emigrant remittances were equivalent to 50 per cent of Morocco's total export earnings in the mid 1980s.
⁶¹ European Commission (1979) *Report on the Global Mediterranean Policy and Enlargement of the Community*, SEC 79/103, April.
⁶² European Commission (1979) op. cit., p. 6; European Parliament (1988) (Committee on External Economic Relations) *Report on Economic and Trade Relations Between the EEC and the Mediterranean Countries Following Enlargement of the Community*, A2-325/88, December, p. 11.
⁶³ European Commission (1979), op. cit., p. 12.
⁶⁴ Cova, C. (1985) 'La politique communautaire en faveur de la zone méditerranéenne', *Revue du Marché Commune*, No. 291, pp. 525.
⁶⁵ Tovias, A. (1996) op. cit., p. 12.
⁶⁶ Crouzatier, J. (1988), op. cit., p. 202.
⁶⁷ Tovias, A. (1990) *Foreign Economic Relations of the European Community: The Impact of Spain and Portugal*, London: Lynne Rienner Publishers, pp. 79-80.
⁶⁸ Bulletin EC11-1985, point 2.3.16, p. 87.
⁶⁹ For a Maghrebi perspective on this issue, see Sid Ahmed, A. (1993) 'Les relations économiques entre l'Europe et le Maghreb', *Revue Tiers Monde*, Vol. 34, No. 136, Oct-Dec, pp. 759-780; Mezdour, S. (1993) 'Les desequilibres economicos en economie ouverte (cas du Maghreb)', *Revue Algérienne des Sciences Juridiques, Economiques et Politiques*, Vol. 31, No. 3, pp. 511-529.
⁷⁰ Spencer, C. (1993) *The Maghreb in the 1990s: Political and Economic Developments in Algeria, Morocco and Tunisia*, Adelphi Paper No. 274, London: International Institute for Strategic Studies, February, p. 17. A good analysis of the economic problems faced by the Mediterranean non-member countries is provided by Bourrinet, J. (1994) 'Aspects économiques: trios défis majeurs pour la cooperation' in J. Bourrinet (ed.) *La Méditerranée: Espace de Coopération*, Centre d'Etudes et de Recherches Internationales et Communautaires, Université d'Aix-Marseilles III, Paris: Economica, pp. 201-217. For detailed statistics, see Ayari, C. (1992) op. cit., esp. pp. 198-9.
⁷¹ Marks, J. (1989) ' The Concept of Morocco in Europe' in G. Joffé (ed.) *Morocco and Europe*, Occasional Paper 7, London: School of Oriental and African Studies, p. 14.
⁷² Bahaijoub, A. (1993) 'Morocco's argument to join the EC' in G. Joffé (ed.) *North Africa: Nation, State and Region*, London: Routledge, pp. 235-246.

Chapter 3

# Old Wine in New Bottles? The Renovated Mediterranean Policy and the Euro-Mediterranean Agreements

**Introduction**

The end of the 1980s saw the emergence of a clearer strategic imperative for EU Mediterranean policy. The fragile economic situations in several North African and Middle Eastern states became increasingly apparent as spiralling external debts and unpopular austerity measures further exposed the weaknesses of incumbent governments and underlying social problems that their policies were failing to address. Iraq's invasion of Kuwait in 1990 and the brief conflict that followed provoked renewed anxiety in Europe about the security of energy supplies from the Middle East. Projections of substantial population growth in North African and Middle Eastern states sparked fears about the potential for an upsurge in illegal immigration into the EU. Linked together, this new set of threat perceptions persuaded key players in the Union of the need to devise policies that were targeted at the root causes of instability. Minor policy changes were initially agreed, but they were followed by an extensive repackaging exercise that culminated in the Euro-Mediterranean Partnership (EMP) and a third generation of bilateral agreements (the Euro-Mediterranean Agreements). The Union's impressive-sounding objective was to turn the Mediterranean into an area of 'peace, stability and prosperity'.[1]

This chapter charts the rise of Mediterranean policy up the EU's foreign policy agenda and the main steps in the development of the EMP. Section one shows how the major stimuli for change were both internal and external, a combination of concerns about the risks of instability in the Maghreb and Mashreq, the higher salience attached to Mediterranean security in the aftermath of the Cold War and political pressure from southern member states. Section two assesses the Renewed Mediterranean Policy (RMP), the largely ineffectual outcome of the Union's attempt to upgrade its relationships with the Mediterranean third countries.[2] Section three discusses the origins of the Euro-Mediterranean Partnership and outlines its key features. The final section examines some of the main problems that arose during the negotiation of the Euro-Mediterranean Association Agreements, the principal policy instrument attached to the EMP.[3] The design of the agreements and the Union's handling of the negotiations were indicative of the gap between its ability to identify strategic objectives and the means to pursue them on paper, and its capacity to deliver effective policies.

## The Changing Definition of Mediterranean Security

The sudden political transformation of Europe in 1989 had a profound impact on both the EU's external environment and its internal order. Its instinctive reaction to this geo-strategic upheaval was to turn to its eastern boundary and begin considering ways to bring back the CEECs into the European fold.[4] Although the Union initially failed to come up with a coherent eastern strategy, it did take the lead in starting the process of economic and political transition in the region. At the same time, however, awareness was growing of the vulnerability of the EU's 'soft underbelly'.[5] With the uneasy balancing effect of US-Soviet competition removed, the challenges of Mediterranean security and the limited political influence of European states in the region were thrown into sharp relief. Nevertheless, the EU found itself expected to assume a bigger share of the responsibility for security in its own back yard, a role it was ill-equipped to perform.

For Mediterranean non-member countries, developments at the end of the 1980s reinforced their sense of marginalization in the international economic and political order. Fearing that they would be overlooked in East-West *rapprochement*, several governments issued warnings about the risks of social and political instability and future conflicts if the widening prosperity gap between North and South was not addressed.[6] Morocco's unsuccessful application for EU membership in 1987, for instance, could be interpreted as a plea for a more equitable economic relationship.[7] States whose economies were already under severe strain were faced with the prospect of being crowded out in the allocation of financial aid, foreign direct investment and other resources to central and eastern Europe. The message to western Europe was simple but powerful: the neglect of its Mediterranean neighbours was no longer sustainable.

A brief analysis of trade and debt statistics for 1989 highlights the gravity of the problems facing much of North Africa and the Middle East. External debts rose throughout the decade on the back of dramatic falls in oil revenues, the global collapse of commodity prices and the failure of domestic economic policies.[8] In 1989, the total external debt of the Maghreb states stood at 41 billion ECUs, while that of the Mashreq countries stood at 53 billion ECUs, figures that represented between 18 and 40 per cent of GNP.[9] For Algeria, debt repayments amounted to 70 per cent of export receipts; for Morocco 45 per cent.

The Mediterranean debt crisis underlined the need for any reform of EU policy to confront the structural asymmetry of its relationships with the non-member states. Sporadic popular demonstrations across the Maghreb in 1988, partly a reaction to austerity measures imposed by the IMF, served as an uncomfortable reminder of the difficulties associated with political reform and economic liberalisation in the region.[10] National governments and private banks in western Europe were collectively the biggest creditors of Mediterranean countries, accounting for around 50 per cent of the region's total debt.[11] A strong case arguably existed for improved coordination among European creditors and the EU was identified as a potential locus for such coordination. Tentative suggestions were made that a new Mediterranean financial institution should be established to channel macro-economic assistance to third countries. Yet the Union had no explicit powers in the Treaties to formulate common policies on the debt issue. Nor was any meaningful political initiative taken by the member states to bring together public and private creditors to consider either substantial restructuring or the writing off of debts. Collective action on an issue of critical importance was therefore excluded from the ambit of Mediterranean policy.

**Table 3.1 Debt Statistics for the Mediterranean Associates**

| Country | 1980 Debt/GNP (%) | 1989 Debt/GNP (%) | 1980 Debt/Exports * (%) | 1989 Debt/Exports * (%) |
|---|---|---|---|---|
| Cyprus | 25.0 | 47.0 | 49.0 | 82.0 |
| Maghreb | 47.2 | 74.9 | 150.1 | 237.9 |
| Malta | 8.8 | 20.7 | 9.1 | 24.3 |
| Mashreq | 52.0 | 102.7 | 110.0 | 229.3 |
| Turkey | 34.3 | 53.8 | 332.9 | 189.8 |

* Earnings from exports of goods and services.
No figures quoted for Israel. Debt stood at 19 billion ECUs in 1989.

*Sources*: World Bank (1996) *World Debt Tables*; Ayari, C. (1992) *Enjeux Méditerranéens: Pour Une Coopération Euro-Arabe*, Paris: CNRS, p. 199.

The Union's trade policy in the Mediterranean was another obvious target for criticism. Despite the association and cooperation agreements and a modest overall expansion of commercial activity during the 1980s, trade with the EU clearly failed to act as a motor for economic growth in most of the associate countries. Indeed, the non-members' share of total EU imports declined from 11 per cent in 1980 to 8.2 per cent by 1988, as trade with the Far East and other trading partners gained ground. Table 3.2 shows that the Union's trade surplus with the Mediterranean non-members decreased only marginally – from 3.2 billion ECUs in 1980 to 2.8 billion ECUs in 1989. As European economies slipped into recession in 1990 a further contraction of trade was expected and the long-standing issue of improving market access assumed greater significance.

However, there seemed little prospect in the early 1990s of an improvement in the trading position of the partner countries. Further erosion of selective trade preferences – a means to protect established markets and trade patterns – through measures agreed in the Uruguay Round of the GATT process led

**Table 3.2 Trade with the EU (Million ECUs) (1980-1989)**

| Country | Imports 1980 | Imports 1989 | Exports 1980 | Exports 1989 |
|---|---|---|---|---|
| Algeria | 4435 | 5848 | 5093 | 4715 |
| Cyprus | 269 | 524 | 601 | 1438 |
| Egypt | 2385 | 2441 | 3397 | 3764 |
| Israel | 1660 | 3197 | 1719 | 5101 |
| Jordan | 21 | 102 | 760 | 905 |
| Lebanon | 45 | 101 | 1139 | 829 |
| Libya* | 7478 | 6304 | 4530 | 2911 |
| Malta | 253 | 568 | 503 | 1064 |
| Morocco | 1356 | 2674 | 1764 | 3226 |
| Syria | 969 | 775 | 1400 | 780 |
| Tunisia | 1380 | 1980 | 1684 | 2531 |
| Turkey | 1053 | 5536 | 1917 | 5609 |
| TOTAL | 21304 | 30050 | 24507 | 32873 |

* Libya, though it did not have 'associate' status, is included in the table because of the sizeable volume of its trade with the EU.

*Source*: Data extrapolated from Eurostat, various publications.

observers to predict stagnation rather than growth. Businesses in the mediterranean third countries would face increased competition for European markets and capital. As Henri Regnault put it, 'when we prefer the whole world, we no longer prefer anyone'.[12] Projections made during the Uruguay Round suggested that the non-members' trade revenue would contract by 510 million ECUs once the Round was completed.[13] Coupled with the effects of liberalisation programmes demanded by international creditors, the pace and direction of global economic change was outstripping the capacity of governments to implement reforms. They looked to the EU for assistance, including help with economic restructuring, small business and financial market development, and the modernisation of production facilities.[14] Conversely, if the Union was to protect its dominant economic position, some form of 'deepened regionalism' seemed to be the most appropriate method of binding Mediterranean states to it.[15] That concept implied improved terms of trade, an expansion in the number of issues covered by formal agreements and measures to encourage closer political relations.

The consequences of the Single European Market (SEM) also had to be factored into the Mediterranean economic equation. For the Union's trading partners, the potential trade creating effects of the 1992 project were likely to be outweighed by its diversionary effects on trade and investment.[16] Studies predicted that any expansion of imports into the EU from the single market initiative would centre on manufactured goods rather than primary commodities'.[17] Those states that were experiencing modest success in developing manufactured export sectors, such as Morocco, Tunisia and Turkey, might benefit from the SEM. But there were serious concerns that the single market project would generate new import barriers, lead to a further contraction of trade preferences, create additional disincentives to already slow rates of inward FDI, and impose tighter and more strictly policed rules of origin.[18] Ahead of the 1992 deadline, the Union felt it necessary to issue assurances that its Mediterranean trading partners would not be sidelined. Commissioner Abel Matutes claimed that 'we have a vital interest in being open to imports and being able to export to the rest of the world. The risks of the Community being closed to the rest of the world when it completes the single market in 1992 are non-existent'.[19]

The Union's attention to the poor economic performance of the partner countries must also be attributed to perceptions about the potential political and social fallout. Since the 1960s, economic growth had lagged far behind rapid population expansion in the Maghreb, Mashreq and Turkey, resulting in a significant drop in GDP per capita from 1974-1990.[20] In 1990, per capita GDP in the EU stood at 16,500 ECUs, while in the Maghreb and Mashreq countries it stood at less than 1,500 ECUs.[21] With economies (and governments) unable to generate sufficient employment to keep up with the demand for work from burgeoning young populations, pressure built up behind a number of safety valves, of which migration and the possibility of radical challenges to 'friendly' governments had the most far reaching implications.[22] Several studies had identified the potential for an upsurge in illegal immigration, particularly from the Maghreb and South East Europe.[23] As a former Moroccan ambassador to the UK put it, 'if we want to keep people in our country, we have to find a way to give them jobs'.[24]

For many EU member states, and for Middle Eastern and North African governments, the growing popularity of Islamic opposition movements across the region was regarded as a new 'threat' to security. France, for instance, identified the rapid expansion of militant Islamic organisations as one of its key foreign policy challenges of the 1990s.[25] Young unemployed people, particularly in the poorest areas of major urban centres, were increasingly turning to Islamic movements which offered appealing ideological visions and a challenge to the inequities generated by western domination of the global economy. The paring back of welfare states and disillusionment with the lost ideals of the post-independence period provided fertile ground for radical alternatives to the existing order.

The Union's response to the rising popularity of Islamic groups had to be carefully measured. On the one hand, large populations of Muslims in France, Germany and the UK made relations with the Islamic world as much an internal issue as an external one for member governments.[26] Considerable pent-up hostility existed towards a 'West' that proclaimed its support for democratisation and pursued it in foreign policies while at the same time using its influence to prevent Islamic opposition movements coming to power. On the other hand, many regimes in North Africa and the Middle East enjoyed the overt support or tacit approval of EU member states and the west in their anxiety to safeguard commercial and political interests. Furthermore, as Cold War armoury started to be dispersed in the former Soviet Union, it was feared that 'rogue' governments or Islamic groups hostile to the West might illicitly acquire chemical, biological or nuclear weapons. Anti-government violence might in turn trigger unrest in western Europe, with Islamic activists exploiting links between groups on both sides of the Mediterranean and their ability to operate inside an EU whose borders were becoming increasingly porous.

This combination of destabilising economic, political and social forces in the Mediterranean pointed to the need for a multi-dimensional, holistic approach to regional security, consistent with a broader trend evident in the security studies literature towards re-defining the concept of security itself.[27] Policies would have to encompass, *inter alia,* cultural, economic, environmental and social issues – and address the interdependency of the factors influencing security.[28] As Barry Buzan argues, economic underdevelopment and poverty were causal factors in the type of social disorder that might threaten the stability of failing states.[29] Weak, insecure states were in turn more inclined to resort to violence in the face of perceived or real threats and challenge the prevailing international order.

The shift of emphasis from traditional politico-military security towards soft security implied a more prominent role for organisations with very broad remits, such as the EU, the OSCE and the United Nations, and an increase in activities that brought governments and non-governmental organisations together to address common problems. A 1990 UN General Assembly resolution, for example, invited governments, regional organisations and sub-regional groupings to submit to the Secretary General ideas and suggests for intensified cooperation across a variety of fields.[30] The changing agenda of NATO indicated how deeply this new thinking had penetrated. The 'Strategic Concept' agreed by the North Atlantic Council in 1991 called for 'interlocking institutions' that would pursue a 'broad approach to security'.[31] It referred to the political, economic, social and environmental elements of security and to the need for 'complementary' action by the OSCE and the European Community.

The Mediterranean region at the turn of the decade appeared to be an ideal test of the capacity of the EU's external policy-making system to apply the concept of soft security. From the point of view of the EU and its member states, the socio-economic and political signals emanating from the region were providing a stream of largely negative policy feedback and creating a strong case for policy change.[32] The apparently diminishing relevance of traditional balance of power politics and military capability after 1989 brought renewed interest in the notion of the Union as a benevolent 'civilian superpower', contributing financial aid and its functional expertise to the construction of a revised model of international relations. However, the extent to which the Union was capable of performing the role of benefactor again hinged on the willingness of the member states to sacrifice short-term political expediency for long-term strategic action. In broader terms, the policy discourse that developed around Mediterranean security tended to be long on rhetoric and short on substance, a problem not confined to the EU. Terminology such as 'co-development', 'cooperation' and 'dialogue' abounded without any clear sense either of how such concepts might be operationalized. Whether or not 'new security' would acquire more than superficial meaning remained to be seen.

## The Renewed Mediterranean Policy

With a former Spanish MP – Abel Matutes – taking charge of the Mediterranean brief from 1989, the EU's re-evaluation of its policy started with the Commission.[33] Matutes' approach was to work on the argument that Europe's security was inseparable from the prosperity and stability of the wider Mediterranean region.[34] Exploratory proposals were presented to the heads of government at the Strasbourg European Council in 1989. The paper acknowledged the poor economic performance of the majority of Mediterranean associates and highlighted their failure to meet the demand for jobs as a major threat to social stability.[35] The deteriorating quality of the Mediterranean environment, growing food shortages and chronic balance of payments deficits were also identified as issues which EU policy had to address.[36]

The European Parliament and the Economic and Social Committee (ESC) joined the debate at the tail end of 1989, calling for 'joint economic development', 'institutionalized economic integration' and more effective management and distribution of EU financial resources.[37] The ESC was especially critical of the member states, taking them to task for 'protectionist practices' and arguing that the most damage had been done by 'the inherent limits and contradictions of the Community's general Mediterranean strategy and by outstanding problems within the Community itself'.[38] It singled out the failure of the member states to open up their agricultural markets, pointing out the paradox that those governments with the most interest in Mediterranean security also tended to be the most protectionist.[39]

The Matutes document came before the Council at an opportune time. Spain and France held the Council gavel in 1989, while Italy took over in the second half of 1990, giving one of the EU's key agenda-setting venues a distinctly Mediterranean bias. As Alvaro de Vasconcelos argues, the region had become a 'common foreign policy priority' for France, Italy and Spain, whose foreign ministries had established a mechanism for regular consultations between their Political Directors.[40] In 1989, Italian Foreign Minister Gianni de Michelis demanded a wholesale rebalancing in the distribution of Community resources to the Central and Eastern European countries and the south, arguing that the Union should 'combine its aid policy to Eastern and to Mediterranean countries with each member country dedicating 0.25 per cent of its GNP to these two areas'.[41] In 1990, Spanish Foreign Minister Fernández Ordóñez called for a new regional security system based on economic development and inter-cultural dialogue. Together, this Mediterranean coalition ensured that the Commission's proposals were not lost in the EU's crowded agenda at this time. It also created a temporary political counterweight against those member states whose priorities lay to the east.

The outcome of Matutes' policy review was the Redirected Mediterranean Policy (RMP), a mixture of promises to improve the terms of the bilateral agreements, additional funding and new financial instruments (See below).[42]

- Revision of the 12 existing bilateral agreements with proposals to improve market access in a number of 'sensitive' sectors including agricultural products and textiles.

- A near tripling of funds from the Community budget and European Investment Bank to Mediterranean third countries in the fourth generation of financial protocols (1992-1996).

- A regulation providing 2.3 billion ECUs for 'decentralized, horizontal or regional cooperation'.[43] The proposed regulation earmarked 230 million ECU in budgetary funds, and 1.8 billion ECU in EIB funds, to be distributed in loans for regional projects in the following areas: inter-university programmes; assistance to small and medium-sized enterprises; joint local authority ventures; environmental projects (500 million ECU of the total, to which a 3 per cent interest rate subsidy would apply); demographic matters; investment creation; the 'cultural dimension of development'.

**Figure 3.1 Main Commitments of the Renewed Mediterranean Policy**

What were the strategic implications of the RMP? On the face of it, the decision to supplement the bilateral financial protocols with a new budget line for regional integration projects met several objectives. First, the low level of trade between the Mediterranean associates was widely regarded as an impediment to economic growth and the liberalisation process.[44] By offering financial incentives, the Union sought to kick-start cross-border economic activity. From its own point of view, a more favourable intra-regional trading environment would help cement the positions of European companies in the associates' markets and facilitate strategically important investments in the transnational oil and gas supply network linking the Maghreb to southern Europe.

Second, regional political integration, a predicted spin-off from economic integration, was seen as a positive development in the security context. As Elfriede Regelsberger argues, 'such developments are judged as stabilising factors in world politics, particularly where such trends are accompanied by internal political reforms in third countries centred on democratic values'.[45] In 1989, the five Maghreb states had launched their own regional organisation – the Arab Maghreb Union – modelled on the EU with joint decision making bodies and an agenda for functional cooperation on a wide range of issues.[46] Although the Union provided no direct financial assistance to the fledgling organisation, the regional integration funds were intended to contribute to cross-border diplomatic activity in the Maghreb.[47]

Third, with the Mediterranean aid budget up for re-negotiation and substantial claims on the Union's coffers from Central and Eastern Europe, the Commission had to make a watertight case in the Council to secure extra money for the Mediterranean. That the RMP earmarked financial aid for internal economic reforms persuaded sceptical northern member states, particularly Germany, to endorse the package, albeit with a 35 per cent cut in the figure originally requested.[48]

However, on closer inspection, the limitations of the new financial instrument were clear. The allocation of the funding was to be decided on a project specific basis, rather than as part of a pre-determined programme. Long delays in the approval of projects coupled with a poor take up rate of funding were persistent problems for the Commission, with available financial resources rarely being fully committed.[49] Promoting cooperation between Mediterranean NGOs – the civil society dimension of the RMP – relied on projects bypassing governments that were often suspicious of political activities outside the control of the state. The upshot was that the new measure had an impact only on very specific types of activity and few spin-off effects.

Other elements of the RMP proved equally disappointing. A Commission suggestion that the EU should coordinate debt policy unsurprisingly fell on deaf ears.[50] Member states were unwilling to stray from a system in which decision-making responsibilities rested with the multilateral financial institutions and collective management among the biggest creditor states in the G7/G10. Despite gestures by individual member states to unilaterally reduce the debt-servicing burden for Mediterranean countries, the Council chose to directly link assistance with debt servicing to the implementation of structural adjustment measures and economic reform programmes imposed by the IMF. Indeed, the segment of EU aid designated to support structural adjustment and macro-economic reforms was made conditional upon adherence to IMF programmes. The Union's only concession over this issue was its offer to provide money for projects in 'sectors particularly affected by structural adjustment'.[51]

On the trade front, the RMP inevitably ran into obstacles in the Council and the constraints associated with the ongoing GATT negotiations. Looming recession in Western Europe made the southern member states particularly sensitive to increased competition. Access for agricultural produce was only marginally improved by an agreement to bring forward by three years the tariff reductions promised after the end of Portugal and Spain's transitional periods. Morocco's Ambassador to the EU responded by delivering a strong rebuke to Brussels, deploring the 'timidity' of the Council's decisions.[52] Relaxation of textile import restrictions, another key sector for Mediterranean third countries, was forced on it by the Uruguay Round rather than by any altruistic intent. A Council decision of December 1990 to eliminate quantitative limits on textile imports simply pre-empted the abolition of the Multi-Fibre Agreement.[53] The overriding impression during this period was that the Union had more important internal and external priorities.

In hindsight, the RMP did little more than act as a legitimating device for increased aid to the Mediterranean. As an example of strategic thinking, it was afflicted with the same faults that impaired the GMP: the gap between policy objectives and concessions that the member states would sanction, the ineffectiveness of policy in addressing the structural asymmetry of Euro-Mediterranean economic relations, and the reliance on existing policy instruments which were manifestly failing to stimulate trade and investment. But the RMP at least ensured that Mediterranean policy stayed on the EU's external relations agenda at a time when the organisation was preoccupied with its own internal transition and with the rapidly evolving situation in eastern Europe. In a very limited way, the regional integration element could be seen as an attempt by the EU to put into practice the notion of soft security. This move to 'regionalise' Mediterranean policy was to be a building block of the Euro-Mediterranean Partnership.

**Towards a Euro-Mediterranean Partnership**

The Gulf crisis of 1990-1 provided a harsh reality check for European policy towards the Middle East and North Africa. The conflict left 'a gaping hole between the North and South' and reinforced the impression of the Union's powerlessness in the politico-security sphere.[54] Anti-war and anti-west demonstrations throughout the Arab world and in a number of European capitals alarmed the member governments, which feared a backlash against commercial interests in the region and hostility from Muslim citizens in Europe.[55] In particular, France's role in the coalition was viewed as tantamount to treason by its sizeable population of Arab immigrants, provoking mass demonstrations in Paris.[56] The burning of French flags during protests in Rabat had a profound psychological effect, prompting some commentators to observe that France had finally 'lost the Maghreb'.[57] One French *député* even called for a 'Marshall Plan for the Mediterranean'.[58] For some, the conflict presented the Union with an opportunity to put its relationship with the Arab world on a new footing.[59] However, as Christopher Piening argues, 'the Gulf crisis was of the sort that the EU was least able to deal with', demanding a rapid political response to Iraq's invasion of Kuwait as well as a nuanced position that took into account politico-cultural sensitivities in Euro-Arab relations.[60] Its failure to project a unified political position on the conflict and the participation of member states in the military campaign against Iraq in a US-led coalition undoubtedly damaged its credibility in the eyes of the Arab world.[61]

Only in the aftermath of the Gulf conflict did the Union's external relations machinery grind into motion. The immediate task was to 'desensitize' relations with the Arab countries, an assignment entrusted to the Troika (Italy, Luxembourg, The Netherlands), which embarked on a conciliatory tour of the region.[62] The ministers involved in the mission returned to Brussels with requests for substantial financial assistance to offset the loss of trade that resulted from the conflict.[63] Since the Union had already contributed 1.5 billion ECUs in balance of payments support to the 'front line' states in the conflict in August 1990, the only additional assistance it was prepared to offer was loan capital of 250 million ECUs to Israel and the Palestinian Territories to help rebuild communications and other infrastructure networks.[64] The Union's behaviour during this period was that of an irresolute organisation, unable to hide divisions among the member states over military action and unsure of how best to respond at the end of the conflict.

With no immediate prospect of mobilising the EU as a whole, the 'big three' southern EU member states – France, Spain and Italy – along with several non-member states explored other avenues for regional cooperation. The most ambitious of these was a Spanish/Italian proposal for a Conference on Security and Cooperation in the Mediterranean (CSCM), unveiled at a CSCE summit in Palma during September 1990. Modelled on the Helsinki agreement, the CSCM was to have the same wide-ranging remit as the CSCE, bringing together Mediterranean Arab states, Gulf states and EU member states.[65] Spain and Italy viewed the proposal primarily as a conflict prevention mechanism and a vehicle for multilateral dialogue between the Islamic world and the West.[66] However, the USA, which was left off the list of prospective CSCM members, dismissed the initiative as a thinly veiled attempt by the Europeans to challenge its position as the lynchpin of international security in the region. By mid-1992, the proposal had dropped off the CSCE agenda, replaced instead by a vague offer to 'exchange information' with Mediterranean states.[67]

An alternative route was followed by France, which favoured a narrower sub-regional approach centred on North Africa and the western Mediterranean, its traditional *chasse gardée*. In December 1990, it launched an initiative to instigate political dialogue between five northern Mediterranean states and the five states of the AMU. The '5+5' process was formally launched at a conference of Foreign Ministers in Rome. The agreement provided for annual meetings between Foreign Ministers, and established several working groups to cover issues such as economic development, food self-sufficiency and environmental management. As was the case with the CSCM, the 5+5 dialogue quickly foundered when political tensions surfaced among the participating states.[68] In a rare show of diplomatic unity within the EU, the European participants refused to sit at the same table as Libya, which had recently been formally condemned for refusing to release the suspects in the Lockerbie bombing for trial. The death knell of the venture was sounded by the Algerian military's decision to annul national elections in January 1992.

The failure of these multilateral diplomatic initiatives refocused attention on EU foreign economic policy. At the start of 1992, Spain was given the task of producing a report on how relations between the Union and the Maghreb states could be improved.[69] Working closely with Commissioner Matutes, the Gonzalez government suggested a 'partnership' with the Maghreb states which would include a free-trade area and an extensive agenda for cooperation on everything from the common management of natural resources and energy policies to food supplies. The paper also called for the institutionalisation of meetings between the Union and the Arab Maghreb Union at both the governmental and parliamentary levels.[70] The tone of the report was firmly neo-liberal, arguing that free-trade, increased private investment and macro-economic reform were the most effective means to socio-economic development and modernisation, and that Association Agreements and EU financial aid should be used in support of these objectives.[71] On the basis of the Spanish paper, the Commission was assigned the task of preparing a set of policy proposals.

This latest drive to revise Mediterranean policy gained some of its momentum from the creation of the CFSP. One effect of the CFSP had been to force the member states to identify common foreign policy interests and the post-Gulf war Mediterranean was seen as a potential focal point for common foreign policy actions. A report on the CFSP presented at the 1992 Lisbon European Council divided the Mediterranean into two geographical areas for strategic actions aimed at economic development, security and stability: the Maghreb and the Middle East.[72] While the detail of these common interests was imprecise, the Lisbon text nevertheless listed the broad objectives that the Union should pursue. On EU-Maghreb relations, the heads of government called for 'upgraded partnership' and loosely defined 'constructive dialogue' covering immigration, drug trafficking, Islamic fundamentalism, population growth and terrorism. It was a direct endorsement of the joint Commission-Spanish proposals and the Commission's exploratory communication on the subject presented at the summit.[73] On the Middle East, the text called for the Union's 'full involvement' in the Peace Process and for efforts to persuade Israel to change its policy in the Palestinian territories.

The transition to the CFSP also had an impact on the institutional division of labour in Mediterranean policy. As Forster and Wallace put it, 'for the European Commission, external relations and foreign policy had now become one of its most important fields of operation'.[74] Article J.8 (Title V, Maastricht Treaty) gave the Commission a right to submit proposals to the Council on CFSP matters. To make the most of its new powers, the Commission re-structured itself. Directorate General 1B was given responsibility for the southern Mediterranean and the Middle East, while DG1A acquired a CFSP directorate. The Commission duly prospered by virtue of its permanency in both the EC and CFSP structures, a development intended to improve the coherence of EU external policy-making by bridging the divide between pillars I and II. It was optimistically anticipated that the new machinery might enable the Union to harness the substantial leverage it possessed through its external trade and aid policies to an enhanced foreign and security policy.

Consistent with the Lisbon text, the Commission's work continued to focus on the Maghreb.[75] By the end of 1992, several months of exchanges between the Commission and the Moroccan and Tunisian governments had laid the foundations for new agreements with the EU based on three distinct lines of action. First, both sides agreed to further renegotiation of the terms of trade in the agreements, with Morocco and Tunisia pressing for full free-trade in all sectors.[76] Second, provisions would be included in each agreement covering rights of establishment for businesses, rules on the movement of services and capital, and the possibility of joint research and development projects. Third, in a concession to the non-member governments, the agreements would include provisions for 'social cooperation', essentially ministerial-level dialogue on issues such as migration and living and working conditions for Maghrebi citizens in the EU. At a meeting of EU foreign ministers in December 1992, the Commission's recommendations were given the green light by the member states and work began on mandates for the Commission to begin negotiations.

However, the rapidly evolving peace process in the Middle East persuaded DG1B that the model for the Euro-Maghreb partnership could be used as a means to stimulate 'post-conflict' economic cooperation between the Arabs and Israelis.[77] There was also a sense among other Mediterranean partners that too much of the EU's attention was being devoted to the Maghreb. At a meeting of the EU-Egypt Cooperation Council in July 1992, an Egyptian official urged the Union to 'embrace the Mediterranean region as a single entity'.[78] When it appeared during 1993 that there might be a peace dividend from the Israel-PLO negotiations, the partnership proposals were duly extended to embrace the Mashreq and take in the Union's relationships with Cyprus, Malta and Turkey.[79] By 1994, the EU's relationships with the Mediterranean non-member countries had been subsumed under a single policy framework labelled the Euro-Mediterranean Partnership.[80]

The main policy instrument attached to the EMP was the Euro-Mediterranean Association Agreement, which incorporated the majority of the proposals made in the joint Commission-Spanish paper.[81] The basis of these revised agreements was the gradual liberalisation of trade over a transitional period of up to 12 years.[82] The precise provisions of the trade component of the agreements varied from one partner country to another but contained certain common features, set out in Figure 3.2.

---

- Customs duties on EU exports of industrial products to the partner to be eliminated gradually during the transitional period. The partners' exports of these products already benefited from duty-free access to the EU.
- Some liberalisation of trade in agricultural products through reciprocal granting of preferential access to markets.
- The extension of trade preferences based on existing arrangements, with the Mediterranean partners extending more limited preferences to EU exports. The situation was to be reviewed after January 1 2000.

---

**Figure 3.2 Common Provisions of the Euro-Mediterranean Agreements**

Crucially, the Council again ruled out substantial liberalisation of agricultural trade. Instead, decisions on market access for specific products were to be based on 'traditional' trade flows, although the Union promised to review the market situation for Mediterranean agricultural products by the end of the 1990s after pressure from the Moroccan and Tunisian governments. Other sectors, such as services, were excluded altogether from the proposals. All the agreements were to include provisions for the discussion of issues such as energy policy, transnational crime and immigration. Formalized political dialogue, superseding the system of Cooperation Councils and Committees, gave the agreements a stronger institutional structure. Implementation was to be overseen by regular meetings of ministers and foreign ministry officials. In terms of both their scope and the machinery to oversee their implementation, the Euro-Med agreements represented a modest advance on previous accords.

The delivery of tangible benefits such as increased export earnings and rising inward investment to the partner countries from the Euro-Mediterranean Agreements was essential to the long-term success of the EMP and to its centrepiece, the creation of a Mediterranean free-trade area. Free-trade was a high stake game for states which had few resources at their disposal to counter the negative impact of increased competition on domestic producers. The upsurge in investment that was seen as a precondition for sustained economic growth in the region required the political commitment of governments to create a more conducive trading environment.[83] Concessions by the EU in the negotiation of the agreements, particularly steps to open up its lucrative agricultural markets, therefore had both symbolic and practical significance. In the event, the Union was to prove resolutely defensive.

## Negotiating the Euro-Mediterranean Agreements

When negotiations opened with Tunisia and Morocco in 1994, it was immediately clear that the member states would again hold sway over the final terms of the agreements. The Council attached footnotes to each of the Commission's initial negotiating mandates stipulating that traditional trade flows should be the guiding principle and setting upper limits to new concessions on import quotas.[84] In addition to keeping to those targets, the Commission was 'asked to avoid proposing additional concessions which could worsen the situation of the EU market for sensitive products'.[85] The ability of Commission negotiators to 'push the envelope' during negotiations was consequently subject to strong formal constraints from the outset. Such decisions reflected the EU's underlying interest in boosting exports to the partner countries while restricting the scope for increased imports.[86] They also highlighted the politically charged nature of measures that might lead to additional competition for the Union's agricultural sector.

Completing the liberalisation of trade in industrial products posed comparatively few problems. The Mediterranean partner countries conceded that their markets would have to be fully opened to imports of European manufactured goods, although some demanded transition periods beyond the 12 years stipulated in the original proposals. Such was the dominance of European manufactured exports in the region that member governments saw little danger from new competition. But the Union stuck to its firm line on agricultural trade, even when the partners themselves demonstrated that they had the ability to take up, or even exceed, their maximum quotas. Egypt, for instance, had developed substantial new agricultural production capacity during the early 1990s. Having been promised free-trade, many of the Mediterranean partners' opening demands were far in excess of existing import quota levels. Even allowing for 'over-asking and under offering', standard techniques in international negotiations, the differences in the starting positions of the two sides pointed to lengthy, hard-fought and highly political bargaining.[87]

As the Euro-Med talks unfolded, two features of the process illustrated the importance of reaching internal agreement to the EU's conduct in external negotiations. First, the Commission found itself in the difficult but familiar position of pivot between the member and non-member governments. Switching between parallel negotiations – internally with the member states, externally with the partner countries – DG1B had to ensure that it could sell concessions and measures included in the agreements to the partners at the same time as extracting concessions from individual member governments and assembling deals that would pass through the Council. One official described the Commission-Council relationship in these simplified terms:

> The Commission informs constantly the Council on the negotiating process. When it considers that the negotiations are over, [it] goes to the Council and says that "ten per Cent of the mandate is not fulfilled because our partners didn't accept this and this". The Council says 'try and try again', and the Commission says 'that's all, now you decide''.[88]

Second, the Commission's role as lead negotiator was complicated by divisions among its own DGs. For instance, DG1B was responsible for driving forward the EMP while the priorities of DGVI (Agriculture) were to defend the EU's agricultural interests and ensure that the agreements complied with the Common Agricultural Policy. The process of adopting EU negotiating lines was thus a complex exercise. It involved finding compromises which were acceptable to both individual member governments and the partners, settling differences inside the EU's institutions and reconciling the conflicting objectives of different Union policies.

Broadly speaking, the member states split into two camps in the Euro-Med negotiations. A 'northern', liberalising tendency including Germany, the UK and the Scandinavian states took the view that the benefits of increased competition outweighed the costs to producers. The 'southern' camp, which included Italy, Portugal and Spain, adopted a protectionist, producer-orientated line. As a national official put it:

> We have tried quite hard to make things as liberal as possible. But it is an uphill struggle. In the EU, it is a producers market. Their interests are valued much more highly than consumers' interests.[89]

The likely impact of this fault line had been flagged by the Economic and Social Committee well before the negotiations began. Its argument was a prescient one:

Until these two positions are superseded by new thinking which combines trade policy with economic and financial policy, as part of a joint development policy – of mutual, Euro-Mediterranean interest – the only common ground will remain the purely negative position of not strengthening Community Mediterranean policy, leaving the bulk of cooperation work in the Mediterranean basin to the member states.[90]

The problematic task of finding 'middle ground' between the two standpoints was left to the Council working groups which followed the negotiations.

The positions of the 'southern' member states were consistent with the intensity of their preferences on the issue of import quotas. With EU agricultural markets already saturated with 'Mediterranean' products, it was politically inexpedient for southern governments to sign up to agreements whose net effect would be an increase in competition. Farm lobbies were extremely powerful domestic constituencies in France, Italy, Portugal and Spain, using established formal channels to national ministries as well as blockades and demonstrations to exert pressure on their respective governments. In at least two cases – the negotiations with Morocco and Tunisia – protests by European farmers that involved the destruction of imported produce led to discussions being temporarily halted.[91] Since the agreements had to be ratified by national parliaments, governments were inevitably cautious about being seen to concede ground in the negotiations.

However, the Euro-Mediterranean Agreements were notable for the politicization of concessions on import quotas by northern member states. Governments that previously had not had cause to block negotiations suddenly found themselves under pressure to safeguard domestic interests over apparently small quota increases. A dispute over cut flowers in the Moroccan agreement was a case in point. Germany and the Netherlands questioned the Commission's offer on cut flowers (5000 tonnes per annum), arguing that it had exceeded its mandate.[92] The German government's claim that the tonnage offered would harm domestic growers was a puzzling one given its strong preference for trade liberalisation. Under the agreement, Germany would receive only 700 tonnes of flowers per annum with a market value of 1 million ECUs, a tiny percentage of its total production. The Netherlands adopted a similar line. The problem for both was that representatives of the flower growing industries had mobilized in opposition to the Euro-Med agreements. One official summarised the situation in the following way:

> Trade is bigger than production, but the point is that it is a traditional industry. You can't retrain flower growers overnight.[93]

A measure of the sensitivity of the Dutch government on this issue was its decision to engage in direct talks with the Moroccan government.[94]

Predictably, the Commission found itself unable to contain the Euro-Med negotiations at the so-called 'technical level', where agreements on the figures for import quotas and other clauses were thrashed out by diplomats in Brussels. Instead, discussions about the most sensitive issues for both the member states and the partner countries often became politicised to such a degree that direct intervention at the highest political level was required. During negotiations with Egypt in 1998, for instance, Commission President Jacques Santer met with President Hosni Mubarak in an attempt to find a solution to protracted disputes over import quotas for oranges, rice, cut flowers, rules of origin and the thorny question of a clause in the agreement requiring Egypt to readmit citizens who had tried to enter the EU illegally.[95] Santer's statement that the Union would 'not let a few oranges stop the negotiations' had a hollow ring to it.[96]

In order to break the increasingly frequent deadlocks in the talks, the Commission was occasionally forced to challenge the limits of its autonomy. After it reportedly offered Morocco an increase in its import quota for tomato paste that exceeded the figure stipulated in the negotiating mandate, it was publicly rebuked by the Portuguese government for tending to 'negotiate free-wheel and to substitute itself in the role of political organs that represent sovereign states'.[97] During negotiations with Jordan, it was criticised for having negotiated, without the approval of COREPER, a revision clause in the agreement which allowed for the re-negotiation of quotas within three years of the accord entering into force.[98] At times, DG1B seemed to be faced with a no-win situation. A request to COREPER from one member state to intervene in the negotiations was rejected on the grounds that the Commission alone should be acting on behalf of the Union.[99] The effects of this institutional wrangling were damaging delays in the Euro-Med process and a lack of flexibility on the EU's part.

When politicisation took disputes in the Euro-Med negotiations to the Council's table, it took a mixture of political pressure from Council Presidencies and pay-offs to individual member states to resolve outstanding issues. In the negotiations with Morocco and Tunisia, the French and Spanish Presidencies used the chair to urge governments to conclude the accords. Spanish Foreign Minister Javier Solana, for instance, repeatedly stressed that the value of the trade concessions at stake amounted to only 20 million ECUs.[100] French ministers showed solidarity with the Spanish, criticising what they saw as intransigence on the part of the other member states.[101] The use of side payments also paved the way for agreements to be concluded. The Guterres government in Portugal had just taken office when it found itself facing increased imports of Moroccan tomato concentrate and canned sardines. These sectors were responsible for the majority of the output of the Portuguese food processing industry, and farmers and fishermen were the traditional constituents of the opposition parties. Anticipating hostility at home to the Morocco agreement and the possibility of an embarrassing row as it passed through the parliament, the government rounded on the Commission. The Portuguese government blocked negotiations until the Commission promised extra funding (from the EU's Structural Funds) to modernize the canning industry and new controls on the marketing of Moroccan imports.[102] Such face-saving compromises were a typical feature of the negotiations.

Despite the 'partnership' label, the Mediterranean non-member countries appeared to be bit players in the Euro-Med negotiations. Only Morocco, which possessed the bargaining chip of access to its fishing grounds, was able to hold out for additional EU concessions and extra funding, securing financial compensation for its fishing fleets in return for improved access for its tomato exports. Others bemoaned the Union's inflexibility but stuck to their demands. One official argued:

> Come 2010, our markets will be open 100 per cent for European industrial products and what we are asking for is equal treatment in agriculture. We are being practical and realistic. We know that there are big problems in the CAP. We said OK, we will not ask for equal treatment at this point. At least at this point we would like to increase our exports to the EU and have some privileges.[103]

The tone of this appeal for equity highlighted the partners' limited effective influence over the Union's key decisions and their low expectations about the final deals that they would be offered. Moreover, further modifications to the terms of the agreements, accepted as necessary by the EU during the negotiations, would be driven by factors outside the scope of the Euro-Med Partnership. Reform of the CAP, for instance, would be a long-term process, impelled by eastern enlargement of the Union in the mid-2000s and a new round of multilateral trade liberalisation under the auspices of the World Trade Organisation.

In view of the numerous problems in completing negotiations with the partners, the Union was forced to admit that the completion date for the free-trade area would be pushed back five years to 2015[104] which was excessively optimistic as the concluded agreements underwent the slow process of ratification by each member state. By 2001, the Union had only concluded agreements with six states, and of those only four agreements had entered into force (see below).

**Table 3.3 Status of Negotiations with Partner Countries, March 2001**

| Partner Country | Negotiations Opened | Agreement Signed | Entry into force |
|---|---|---|---|
| Algeria | 1997 | Negotiations Ongoing | - |
| Egypt | 1996 | Concluded 1999 | - |
| Israel | 1995 | November 1995 | June 2000 |
| Jordan | 1996 | November 1997 | - |
| Lebanon | 1997 | Negotiations Ongoing | - |
| Morocco | 1993 | February 1996 | March 2000 |
| Palestinian Authority | 1996 | February 1997 | July 1997 |
| Syria | 1998 | Negotiations Ongoing | - |
| Tunisia | 1993 | July 1995 | March 1998 |

*Source*: European Commission, DG1B (2001) *Progress of Negotiations on Euro-Mediterranean Association Agreements*, April, http://www.euromed.net.

The impact of the Euro-Mediterranean Agreements would take time to materialize. However, commentators were quick to highlight problems in the design and contents of the EMP that seriously compromised its objectives. Some challenged the underlying assumption that liberalising trade in manufactured goods could produce sustained rather than temporary economic growth.[105] Others pointed to the Union's failure to grant concessions to the partners in a sector (agriculture) in which they enjoyed a competitive advantage over the member states. Moreover, in the short term at least, the major beneficiaries of regional trade liberalisation would be European businesses, cementing their already dominant position in the partners' markets. Projections of positive economic benefits from the free trade initiative prescribed the implementation of a raft of accompanying reforms to taxation systems and other far-reaching administrative changes. Yet one effect of trade liberalisation would be to considerably reduce revenue from import duties. Given the pressure on the partner governments to balance external demands for reform with internal demands for welfare, the Euro-Mediterranean Agreements hardly provided a strong incentive to meet the challenge.

## Conclusions

To a considerable extent, the Euro-Mediterranean Partnership was simply 'old wine in new bottles'. The basic structure of Mediterranean policy was retained, with new provisions for cooperation across a range of issues built into modified Association Agreements. While there was a clearer definition of the Union's strategic interests and objectives in the region, neither the Redirected Mediterranean Policy nor the EMP seriously addressed the 'big' questions: the deep-seated asymmetry in trade relations, the debt crisis and the risks of political and social instability posed by poverty, high unemployment and poor economic performance. Under pressure to respond expeditiously to events in the Gulf and the re-launch of the Middle East Peace Process, the partnership concept amounted to a declaration that the Union would engage with the partner countries on a more systematic basis.

Beyond the partnership rhetoric, however, the Union once again proved stubbornly protectionist on the issues that really mattered to the partner countries. As one diplomat put it, 'it is sad to see how much political mileage there is out of 1 tonne of cut flowers. But [EU] politics works like that – very short-sighted'.[106] The Commission inevitably found itself caught between its role as a servant of the member states, its responsibilities for regulating EU markets, and the need to reach deals with the Mediterranean partner countries which represented an improvement on the status quo. The partners were not unique in finding the EU a tough and defensive negotiator. The 1990s saw the EU embroiled in protracted rows over agricultural trade in the Uruguay Round of the GATT. Its 'Europe Agreements' with the Central and Eastern European countries were notable for the numerous protocols and annexes attached to the accords that allowed for trade barriers to be re-imposed if EU producers faced unacceptable competitive pressure from imports.

The politicisation of trade diplomacy has been an enduring characteristic of the Union's behaviour in the international system.

What does the negotiation of the Euro-Mediterranean Agreements tell us about the pursuit of strategic action through the EU's external economic policies? First, it suggests that the organisation was more adept at consolidating and promoting European commercial interests than it was at taking a progressive lead in regional economic development. Second, it highlights the complex characteristics of the EU as a strategic actor. Authority is diffused across different institutions, a wide range of forces vie for influence on policy and the member states bring diverse and often conflicting interests and objectives to the negotiating table. The result is that, even when the Union is able to settle on a reasonably coherent set of objectives, they are prone to being undermined by the assertion of national interests. Third, it calls into question the Union's capacity to pursue soft security through the EMP. That the central plank of the initiative – the free-trade area – got off to such a hesitant and controversial start did not augur well for its capacity to remedy the fundamental economic inequality of Euro-Med relations.

## Notes

[1] European Commission (1994) *Strengthening the Mediterranean Policy of the European Union: Establishing a Euro-Mediterranean Partnership*, COM (94) 427 Final, 19 April, p. 1.
[2] The RMP has variously been referred to as the Renewed Mediterranean Policy, Reformed Mediterranean Policy and Redirected Mediterranean Policy.
[3] The negotiations with Algeria, Israel and the Palestinian Territories are dealt with in more detail in Chapters 5 and 6.
[4] Croft, S., Redmond, J., Wyn Rees, G. and Webber, M. (1999) *The Enlargement of Europe*, Manchester: Manchester University Press, p. 65; Friis, L. and Murphy, A. (1999) 'The European Union and Central and Eastern Europe: Governance and Boundaries', *Journal of Common Market Studies*, Vol. 37, No. 2, pp. 211.
[5] See, for example, International Institute for Strategic Studies (1988) *Prospects for Security in the Mediterranean, Parts I-II-III*, Adelphi Papers, Nos. 229-230-231, London: IISS; Aliboni, R. (1990) 'The Mediterranean scenario: Economy and Security in the Regions South of the European Community, *The International Spectator*, Vol. 25, No. 2, pp. 138-54; Aliboni, R. (1991) *European Security Across the Mediterranean*, Chaillot Papers, No. 2, Paris: Institute for Security Studies, WEU; Laipson, E. (1990) 'Thinking about the Mediterranean', *Mediterranean Quarterly*, Vol. 1, No. 1, pp. 50-66.
[6] See Ravenel, B. *Mediterranée, le Nord contre le Sud?*, Paris: L'Harmattan; Ravenhill, J. (1990) 'The North-South balance of power', *International Affairs*, Vol. 66, No. 4, pp. 39-51.
[7] Marks, J. (1989) 'The Concept of Morocco in Europe' in G. Joffé (ed.) *Morocco and Europe*, Occasional Paper 7, London: Centre of Near and Middle Eastern Studies, S.O.A.S., p. 17.
[8] See CEPII (1988) 'La dette des pays méditerranées', *Problèmes économiques*, No. 2062, Paris: La Documentation Française, 17 February, pp. 28-31.
[9] As for the position of the other Mediterranean associates in 1989, Cyprus carried a debt of 1.7 billion ECUs, Malta 0.25 billion ECUs and Turkey 35 billion ECUs.

¹⁰ Nigoul, C. (1991) 'Quelques remarques sur les facteurs économiques et sociaux de l'insécurité en méditerranée' in H. El Malki (ed.) *La Méditerranée en question: Conflits et interdépendances*, Casablanca: Fondation du Roi Abdul-Aziz and Paris: Editions du CNRS, p. 135.
¹¹ Khader, B. (1997) *Le Partenariat Euro-Méditerranéen*, Louvain-la-Neuve: Centre d'Etudes et de Recherches sur le Monde Arabe Contemporain (CERMAC), p. 45.
¹² Regnault, H. (1995) Address to Conference, *GATT-Europe-Méditerranée*, Club Financier Méditerranéen, Nice, 31 March-1 April, p. 23.
¹³ Ibid., p. 24.
¹⁴ Koubaa, N. (1995) (Banque arabe tuniso-libyenne de développement et de commerce extérieur) 'Address to conference', Club Financier Méditerranée, *GATT, Europe, Méditerranée*, Nice, 31 March-1 April, p. 34.
¹⁵ Aliboni, R. (1992a) 'Southern European Security in the 1990s: Perceptions and Problems' in R. Aliboni (ed.) *Southern European Security in the 1990s*, London: Pinter, p. 8.
¹⁶ Stevens, C. (1990) 'The Impact of Europe 1992 on the Maghreb and Sub-Saharan Africa' *Journal of Common Market Studies*, Vol. 24, No. 2, p. 225.
¹⁷ Ibid., p. 239.
¹⁸ Dimeglio, W. (1995) *Pour un Partenariat Industriel avec le Maghreb et les PECO: Rapport au Premier Ministre*, Paris: La Documentation Française, p. 61.
¹⁹ Abel Matutes, quoted in Islam, S. (1989) 'Exploring the EEC dimension', *Middle East Economic Digest*, 2 June, p. 4.
²⁰ Bourrinet, J. (1993) 'Aspects Economiques: Trois Défis Majeurs pour la Coopération' in J. Bourrinet (ed.) *La Méditerranée: Espace de Coopération?*, Paris: Economica, p. 205; Escallier, R. (1991) 'La transition démographique', *Etat du Maghreb*, Paris: La Découverte, p. 83.
²¹ Figures extrapolated from World Bank (1992) *World Development Report*, Washington: World Bank.
²² The heavy reliance of Arab Mediterranean states on the public sector as a source of employment made them all the more sensitive to outside pressure to cut public spending.
²³ Salt, J. (1991) *Current and Future International Migration Trends Affecting Europe*, Strasbourg: Council of Europe; Lopez García, B. (1992) 'Les mouvements de population en Méditerranée' in M. Dumas (ed.) *Méditerranée Occidentale: Sécurité et Coopération*, Paris: Fondation pour les études de défense nationale, pp. 45-56; Haddaoui, R. (1993) 'Le nouveau visage de l'émigration marocaine' in The Philip Morris Institute, *Vers un Politique Européenne de l'Immigration*, Brussels: The Philip Morris Institute, p. 23; Lahav, G. (1993) 'Immigration, Hypernationalism and European security' in J. Philip Rogers (ed.) *The Future of European Security*, Basingstoke: Macmillan, pp. 74-81.
²⁴ Haddaoui, K. (1995) 'Evidence to the House of Lords', *Eleventh report from the House of Lords: Relations between the EU and the Maghreb Countries*, 11 November, London: HMSO, p. 39.
²⁵ Juppé, A. (1995) 'Quel horizon pour la politique étrangère de la France?', *Politique Étrangère*, Vol 60, No. 1, p. 245.
²⁶ For France in particular, relations between its Maghrebi immigrant communities and the state were already tense and were being aggravated by the defiant racism of the *Front Nationale*.
²⁷ Booth, K. (1991) 'Introduction. The Interregnum: World Politics in Transition' in K. Booth (ed.) *New Thinking About Strategy and International Security*, London: HarperCollins, pp. 1-23; Miall, H. (1991) 'New visions, new voices, old power structures'

in K. Booth (ed.) *New Thinking About Strategy and International Security*, London: HarperCollins, pp. 293-312; Grasa, R. (1995) 'El Mediterráneo desde una perspectiva globalizadora de la seguridad: Una mirada a a dimensión cooperativa de la conflictividad', *Papers: Revista de Sociologica*, No. 46, Bellaterra: Universidad Autònoma de Barcelona, pp. 25-42; Algieri, F. (1996) 'In Need of a Comprehensive Approach: The European Union and Possible External Security Challenges' in F. Algieri, J. Janning and D. Rumberg (eds) *Managing Security in Europe*, Gutersloh: Bertelsmann, pp. 189-207.
[28] Peterson, J. (1996) *Europe and America: The Prospects for Partnership*, London: Routledge, p. 158.
[29] Buzan, B. (1991b) 'Is international security possible?' in K. Booth (ed.) op. cit., p. 46.
[30] United Nations General Assembly (1990) *Strengthening of Security and Cooperation in the Mediterranean Region*, Resolution A/RES/45/79, 12 December, http://heimedac.unige.ch/V/T/1310.html.
[31] NATO (1992) *The Transformation of an Alliance: The Decisions of NATO's Heads of State and Government*, Brussels: NATO Office of Information and Press, pp. 29-54.
[32] Cremasco, M. (1990) 'The Mediterranean Area in Perspective', *The International Spectator*, Vol. 25, No. 2, p. 119.
[33] European Commission (1989a) *Redirecting the Community's Mediterranean Policy*, SEC (89) 1961, 23 November. The background of Commissioner Abel Matutes, an Ibizan businessman and former MP, made him well aware of the relationship between socio-economic conditions in North Africa and migration into southern Europe. See Echeverría Jesús, C. (1993) 'La Reforma de la Politica Mediterranea de la Comunidad Europea', in Marquina, A (ed.), *El Flanco Sur de la Otan*, Madrid: Editorial Complutense, p. 119.
[34] Matutes, A. (1989) 'Commissioner Matutes reviews issues for the Community in the Mediterranean', *Speech to Pio Manzu Conference*, Rimini, Press Release IP/89/776, Rapid Database, http ://europa.eu.int/rapid/cgi.
[35] European Commission (1989b) *Commission Proposes Renewed Mediterranean Policy*, Press Release, P/89/71, Rapid Database, «http ://europa.eu.int/rapid/cgi».
[36] European Commission (1989c) *Redirecting the Community's Mediterranean Policy*, SEC (89) 1961 Final, Brussels: Office for Official Publications of the European Communities.
[37] Economic and Social Committee (1989) *Opinion on the Mediterranean Policy of the European Community*, Official Journal C221, 28 August, pp. 16-28.
[38] Ibid., p. 17.
[39] Ibid., p. 18.
[40] De Vasconcelos, A. (1993) 'Disintegration and Integration in the Mediterranean', *The International Spectator*, Vol. 28, No. 3, p. 69. See also Gambles, I. (1989) 'Prospects for West European Security Cooperation', *Adelphi Papers*, No. 244, London: IISS, p. 55.
[41] Aliboni, R. (1992b) 'Italian Security Policy in a Changing International Environment, *Jerusalem Journal of International Relations*, Vol. 14, No. 2, p. 100.
[42] European Commission (1990a) *Towards a New Mediterranean Policy*, SEC (90) 812, Brussels, 1 June.
[43] European Commission (1991a) *Proposal for a Council Regulation (EEC) concerning financial cooperation in respect of all the Mediterranean non-member countries*, COM (91) 48 Final, 19 February. Article 3, Council Regulation 1763/92, Official Journal L181, 1 July, pp. 1-8.
[44] Kebabdjian, G. (1995) 'Le libre-échange Euro-Maghrebin: Une évaluation macro-économique', *Révue Tiers Monde*, Vol. 36, No. 144, p. 31. Intra-regional trade accounted for around only 4% of exports and imports.

⁴⁵ Regelsberger, E. (1991) 'The Twelve's Dialogue with Third Countries - Progress Towards a *Communauté d'Action*' in M. Holland (ed.) *The Future of European Political Cooperation: Essays on Theory and Practice*, Basingstoke: Macmillan, p. 174.
⁴⁶ The Members of the Arab Maghreb Union were Algeria, Libya, Mauritania, Morocco and Tunisia.
⁴⁷ European Commission (1990b) *Relations Between the European Community and the Arab Maghreb Union*, Memo/90/58, Rapid Database, http://europa.eu.int/rapid/cgi.
⁴⁸ The Commission originally asked the Council for a total of 6.775 billion ECUs (2.855 billion ECU in the bilateral protocols; 3.920 billion ECUs for regional financial cooperation), but secured only 4.405 billion ECUs. See Economic and Social Committee (1992) *Opinion on the Mediterranean Policy of the European Community*, Official Journal C40, 17 February, pp. 67-86.
⁴⁹ Interview, Brussels, 19 December 1996.
⁵⁰ European Commission (1990a) op. cit., p. 11.
⁵¹ Council Regulation (EEC) No. 1762/92 on the implementation of the Protocols on financial and technical cooperation concluded by the Community with the Mediterranean non-member countries, *Official Journal L181*, 1 July 1992, p. 2.
⁵² *Agence Europe*, 16 May 1991, p. 8.
⁵³ Even then, the Union still ensured that safeguard measures were built into its new textile import regime to protect European manufacturers from competition.
⁵⁴ Daguzan, J. (1992) 'Coopération régionale et sécurité collective en Méditerranée', *Revue d'Economie Régionale et Urbaine*, Vol. 4, p. 569; See also Mortimer, E.J. (1991) 'New Fault Lines: Is a North-South Confrontation Inveitable in Security Terms?' in International Institute for Strategic Studies, *New Dimensions in International Security*, Adelphi Paper 296, London: IISS, pp. 80-81.
⁵⁵ Spencer, C. (1993) *The Maghreb in the 1990s: Political and Economic Developments in Algeria, Morocco and Tunisia*, Adelphi Paper No. 274, London: Brasseys/IISS, p. 35.
⁵⁶ Khader, B. (1997) *L'Europe, le proche-orient et la Palestine, 1957-1999: Synthèse et enseignements*, Paper presented to Seminar: The EU's Common Foreign and Security Policy and World Responsibilities, Institut d'Etudes Européennes, Brussels, 3-5 October.
⁵⁷ 'La France en train de Perdre le Maghreb?', *Le Canard Enchaîné*, 23 January 1991, p. 1.
⁵⁸ Jacques Blanc (UDF) (1990) 'Debate on the Middle East and the Future of Europe', Débats Parlementaires, Assemblée Nationale, *Journel Officiel*, Session 89/90, Fiche no. 90-03, 11 April, p. 227.
⁵⁹ European Parliament (1991) (Committee on External Economic Relations) *Report on a Revamped Mediterranean Policy*, Brussels, 3 May, p. 9.
⁶⁰ Piening, C. (1997) *Global Europe: The European Union in World Affairs*, Boulder and London: Lynne Rienner, p. 76.
⁶¹ Anderson, S. (1992) 'Western Europe and the Gulf War' in R. Rummel (ed.) *Toward Political Union: Planning a CFSP in the EC*, Boulder and Oxford: Westview, p. 157.
⁶² Basfao, K. and Henry, J-R. (1991) 'Le Maghreb et l'Europe: Que faire de la Méditerranée?', *Vingtième Siècle Revue d'Histoire*, Vol. 32, Oct-Dec, p. 44. See also Guelton, F. (1996) *La guerre américaine du Golfe*, Lyon: Presses Universitaires de Lyon.
⁶³ The main economic consequences of the Gulf War were sharp falls in revenues from exports, tourism and remittances from migrant workers, sharp depreciations of currencies, and increased costs from supporting returning migrant workers and the reconstruction of infrastructures.

⁶⁴ European Commission (1991b) *Additional financial aid for countries in the Middle East and Mediterranean affected by the Gulf War*, COM (91) 61 Final, 28 February; *Agence Europe*, 14 March 1991, p. 3.
⁶⁵ Domestici-Met, M and Dubois, L. (1990) 'Le Rôle de l'Europe: La Communauté Européenne' in J. Bourrinet (ed.) *La Méditerranée: Espace de Coopération?*, Paris: Economica, p. 141.
⁶⁶ In March 1991, US Secretary of State James Baker reportedly told Italian Foreign Minister Gianni di Michelis that there was 'no question of discussing the CSCM'. Khader, B. (1997) *Le Partenariat Euro-Méditerranéen Apres la Conférence de Barcelone*, Paris: L'Harmattan, p. 56; Ghebali, V.Y. (1993) 'Toward a Mediterranean Helsinki Type Process', *Mediterranean Quarterly*, Vol. 4, No. 1, p. 98.
⁶⁷ Xenakis, D. (1998) 'The Barcelona Process: Some Lessons From Helsinki', *Jean Monnet Working Papers in Comparative and International Politics*, No. JMWP 17.98, Catania: University of Catania, p. 7.
⁶⁸ Ghebali, V.Y. (1993) op. cit., p. 98.
⁶⁹ *Agence Europe*, 29 February 1992, p. 7.
⁷⁰ *Agence Europe*, 3 March 1992, pp. 9-10.
⁷¹ Ibid.
⁷² European Council (1992) *Conclusions of the Presidency*, Rapid Database, http://europa.eu.int/rapid/cgi/.
⁷³ European Commission (1992) *The Future of Relations Between the Community and the Maghreb*, SEC (92) 401, Brussels, 29 April.
⁷⁴ Forster, A. and Wallace, W. (1996) 'Common Foreign and Security Policy: A new policy or just a new name?' in H. Wallace and W. Wallace (eds) *Policy-Making in the European Union*, Oxford: Oxford University Press, p. 431.
⁷⁵ European Commission (1992) op. cit.
⁷⁶ *Agence Europe*, 15 July 1992, p. 10.
⁷⁷ European Commission (1993) *Future Relations and Cooperation between the Community and the Middle East*, COM (93) 375 Final, Brussels, 8 September; Rhein, E. (1994) *The European Contribution to the Middle East Peace Process*, Speech to Dialogo Mediterraneo, Venice, 23-24 January.
⁷⁸ *Agence Europe*, 24 July 1992, p. 9.
⁷⁹ The Mashreq includes Egypt, Lebanon, Jordan.
⁸⁰ European Commission (1994) *Strengthening the Mediterranean Policy of the European Union: Establishing a Euro-Mediterranean Partnership*, COM (94) 427 Final, 19 April.
⁸¹ *Agence Europe*, 26 September 1992, p. 3.
⁸² European Commission (1995c) *Proposal for a Council and Commission Decision on the conclusion of a Euro-Mediterranean Agreement establishing an Association between the European Communities and the Member States on the one part, and the Kingdom of Morocco, on the other part*, COM (95) 740 Final, Brussels, p.2.
⁸³ Petri, P. (1997a) *The Case of Missing Foreign Investment in the Southern Mediterranean*, OECD Technical Papers, No. 128, Paris: OECD, p. 11.
⁸⁴ Interview, Brussels, 16 October 1998.
⁸⁵ *Agence Europe*, 8 December 1993, p. 7; *European Report*, No. 1908, December 8 1993, Sect. V, p. 6.
⁸⁶ Tovias, A. (1999) Regionalism and the Mediterranean in G. Joffe (ed.) *Perspectives on Development: The Euro-Mediterranean Partnership*, London: Frank Cass, p. 82.
⁸⁷ Kaufmann, J. (1988) *Conference Diplomacy: An Introductory Analysis*, Dordrecht: Martinus Nijhoff, p. 161.

[88] Interview, Brussels, 16 October 1998.
[89] Interview, Brussels, 12 December 1996.
[90] Economic and Social Committee (1992) *Opinion on the Mediterranean Policy of the European Community*, Official Journal, C40, 17 February, p. 72.
[91] *El País*, 24 November 1995, p. 3.
[92] *European Report*, No. 2081, November 4 1995, Sect V, p. 16. In 1994, Morocco exported only 2100 tonnes of cut flowers.
[93] Interview, Brussels, 11 December 1996.
[94] Interview, Brussels, 11 December 1996.
[95] *European Report*, No. 2290, February 11 1998, Sect. V, p. 3.
[96] *Agence Europe*, 12 February 1998, p. 4.
[97] *Reuters*, 10 November 1995, http://wvnms.wvnet.edu/~boukhli/c2.
[98] Jordan had specifically requested that this modification clause be included to allow for increases in quotas according to its production capacity and the Commission had accepted its request. The southern member states subsequently used threats of non-ratification to force the Commission back to the negotiating table. In exchange for a 14 per cent increase in its quota for tomato concentrate, and after a further delay of 8 months, the Jordanians finally accepted the withdrawal of the revision clause
[99] Interview, Brussels, 25 March 1997.
[100] *European Report*, No. 2084, 14 November 1995, p. 13.
[101] *Marchés Tropicaux et Méditerranéens*, 17 November 1995, p. 2521.
[102] *European Report*, No. 2085, 18 November 1995, p. 9; Abouyoub, H. (Moroccan Minister of Agriculture), 'Interview', *Jeune Afrique*, No. 1820, 7-13 November 1995, p. 40.
[103] Interview, Brussels, 5 December 1996.
[104] *Agence Europe*, 4 March 1998, p. 10.
[105] Sid Ahmed, A. (2000) 'Economic convergence and "catching up" in the Mediterranean: Diagnosis, Prospect and Limitations of the Barcelona process and elements for a strategy' in G. Brauch, A. Marquina and A. Biad (eds) *Euro-Mediterranean Partnership for the 21$^{st}$ Century*, Basingstoke: Macmillan, p. 155.
[106] Interview, Brussels, 12 December 1996.

Chapter 4

# The Barcelona Process

**Introduction**

If the Euro-Mediterranean Agreements represented 'more of the same', then the Barcelona process was a new departure in EU Mediterranean policy. This multilateral dimension of the Euro-Mediterranean Partnership, based on a Declaration and Work Programme, secured the approval of 27 governments and spawned a rolling programme of cooperation among governments and non-governmental actors across an extensive range of issues.[1] The Declaration committed the signatories to dealing with highly sensitive subjects such as arms control, democratic reforms and human rights in a format resembling that of the Organisation for Security and Cooperation in Europe (OSCE). The participation of Israel, Lebanon, the Palestinian Authority and Syria gave the Barcelona process a unique status in the region as the only forum in which their politicians and officials would routinely sit together at the same table.

This chapter examines the negotiation of the Barcelona conference and assesses its contribution to the EU's strategic behaviour in the Mediterranean region. Section one discusses the rationale behind the EU's decision to convene the conference, which was taken at a propitious time in Euro-Med relations. Section two analyses the preparation of the Conference during 1995, illustrating how the process was dominated by the EU and by the Mediterranean member states in particular. The third section focuses on the content of the Barcelona Declaration and Work Programme and the early stages of the implementation process. It briefly considers some of the key measures that developed out of the Declaration's three chapters and the problems that arose as differences between the signatories, particularly over the Middle East Peace Process, caused the EMP to stall.

**The Road to Barcelona**

It is difficult to pinpoint either a 'big idea' or a main sponsor behind the decision to initiate the Barcelona process. The political opportunity space for the conference arose out of a combination of favourable circumstances. In the post-Cold War environment governments and non-governmental actors acknowledged the potential benefits of collective action to manage 'common' Mediterranean problems. Interest in multilateralism was sparked by the short-lived period of

Arab-Israeli rapprochement in the early 1990s and the brief reduction of tension in the region. The seeds of the conference also germinated in the vacant ground left by the abortive attempts to create the CSCM and 5+5 regional diplomatic forums. Both schemes had demonstrated the presence of political support among governments in the Mediterranean for new institutional architecture.[2] High-ranking politicians from several Mediterranean states put the case for an adapted OSCE model, with the emphasis on a comprehensive approach to security, in the region.[3] The arguments of Guido de Marco, Malta's Foreign Minister and a leading proponent of multilateralism, were typical:

> We cannot close an eye to regional flash points that must be contained and possibly diffused, if our own security is not to be put in jeopardy. We should all try to create the facilities to involve all the parties concerned in a dialogue.[4]

De Marco's assumption, one also publicly expressed by Italian foreign minister Gianni de Michelis and Spain's Fernandez Ordoñez, was that regular 'dialogue' – in other words, meetings of ministers, diplomats and other national representatives – would be the starting point for conflict prevention and confidence building.[5]

Consistent with its own advocacy of deeper regional integration, the European Commission's 1992 proposals for a Euro-Maghreb partnership called for the bilateral track of the EMP to be complemented by dialogue on 'all matters of common interest' between the EU, Algeria, Morocco and Tunisia.[6] By 1993, participation by the Union in the 'stop-start' multilateral track of the Middle East Peace Process had convinced DG1B that the partnership concept should be extended to Israel and the Mashreq countries.[7] The Commission's optimistic expectation was that the Union might come to play a leading role in normalising inter-governmental relations between Israel and the Arab states. In a follow-up communication to the Council, the Commission argued that multi-sectoral, functional cooperation between governments and private actors was essential to the consolidation of the Peace Process and raised the possibility of establishing 'joint institutions'.[8] This bid for increased influence over Arab-Israeli relations was an important motive behind EU activities in the region during the early 1990s.

The idea of convening a conference was first openly mooted under the Greek Council Presidency at the Corfu Summit in June 1994, with Spain offering to host the event at the end of 1995.[9] Once again, the agenda setting power of the Presidency enabled a Mediterranean member state to make the region an external policy priority of the Union. However, the real watershed was the Essen Summit in December 1994. Regardless of the underlying strength of their commitment to it, the heads of government unanimously endorsed the proposal in an outward show of unity.[10] Behind the scenes, the agreement to hold the conference formed part of an inter-governmental deal in which the Mediterranean member states accepted that eastern enlargement had to be the EU's number one priority in exchange for a significant political gesture towards the south.[11]

The prime movers on the Barcelona initiative were France, Italy and Spain. The extent to which the three governments engaged in practical collaboration is unclear, but there was evidently sufficient convergence between their foreign policy positions to generate the necessary political impetus behind the project.[12] A shared interest in finding a better balance between the eastern and southern dimensions of EU external policy was an important uniting factor. According to one official:

> There was no institutional coordination on Mediterranean issues, no contact group, but events in the EU provoked cooperation among France, Italy and Spain.[13]

In a similar vein, another official described the relationship between the Mediterranean member states as 'intuitive', relying more on their 'proximity of interests' than any methodical effort to adopt joint positions.[14]

The most active member of this informal Mediterranean caucus was Spain, which put itself at the forefront of moves to multilateralize EU Mediterranean policy.[15] Having embraced the 'Europeanisation' of its foreign policy after accession, the Spanish government readily accepted the case for pursuing strategic interests through EU action.[16] Given the supposed centrality of trade and aid in the post cold war security – policy areas in which the Union exercised a substantial array of exclusive competencies – the European route was unavoidable. From 1989 onwards, the Gonzalez government had committed itself to the CSCE, rather than NATO, as the most appropriate European and Mediterranean security organisation.[17] But when it became clear that the Ordoñez-De Michelis sponsored CSCM project was destined to fail, Spain turned its attention to promoting EU policy. Its subsequent offer to host the conference in Barcelona was the culmination of several years of quietly effective Spanish diplomacy in the Arab world and confirmation of its vocation as a significant diplomatic player in the Mediterranean.[18]

From the EU's perspective, the decision to develop a multilateral track served several purposes. First, it promised to install new machinery to assist the pursuit of European political and economic interests. Adding a multilateral element to Mediterranean policy would potentially equip the EU with a mechanism to secure 'boundary management' objectives by pulling together a variety of programmes under a single heading.[19] Second, it was the kind of grand political gesture called for by Jacques Delors, who argued that the Union needed to send 'powerful messages to its neighbours' in the east and south.[20] Third, given the economic shocks which were predicted to accompany the Euro-Med free-trade initiative, the conference helped to sell the EMP to the partner governments by creating a façade of diplomatic equality and elevated political status, at least in the short term. Finally, it was also expected that the conference would help to kick start the negotiation of the Euro-Mediterranean Agreements with Morocco and Tunisia which had stalled during 1994. The assumption was that all parties would want to conclude the negotiations before the event as a sign that the EMP was making tangible progress.[21]

If the rationale for holding a conference was reasonably clear, there was far less clarity about how it would 'add value' to the existing Mediterranean policy framework. As one official commented, the member states had agreed to hold the event 'with no idea as to what it should initiate'.[22] The Commission's initial communication on the subject was instructive, being long on rhetoric and short on substance:

> The conference should reach agreement on a series of economic and political guidelines for Euro-Mediterranean policy into the next century, which could be set out in a new Charter. The Conference should thereby contribute to creating a larger awareness, among political and business leaders throughout the world, of the Mediterranean being ready to embark on a courageous journey which will progressively transform it into a region of stability and peace, rapid economic development, social change and, last but not least, political pluralism.[23]

There was no question of the conference producing an international treaty that would impose formal obligations on its signatories. Merely getting all the partners to attend would be an achievement its own right.

## Negotiating the Barcelona Conference

The Barcelona conference was, as Esther Barbé argues, a 'genuinely European project'.[24] The decision to hold the conference was the EU's alone and was effectively presented to the partners as a *fait accompli*. As the agenda-setting phase was to show, the interests of individual EU governments, which periodically manifested themselves in differences of opinion about the contents of the Declaration and Work Programme, dominated the preparations. Moreover, much of the preparatory work was conducted along the lines of a CFSP action, with the Troika undertaking the bulk of the diplomatic legwork. The member governments therefore exercised tight control over the process from the outset.

Drafting of the Barcelona Declaration commenced under the French Council Presidency at the start of 1995.[25] The Balladur government made Mediterranean policy a central plank of its six-month programme for the EU and set out to impose its own vision of the EMP on the conference. Exploratory discussions took place in the relevant Council working-groups with the tabling of detailed *fiches* submitted by individual French ministries which covered a raft of different issues.[26] A discussion document setting out the initial position of the Union was put to the General Affairs Council on April 10. The report was approved by EU Foreign Ministers and served as the basis for consultations between the Troika and the Mediterranean partners, the first time the latter were approached for their input.

The Commission spent the period after the Essen summit working on its own proposals to implement the EMP. Its ensuing communication to the Council, timed to coincide with the member states' first formal discussion of the draft Declaration also called for a substantial increase in financial assistance to the region.[27] The document incorporated a breakdown of prospective spending commitments, an analysis of the EMP's strategic aims and objectives, and guidelines for EU follow-up actions in each policy area. Such thoroughness was intended to reassure sceptical northern member states that the distribution of EU funds would be tightly controlled and strategically targeted. The Commission took the view that the proposals could serve as a useful basis for the Barcelona conference, an attempt by Commissioner Marín to counter the Council's domination of the exercise.[28]

Feedback on these early drafts from the twelve partners was broadly positive. However, there were general concerns about the orientation of the EMP and some very specific concerns about the conference itself. For several governments, any moves to multilateralize Mediterranean policy threatened to water down their 'special' bilateral relationships with the EU and with individual member states. In the words of one official:

> You cannot come up with a policy devised in Brussels and say 'this will apply all the way to Egypt or Israel'. You cannot simply think of any policy that would be fit for all these countries and serve all their interests at the same time, and not be detrimental to a major extent to one group or another.[29]

Another official complained that:

> There was no prior consultation between the EU and the Mediterranean states on what were the real needs. The concept of specificity is important. No structure can be adapted to countries with very different cultural heritages and social cleavages.[30]

Such attitudes were symptomatic of a fundamental problem with the EMP. The concept of a 'Euro-Mediterranean' space was regarded by many as an artificial construction that marked out the geographical boundaries of Europe's project to extend its sphere of influence but failed to take into account intra-regional diversity.[31] In imposing this notional unity on the Mediterranean region, the EMP risked being seen merely as another convenient vehicle for westernisation rather than the basis for putting relations between the Union and the partners on a new footing.[32]

Concern was also expressed about the EU's over-emphasis of the politico-security dimension of the EMP and its lack of attention to a range of socio-cultural issues. The Maghreb countries, for instance, pointed out that sensitive issues such as the status of migrant workers in the Union had been left out of the draft document.[33] On the equally delicate issues of democratisation and human rights, the partners voiced reservations about the perceived imposition of European cultural norms and the possibility of tighter political conditionality being applied to EU aid. The Union's reluctance to make substantial new trade concessions to the partners undermined its attempts to pressurize them over human rights and democracy.[34] Accusations of cultural imperialism, suspicion of the EU's motives and disquiet about western attitudes towards Islam were to be regular points of contention as the Barcelona process unfolded.

By the end of the French Presidency in June 1995, a largely unaltered framework document, incorporating the results of consultations between the troika and the partners, had been adopted by the Foreign Ministers. Of the handful of concessions made to the partners, the most notable was the addition of a passage stating that the Euro-Mediterranean Agreements would 'safeguard the specificity' of the partners' bilateral relations with the Union.[35] The Cannes Summit (June 1995) subsequently approved the document. Its main themes are set out below.

> 1) A political and security chapter, comprising, *inter alia*, measures designed to promote regional political stability, the non-proliferation of weapons, respect for democratisation and human rights, and specific 'confidence building' measures.
> 2) An economic and financial chapter, including the often repeated commitment to establish a free-trade area by 2010, increased economic, financial and technical co-operation and other forms of support for the economic development of the partners' economies.
> 3) A social and human chapter, including dialogue between social organisations, cultural exchanges (between schools and universities, for instance) and other non-governmental forms of co-operation.[36]

**Figure 4.1 Draft Programme for the Barcelona Conference**

Cannes was also significant for the resolution of an internal dispute about the budget for the EMP. Ahead of the European Council meeting, the partner countries had been critical of the Union's indecision in agreeing an increase in financial assistance to accompany the initiative. A protracted and public row among the member states over the budget undoubtedly sent out a negative signal about the Union's commitment to the project. Under pressure to push through a new aid package, the summit saw the member states agree to increase total funding to 4.7 billion ECUs, matched by an almost identical amount in EIB grants and loans.

As the baton passed from France to Spain, differences emerged between the two over the relative importance of each chapter of the Declaration. Having successfully co-sponsored the Stability Pact for Central and Eastern Europe, Balladur's government regarded a similar initiative for the Mediterranean as a means to boost the Union's profile in the Middle East by promoting it as an alternative interlocutor to the USA.[37] French diplomats sought to bring the Political and Security chapter to the fore by proposing that a Mediterranean stability pact should be the centrepiece of the Political and Security Partnership.[38] However, the Spanish government felt that no single chapter should dominate, and that any attempt to establish new codes of conduct for international relations in the Mediterranean region could interfere with the Middle East Peace Process.[39] Asserting its credentials as an 'honest broker', Spain took a more guarded position on the EU's involvement in the Middle East Peace Process, believing that step-by-step confidence building and careful, relatively neutral diplomacy would produce better results in the long run than a high profile political initiative. As the Declaration passed through the Council's working groups, Spanish representatives persuaded their counterparts to heed Commissioner Marín's warning that the Barcelona process should keep its distance from the Peace Process.[40]

In the run up to the Conference itself, more problems surfaced which drew further attention to the EU's lack of unity. The first concerned a request by eight Arab-Mediterranean countries, led by Algeria, to allow Libya to attend.[41] The exclusion of Libya from the EMP left a gaping hole in the Euro-Med construction. As a major supplier of oil to Italy and with a recent history of hostility to the 'West', a Libyan presence at Barcelona made strategic sense. Spanish Foreign Minister Javier Solana hinted that it might be allowed to participate, stating that 'it has not been ruled out that observers may be attending in one form or another'.[42] However, Commissioner Marín appeared unsympathetic, arguing that Libya had not entered into 'contractual relations' with the EU, an unwritten prerequisite of participation.[43] Moreover, in view of the continuing *impasse* over the Lockerbie and UTA bombings, the prospect of British and French Foreign Ministers sitting alongside Libyan leaders was always unlikely.[44] In the end, the problem was resolved when Colonel Gadhaffi retracted his government's request to attend.[45]

A second issue concerned requests by the Arab League, Russia and the USA to attend the conference as official observers. The traditional security interests of the superpowers in Mediterranean, and the involvement of Egypt, Israel, Jordan and Syria in the EMP, elevated the status of the event. France and Spain, however, were especially guarded about a US presence. As a spokesperson for the French foreign ministry put it, 'the Barcelona conference is only for Europeans and Mediterraneans, and the USA is neither'.[46] In the Spanish press, the USA stood accused of trying to get in by the back door.[47] Ultimately, the EU stuck to its guns over the exclusivity of Barcelona, and 'outsiders' were only invited to observe the opening plenary session.

A host of problems arose with the text of the Declaration during the month before the conference, forcing some re-wording of the document. The terms of the Political and Security chapter drew strong objections from the Arab partners. Syria, backed by the Palestinians, questioned the sections on self-determination and the fight against terrorism, arguing that armed conflicts over occupied territories should not be defined as terrorism, but as 'legitimate struggles'.[48] Egypt, along with Syria, also attempted to use the Barcelona Declaration to demand Israel's signature of the Nuclear Non-proliferation Treaty.[49] There was no likelihood of finding agreements on these issues that would satisfy all the participants, and the authors of the Declaration were simply forced to paper over the cracks.

Decisions about the institutional machinery to oversee the Barcelona process were taken in October 1995. A 'Senior Officials Committee' comprising Ambassadors and other high-ranking foreign ministry personnel was established to oversee the Political and Security Partnership. In an attempt to preserve the sanctity of the Union's institutional procedures, Belgium and Luxembourg argued that only the Troika should represent the Union.[50] Others, fearing that they would lack influence on the Barcelona process outside the Troika, argued for the full participation of all the member states.[51] The eventual compromise stipulated that the Troika would represent the Union, but that the other member states could attend meetings and intervene if the chair permitted it.[52] The other two chapters were to be overseen by the 'Euro-Med Committee' on which the member states were to be represented only by the Troika. All twelve partners, and the Commission, would sit on both Committees. The Commission was assigned the role of manager of the Barcelona process and therefore found its position strengthened by its presence on both the key steering committees. The design of this institutional machinery had some significance for EU external policy making. It marked a tentative move to link Union activities in pillars I and II, since it was anticipated that the EMP might be a source of CFSP Joint Actions that would in turn activate Community policy instruments.

The negotiation of the Declaration and Work Programme reinforced the EU's command over the form and content of the Euro-Med Partnership. France and Spain took on the lion's share of the task of drafting the Declaration and produced a document that reflected both the priorities of the Mediterranean member states and the EU's interest in strengthening its economic grip on the region. The peripheral involvement of the partners in the preparations also drove home the illusory nature of the partnership concept. The partners appeared to have little say in the balance between the three chapters of the Declaration which put European concerns about security and the promotion of 'western' values ahead of their demands for fairer treatment in both economic and political terms. For the Arab governments, the failure of the EMP to take on the political situation in the Middle East heightened their scepticism about the value and durability of the Barcelona package. Closing the gap in expectations about what the EMP would deliver was a sizeable challenge.

**The Barcelona Process**

It was hard not to be swept along by the tide of euphoria generated by the Barcelona conference. Pictures of Israeli, Lebanese, Palestinian and Syrian representatives standing together in the Catalan sunshine captured the essence of the so-called 'Barcelona spirit'. One commentator even likened it to the 1955 Messina conference.[53] As Bichara Khader remarks, 'those who dared to express scepticism about the project of "partnership" were described as "Cassandras"'.[54] The diplomatic momentum initially seemed to be sustained when the Council Presidency passed to Italy. Schedules for follow-up meetings covering much of the Work Programme were drafted by the Italians under the energetic chairmanship of Ambassador Antonio Badini.[55]

However, the euphoria was short-lived as the limitations of the process and the sensitive nature of much of its subject matter became apparent. Crucially, and inevitably, the breakdown of the Middle East Peace Process during 1996 and

1997 infected the Euro-Mediterranean Partnership and brought the Barcelona initiative to a virtual standstill. Progress became a matter of ensuring that the partners continued to attend meetings. The second and third meetings of the Euro-Med Foreign Ministers in Malta (April 1997) and Palermo (June 1998) were beset by arguments between the Israeli and Palestinian delegations and produced little more than updates on the EMP. By the time of the Stuttgart ministerial meeting in 1999, simply keeping the process alive had become the priority.

A measure of the EU's disappointment with the Barcelona process was its decision in June 2000 to adopt a four-year 'Common Strategy' for the Mediterranean (CMS) under the provisions of the Amsterdam Treaty, part of an effort to 'reinvigorate' the EMP by giving the package greater strategic coherence.[56] The stated aims of the CMS were to 'undertake a comprehensive review' of the process and make it 'more action-orientated and results-driven'.[57] The document mapped out the Union's common interests in the form of a 'vision' for the region, listed a detailed set of objectives and the instruments for implementing the Strategy. The intention, at least ostensibly, was to pull together the disparate activities of the Barcelona process and to provide a firmer basis to generate specific EU Joint Actions. Stronger political direction would be engendered by entrusting the implementation of the CMS to the European Council and the Council Presidencies.[58]

However, much of the text of the CMS merely restated the original objectives of the EMP, raising questions about its 'value added' and its potential to move the Barcelona process forward.[59] Its most notable break with the Barcelona Declaration was the explicit linkage it made between the EMP and the Middle East Peace Process. Divisions among the member states during the negotiation of the CMS ruled out any possibility of a more decisive statement.[60] The end product was a document that did not 'propose any fundamental re-evaluation of how the Barcelona model may have failed in its conception as well as in its execution'.[61] There was apparently little prior consultation on the Mediterranean Strategy either within the EU or between the EU and the partner countries. With Common Strategies for Russia and the Ukraine already on the table, the CMS was also a product of the internal politics of balancing EU foreign policy action in the east and south. The need to be seen to be doing something in relation to the EMP appeared to count for much more than its substance. This section goes on to examine the three chapters of the Barcelona Declaration and discusses some of the key problems relating to its implementation.

*Political and Security Partnership*

The language of the Political and Security Partnership looked ambitious, pledging the signatories to 'establishing a common area of peace and stability' and to upholding principles of human rights and fundamental freedoms, self-determination, and territorial integrity. Drawing on principles from the OSCE, UN and other international agreements, the first chapter referred to internationally, though not universally, accepted norms and rules of inter-state conduct. The signatories undertook to promote confidence and security building measures, to prevent the proliferation of nuclear weapons and to cooperate in the fight against terrorism. A commitment was included to draw up proposals a Mediterranean stability pact, though it was expressly identified in the text as a long-term goal.

Notwithstanding the ambiguity of terms like 'peace' and 'stability' as strategic objectives, the substance of the Political and Security Partnership clearly touched raw nerves. Indeed, both the Israeli and Syrian delegations reiterated their objections to its content at post-Conference press briefings. Issues such as terrorism, human rights, self-determination and territoriality were at the heart of the conflict in the Middle East. Without any legal basis for the Declaration, it was not clear how the first chapter could generate action on such sensitive topics. As one official conceded:

> We don't know how we are going to proceed. Do we start big discussions on human rights in the Mediterranean? I don't know.[62]

There was a sharp contrast between the rhetoric and tone of the Declaration and the small number of measures on which any progress could be made during the follow-up process.

The fate of the stability pact proposal exemplified the gulf between the signatories on politico-security issues, as well as the difficulty of making the transition from dialogue to action. During the conference, France and Malta – the co-sponsors of the stability pact – had pressed for it to be adopted as a priority measure in the follow-up to Barcelona.[63] However, France's counterparts in the EU were rather less enthusiastic. Most preferred a cautious approach, fearing that formal multilateral commitments over security might rebound on the Union given the unravelling of the Oslo accords.[64] Despite the direct intervention of President Jacques Chirac's office, the French government was forced to lower its sights, conceding that the Charter should simply be 'something to help relations between all the Mediterranean countries'.[65] As the atmosphere between the Arab and Israeli governments further deteriorated, the participants in the 1998 Malta meeting agreed to put their work on the pact on the back burner, to be resumed 'when political circumstances allow[ed]'.[66] When a formal draft of the Charter was finally put to the Euro-Med Foreign Ministers meeting in November 2000 (Marseille), they could only agree to indefinitely defer a decision on its adoption and make a tentatively worded reference to the utility of the initiative in 'deepening political dialogue'.[67]

While Arab-Israeli tension was the overriding reason for the failure to agree a Stability Charter, wariness within the EU about new security arrangements was also a significant factor. Critics of the Barcelona process singled out the failure of the EU to channel its input into the first chapter through the CFSP.[68] The European Parliament, for instance, argued that the Political and Security Chapter affected the security of the Union as a whole and that any initiatives taken should be explicitly treated as CFSP actions.[69] The argument was a familiar one: the EU stood a much better chance of achieving its objectives if it spoke with a single voice. However, even in the unlikely event of member states unanimously agreeing specific Joint Actions on Mediterranean security, the EU possessed no independent defence/military capability to back up such measures if the need arose. Mediterranean security experts involved in the first chapter agreed that the presence of 'outsiders' – principally the USA, but also NATO – would remain essential.[70] Bearing in mind the deeply entrenched differences between the member governments over the EU's security and defence identity, the Barcelona process seemed patently unsuited to 'hard' security policy-making.

From the Arab partners' point of view, the idea of a security 'pact' was an unwelcome reminder of European colonialism in the Middle East, stirring memories of the notorious Baghdad pact. Such was their sensitivity to the term that it had to be renamed 'Stability Charter'.[71] A more practical concern was the Charter's relevance in the absence of progress in the Middle East Peace Process. One official expressed their position in the following way:

> We believe that it is premature at this time to talk about a stability pact. How can you talk about a stability pact when conflicts are still rampant in the Mediterranean?[72]

For most of the partners, the Stability Charter was also further evidence of the European side's emphasis on the security strand in the EMP to the detriment the other chapters. An official from a partner country called for:

> A greater balance between the three pillars. Of course, there are problems which occupy Southern Europe, including terrorism and drugs, but the security aspect should not dominate.[73]

Their objections to the Charter were a prime example of the partners' strong resistance to any measure that could be perceived as outside interference in internal affairs.[74] The effects of this polarisation of positions on the first chapter extended beyond the Charter proposal. Work in the Senior Officials Committee had initially been divided into six areas: the strengthening of democracy, preventive diplomacy, confidence and security building measures, disarmament and organized crime. A list of proposed measures gradually emerged (Figure 4.2), which were to be funded and coordinated by the EU. However, the participants retreated from plans to develop confidence and security building measures (CSBMs) with a 'hard' security content.[75] Instead, the emphasis was placed on 'partnership building measures', limiting the first chapter's sphere of activity to soft security.

The downgrading of the Political and Security Partnership saw progress largely confined to the development of a network of security experts comprising academics, diplomats and some military personnel.[76] Frequent conferences, seminars, training sessions and the exchange of information on a variety of security-related subjects, if nothing else, promoted awareness of the EMP among an influential group of specialists. Yet there was a sense that the activities of the network were simply covering old ground. For instance, many of the studies that

EuroMeSCo undertook simply duplicated existing research. Moving beyond the opening of channels of communication presented the participants with a much bigger challenge, a result of the deepening political crisis in the Middle East and 'intransigence' on the part of some northern EU member states.[77]

> - A network of political and security correspondents, functioning via a secure fax network.[78]
> - The compilation of human rights, disarmament and weapons inventories through questionnaires distributed to each government.
> - Exchanges of information on disarmament, arms control, terrorism.
> - The launch of a network of defence institutes.
> - Information and training programme for diplomats.
> - Convening of a network of foreign policy analysts – EuroMeSCo – from foreign policy institutes and other academic establishments in each of the participating countries.
> - Measures in the pipeline included:
> - Exchanges of diplomatic and military personnel.
> - An Egyptian/Italian co-sponsored proposal for a multilateral natural disaster management system.

**Figure 4.2 Programme for the First Chapter of the Barcelona Process**

Why did the notion of confidence building prove to be so problematic? First, as Claire Spencer argues, the agenda was geared towards 'preventing future conflicts' rather than resolving the numerous existing disputes in the region.[79] A passage in the Barcelona Declaration stated that the EMP was not intended to replace 'other activities or initiatives undertaken in the interest of peace'. There was therefore little prospect of the EMP addressing the tense relationship between Greece and Turkey, the Cyprus problem and the conflict in the Western Sahara, all issues that undermined confidence between the Barcelona participants. Confidence building measures which directly related to the Middle East Peace Process were deliberately and explicitly excluded from the first chapter. Second, the dominance of the EU in the Euro-Mediterranean context represented a significant obstacle to the 'symmetric and mutually benefiting relationship' which was necessary for long-term confidence building to take place.[80] The Arab and Turkish governments, for instance, viewed attempts by the European side to promote democratisation and human rights through the first chapter as a 'recipe for interference and certain destabilisation'.[81] But the weak bargaining position of the partner countries limited their opportunities to shape positively the agenda of the Political and Security Partnership. Third, there was insufficient recognition of the connection between the narrow definition of confidence building and 'structural risks' such as economic disparities, international debt, racism and fundamentalism that provoked instability and conflict.[82] Despite the calls for a holistic approach to security, there were few concrete examples of linkage between the proposed measures and work underway in the other chapters.

By 2001, participants in the Political and Security Partnership had little to show for 6 years of activity. After the predictable failure of the 27 to adopt the Charter, the list of achievements was a short one. Examples of concrete results included the holding of regular training seminars for diplomats and a variety of exchanges connected with the civil disaster management initiative.[83] Regular meetings of the Senior Officials Committee continued, although hostility between the Arab partners and Israeli representatives made for a difficult working atmosphere. Behind the scenes, officials and scholars involved in the Euro-Med networks pointed to the beneficial effect of airing fundamental differences about security even if it was hard to find any sign of common ground.[84] Their view was that debating such issues might at least lay the groundwork for more substantive cooperative activity when circumstances allowed it. Nevertheless, without movement on the Israel-Palestine crisis, the first chapter looked destined to remain becalmed.

*The Economic and Financial Partnership*

The Economic and Financial Partnership was the centrepiece of the Barcelona process, and the 'engine' of the EMP, committing the signatories to establishing one of the world's largest free trade zones by 2010 with a potential market place of 800 million people. The measures set out in the Barcelona Work Programme were designed to complement the Euro-Mediterranean Agreements by promoting regional economic integration, increased capital investment and infrastructural development, and by setting out guidelines for the management of common resources (environment, water). The MEDA budget would provide a combination of bilateral financial support for structural adjustment and private sector development in individual partner countries and funding for regional projects. The primary purpose of the second chapter was to lay down the methodology by which a framework of economic governance would be extended to the Mediterranean region. Its content underscored the neo-liberal orthodoxy which permeated throughout the EMP.[85]

The Work Programme for the second chapter earmarked the harmonisation of import/export procedures, rules and standards as priorities for the implementation process. Provisions relating to the extension of existing co-operation in fields such as energy, rural development, technology transfer, technical assistance for business co-operation and investment were all designed to pave the way for increased commercial and investment activity. The main beneficiaries would be firms based in the EU through the award of contracts to provide assistance, opportunities for joint commercial ventures and the opening up of new markets.

For the Mediterranean partner governments, an effective Economic and Financial Partnership was an important component of the Barcelona process, promising further improvements in their access to the EU's markets, increased financial aid and the EU's assistance with economic and administrative restructuring. They were persuaded to accept the argument that a multilateral economic relationship with the EU would 'lock-in' the credibility of domestic reform programmes and enable them to exploit the projected benefits of the free-trade initiative.[86] This view was typical:

> Our national industry will suffer very much from the FTA. We have a very strong lobby against this agreement. Can you imagine competing with the giants in Europe? But we know there's no other way to liberalize.[87]

The expectation was that the multilateral track would facilitate the process of bringing trade, investment and taxation laws into line with those of the EU and the emerging framework of WTO rules.

As was the case with the first chapter, implementation of the Economic and Financial Partnership started with meetings to agree 'common sectoral principles as the basis for the alignment of policies'.[88] Follow-up conferences were organized in a bewildering range of sectors, many of which simply led to further meetings. The initial impact of the second chapter was to encourage the development of loose networks of actors – governments, commercial enterprises and other non-governmental organisations – from among the 27. Some networks sprang up around very broad subject areas such as industrial cooperation and transport. Others, such as the network of employers' associations (UNIMED) and the Euro-Mediterranean Forum of Economic Institutes (FEMISE), had a narrower focus. With the backing of funds from the MEDA budget, this type of activity gradually expanded as the Barcelona process bedded in.

Getting the private sector on board was essential to the success of the free-trade initiative. A good deal of attention was therefore directed at improving the incentives for capital investment and business promotion. For instance, one of the first measures implemented in this area was the compilation of investors' guides for each of the partners, funded by the Commission. Networks of chambers of commerce and economic institutes were mandated with the task of improving the flow of business information and increasing awareness of investment opportunities. MEDA funds were provided for European consultancies to advise small and medium-sized enterprises in the partner countries and to oversee the implementation of joint projects. But as Richard Youngs observes, business had limited involvement in the design of the Barcelona process.[89] There were few mechanisms in place to ensure that it would subsequently support the EMP and become engaged in the process to the extent envisaged.

For the 12 partners, the second chapter failed to address several key issues. Criticism centred on the subjects that had been excluded from the Declaration and Work Programme and the use of bilateral negotiations to dictate the terms of the free trade area, a method that enabled the EU to deal with each partner individually and prevent 'collective' bargaining.[90] Capital and goods would move increasingly freely throughout the region, labour would not. The

Declaration made a brief reference to the liberalisation of trade in services but no provisions for it were included in the Work Programme.[91] On the issue of foreign investment, the Work Programme included only a vague pledge to 'help create a climate favourable to the removal of obstacles to investment by giving greater thought to the definition of such obstacles'.[92] The absence of either a timetable for implementation or a strong statement about the immediate priorities for the programme did not reflect the supposed urgency of reform in the partner countries.

Closer analysis of the provisions of the second chapter exposes its strategic weaknesses. Three problems stand out. First, the debt crisis barely figured in the Declaration. The relevant passage read:

> The partners acknowledge the difficulties that the question of debt can create...They agree, in view of the importance of their relations to continue the dialogue in order to achieve progress in the competent fora.

By implication, the debt issue would continue to be handled by governments in the London and Paris clubs and the multilateral financial institutions, forums and organisations better known for conservatism than forward thinking. An Algerian commentator cogently summed up the partners' views on the subject: 'Can a partnership, in the equal benefit of both parties, be built between a "heavy" creditor and his debtor?'[93]

Second, the EU's defensive stance in the bilateral negotiations with the individual partners sharply contrasted with the expansive language on free-trade in the Barcelona process. Xavier Prats, Commissioner Marín's cabinet spokesman on the Mediterranean, put the issue bluntly: 'the EU is selfish, but then so is everyone. The question is, who gets the better deal?'[94] At the same time as trade and industry ministers were meeting around the Mediterranean to discuss cooperation on industrial and investment policies, so negotiators from both sides were arguing over import quotas for oranges, potato and rice.

Third, there was, arguably, excessive dependence on private capital to meet the objectives of the Economic and Financial Partnership. Some of the partner countries, such as Morocco and Tunisia, were able to point to moderate success in attracting inward investment following extensive privatisations. Nevertheless, the evidence at the turn of the millennium suggested that the Middle East and North Africa continued to lack the competitive advantages of regions such as Latin America, South Asia and the Far East, lagging well behind on a wide variety of indicators.[95] Inward foreign investment in the Mediterranean partner countries stagnated during the 1990s.[96] The region absorbs only 5 per cent of all FDI flows to the developing world, while the proportion of EU FDI going to Mediterranean partners actually fell from 2.2 per cent in 1992 to below 1 per cent in 1999.[97] The apparent disinterest of business in the EMP attested to the difficulties of operating in much of North Africa and the Middle East and to the lure of more lucrative markets elsewhere. With the exception of the scramble to invest in the energy sector in North Africa, the response of European companies to the EMP did not represent the essential injection of commercial activity that the architects of Barcelona had hoped for. More than any other element of the Euro-Med Partnership, the second chapter illustrated the magnitude of the task facing the 27 signatories in delivering economic transformation in the region.

*The Social, Cultural and Human Affairs Partnership*

On the face of it, the incorporation of a socio-cultural dimension in the EMP was a laudable objective and one lacking in previous incarnations of EU Mediterranean policy. The third chapter of the Barcelona Declaration contained a pledge to integrate 'civil society' into the Euro-Med process and instigate 'cultural dialogue' and 'exchanges at human, scientific and technological level'. The range of subjects covered in the Declaration and Work Programme was impressive, setting objectives for cooperation in areas such as education, health, democratic practices, migration, terrorism, drug trafficking, international crime, corruption and racism. Such issues were an integral part of the new thinking on security.

However, multilateral activity in this area was fraught with difficulties, opening up the EU to accusations of neo-colonialism and of a 'continued proclivity for imposing its cultural and social values on the developing world'.[98] The Work Programme struck an uneasy balance between progressive language on cultural and social issues, and tough passages on crime, drug trafficking, migration and terrorism that were arguably the Union's real priorities. Human rights were given greater prominence in the Declaration's first chapter, suggesting that they were seen as a matter for governments rather than the much wider range of actors that the third chapter sought to engage.

Perhaps the major shortcoming of the 'human' chapter was its inability to give civil society the free rein it required for progress to be made in implementing the principles of the Declaration. Given the authoritarian nature of several of the partner governments the latitude of action for non-governmental organisations was invariably narrow. The coopting of certain approved organisations and social movements and the suppression of opposition, for instance, were a feature of political systems across the Maghreb and Mashreq. A good example of this paradox arose during preparations for the Helsinki Ministerial Conference on the Environment in November 1997. Several Arab-Mediterranean governments demanded that NGOs originating from their states should receive official accreditation before being allowed to participate. As one official argued, we have to find a place for NGOs, but in most of these countries NGOs represent the opposition'.[99]

If the third chapter did have a positive impact, it was at the margins of the Barcelona process. On the same day that the Declaration was signed, a Euro-Med Civil Forum was established, organised and funded by Cataluña's *Communidad Autonoma*, the European Commission, the EU's Economic and Social Committee, the Spanish Foreign Ministry and UNESCO. Around 1200 representatives from 700 social bodies participated in the first forum which discussed issues ranging from cooperation between SMEs to religious dialogue and inter-cultural exchanges. Outside the official conference, non-governmental interests organised an 'Alternative Mediterranean Conference' attended by 2000 delegates from 300 associations including anti-racist movements and trade unions. It challenged the state-led nature of the Barcelona process, the dominance of trade liberalisation and the involvement of authoritarian governments.

By the time of the Malta summit, the number of initiatives underway in the third chapter had mushroomed. At the second meeting of the Euro-Med Forum, one participant summarized progress thus:

> Many events, fora, workshops and new networks have cropped up all over the Mediterranean. The difficulty of drawing up a report of activities and initiatives is evident and discriminatory. We are unfortunately unable to establish a complete inventory of all the activities and their development.[100]

The fact that appraising the third chapter was so difficult suggested that at least one of its aims – to stimulate de-centralized cooperation between non-governmental actors – was being realised. However, much of this activity was low key in nature, revolving around themes such as the region's heritage, collaboration on audio-visual projects and programmes designed to encourage exchanges between young people. An attempt to boost the profile of the EMP's socio-cultural dimension at the 1998 Rhodes ministerial meeting signified political recognition that progress was lagging behind the other two chapters but failed to give it fresh impetus.[101]

A balance sheet of the third chapter at the turn of the millennium provides testimony to the sensitivity of operating in this sphere of Euro-Mediterranean relations. Besides the steady expansion of a range of uncontroversial cooperative projects between educational and cultural organisations and the convening of meetings of a Euro-Med Parliamentary Forum, there were few signs that civil society was being integrated into the Barcelona process.[102] As Richard Youngs points out, most of these projects encouraged the participation of elites rather than engaging the broader population.[103] The 'MEDA Democracy' budget line was used to support around 150 projects between 1996 and 1998, with much of the funding directed towards training and education on human rights and democracy, awareness campaigns, womens' rights and the media.[104] Here too, the main beneficiaries were 'western style advocacy groups' and European NGOs which ran programmes in the partner countries.[105] The partner governments themselves continued to strongly resist moves to fund 'capacity-building' among non-governmental organisations both within individual states and across the region.

Nevertheless, the early 2000s also saw moves to strengthen the 'social dimension' of the EMP through changes in its agenda.[106] Belated progress began to be made in the implementation process as the EU and the partners gradually settled on a mutually acceptable programme. Renewed efforts were made to expand the low visibility and small scale networking which was the principal activity of the third chapter. As part of a trade-off which involved the introduction of a justice and home affairs dimension to the EMP, the partners were offered 'positive' concessions on the rights of immigrants who lived and worked inside the EU.[107] This concession in turn enabled the EU to put two issues on the table –

terrorism and illegal immigration – which had become highly politicized for the member states. Such compromises helped to assuage governmental concerns about the third chapter but ensured that civil society would continue to play only a bit part in the Barcelona process.

## Conclusions

For Eberhard Rhein, the Euro-Mediterranean partnership 'underscored the ambition of the EU to speak for the whole of Europe'.[108] The Barcelona process was certainly dominated by the Union at both the agenda setting and implementation phases. Close adherence by the member states to the Commission's 1994 proposals on the EMP gave the outward appearance of a high degree of commitment to the European Union as the most appropriate level at which to pursue a comprehensive Mediterranean policy. That this political investment was backed by a substantial financial commitment and an institutional architecture that promised to harness together the EU's established external economic policy instruments to its weaker CFSP suggested that lessons had been learned about how to construct more effective strategic actions.

A brief overview of the institutional dynamics of the implementation process seems to confirm this point. The Commission emerged from the Barcelona conference as the major beneficiary of the initiative. DG1B was granted responsibility for coordinating the follow-up process in all three chapters alongside the Council Presidency. From the outset, the Commission used its power judiciously, deliberately proposing several actions in the first chapter which required funds from the MEDA budget. In doing so, it exploited with the tacit approval of the member states a backdoor route to circumventing the distinction between pillars I and II of the Maastricht Treaty. In a very limited way, politico-security policy was being made, funded and administered by the Community, rather than by purely inter-governmental agreements among the member states. All could agree that effective co-ordination between first and second pillar matters was crucial to the programme's success.

A look beyond these modest improvements in EU external policy making to the record of the Barcelona process over its first five years, however, tells another story about the EMP as strategic action. Assessments of the EMP from both the inside and outside were almost universally negative. In 2000, the Commission's frank evaluation of progress highlighted fundamental problems with virtually every element of the EMP from the slow negotiation of the Association Agreements and its failure to stimulate 'south-south' trade to the lack of 'serious dialogue' on human rights.[109] Perhaps the most telling criticism was that it concerned 'the management, rather than the transformation, of [EU-Mediterranean] relations'.[110] Any one of a myriad of indicators pointed to a widening of inequalities between the EU and the partner countries and growing potential for instability, while the main 'output' appeared to be the development of cooperative networks.

To be sure, the initially upbeat expectations about the Barcelona process were always unwise, especially given the persisting *impasse* between the Arabs and Israelis and the excessively ambitious objectives of the EMP. One interpretation of the Euro-Med venture is that it was premised on change occurring over the long-term through functional cooperation that would 'spill over' and create a culture of regional cooperation at all levels of government. In this respect, supporters of the process might credibly claim that it is too early to judge whether or not it is capable of transforming the fortunes of the region. But several issues heavily weigh against this view. First, despite the presence of overarching coordination machinery, the implementation process has laid bare the lack of consistency between some of the key objectives of the three chapters. Second, a question mark remains about the extent and durability of the Union's economic and political commitment to the Mediterranean. With costly eastern enlargement approaching and an increasingly crowded foreign policy agenda there is a danger that a faltering Barcelona process may fade into the background. Third, the success of the EMP hinges upon a wide range of 'exogenous' factors such as the mobilisation of private capital, substantive CAP reform and an effective solution to the debt problem. There are, as yet, few signs that these processes are moving in the right direction. Fourth, the geographical scale of the EMP and the scope of the tasks set out in the Barcelona Declaration and Work Programme do not lend themselves to effective strategic action. Strategies tend to be at their most achievable when they are based on a relatively small number of objectives and realistic targets. Finally, and most problematic of all, unity of purpose among the EMP's participants has rarely been in evidence. Until relations among the 27 are 'normalised' – and that extends beyond the Arab-Israeli problem – the Barcelona process is unlikely to make significant headway.

## Notes

[1] The Palestinian Authority was effectively treated as a sovereign government for the purposes of the Barcelona conference. The other 26 included the 15 EU Member States along with Algeria, Cyprus, Egypt, Israel, Jordan, Lebanon, Malta, Morocco, Syria, Tunisia and Turkey.

[2] Barbé, E. (1996) The Barcelona Conference: Launching Pad of a Process', *Mediterranean Politics*, Vol. 1, No. 1, p. 26.

[3] Victor Yves Ghebali's work on the OSCE-CSCM link is particularly useful. See, for example, Ghebali, V. (1993) 'Towards a CSCE in the Mediterranean: The CSCM' in M.R. Lucas (ed.) *The CSCE in the 1990s: Constructing European Security and Cooperation*, Baden-Baden: Nomos, pp. 335-43.

[4] De Marco, G. (1997) Speech to Annual Ambassadors' Conference, Valletta, August 1992, cited in Ministry of Foreign Affairs of Malta, *Malta's Foreign Policy in the Nineties*, Valletta: Ministry of Foreign Affairs of Malta, p. 71.

[5] Interview, Valletta, 18 December 1997.

[6] European Commission (1992) *The Future of Relations Between the Community and the Maghreb*, SEC (92) 401, Brussels, 30 April, p. 3.

[7] In 1993, Manuel Marín, another Spaniard, succeeded Abel Matutes as Commissioner in charge of DG1B. By all accounts, Marín devoted a great deal of time to the EU's role in the Middle East Peace Process, which may explain why the Euro-Maghreb partnership temporarily seemed to be put on the back burner.

[8] European Commission (1993) *Future Relations between the Community and the Middle East*, COM (93) 375, Brussels, 8 September, p. 6.

[9] Barbé, E. (1996) op. cit., p. 28.

[10] Gillespie, R. (1997) 'Northern European Perceptions of the Barcelona Process', *Revista CIDOB d'Afers Internacionals*, No. 37, Internet Version, http://www.cidob.es/Castellano/Publicaciones/ Afers/37.html.

[11] Prior to the Essen summit, Felipe Gonzalez threatened to block eastern enlargement in the absence of a meaningful gesture on east-south rebalancing in EU foreign policy. See Gillespie, R. (1997) Ibid.; Joffé, G. (2001) 'European multilateralism and soft power projection in the Mediterranean' in F. Tanner (ed.) *The European Union as a Security Actor in the Mediterranean: ESPD, Soft Power and Peacemaking in Euro-Mediterranean Relations*, Zürcher Beiträge zur Sicherheitspolitik und Konfliktforschung, No. 61, Zürich, http://www.fsk.ethz.ch/documents/Beitraege/zu_61/ zu_61_chapter2.pdf.

[12] Antonio Marquina, for instance, points to the establishment of bilateral strategic groups by the big three (France-Spain and Italy-Spain) in 1989 as concrete examples of security cooperation. Marquina, A. (1991) 'Spain' in M. Jopp, R. Rummel and P. Schmidt (eds) *Integration and Security in Western Europe: Inside the European Pillar*, Boulder and Oxford: Westview, p. 201. By contrast, Roberto Aliboni argues that there was 'reactive solidarity' rather than an 'active solidarity' among the southern EU states. Aliboni, R. (1992) 'Southern European security: Perceptions and problems' in R. Aliboni (ed.) *Southern European Security in the 1990s*, London: Pinter, p. 2. See also Gallino, D. (1991) 'Security challenges as perceived in the Mediterranean NATO countries' in M. Jopp, R. Rummel and P. Schmidt (eds) *Integration and Security in Western Europe: Inside the European Pillar*, Boulder and Oxford: Westview, p. 112.

[13] Interview, Madrid, 6 November 1996.

[14] Interview, Brussels, 11 December 1996.

[15] For instance, the Spanish government was instrumental in setting up a Maghreb Working group in EPC. Marquina, A. (1993) 'Security and cooperation in the Western Mediterranean: The Spanish Policy; in A. Marquina (ed.) *El Flanco Sur de la OTAN*, Madrid: Editorial Complutense, p. 66; Barbé, E. (1996) 'Spain: The Uses of Foreign Policy Cooperation' in C. Hill (ed.) *The Actors in Europe's Foreign Policy*, London and New York: Routledge, p. 118.

[16] Barbé, E. (1995) 'European Political Cooperation: The upgrading of Spanish foreign policy' in R. Gillespie, F. Rodrigo and J. Story (eds) *Democratic Spain: Reshaping External Relations in a Changing World*, London and New York: Routledge, p. 121.

[17] Heywood, P. (1995) *The Government and Politics of Spain*, Basingstoke: Macmillan, p. 279.

[18] Prime Minister Felipe Gonzalez also had domestic motives for offering to host the conference. From 1994, his government had relied on Catalan leader Jordi Pujol's support to preserve its parliamentary majority. Giving the conference to Barcelona could be seen as a reward for Pujol's support. At a time when the Socialist government was being blamed for Spain's economic downturn, and Gonzalez himself was under fire over a corruption scandal, a big foreign policy success had the potential to divert attention away from domestic politics.

[19] See Calleya, S. (1997) *Navigating Regional Dynamics in the Post-Cold War World: Patterns of Relations in the Mediterranean Area*, Aldershot: Dartmouth. The crux of Calleya's argument is that the underlying purpose of the EMP is 'boundary management' rather than 'boundary transformation'.
[20] Quoted in Barbé, E. (1996) op. cit., p. 27.
[21] *European Report*, No. 1968, July 20 1994, Section V, pp. 8-9.
[22] Interview, Brussels, 26 April 1996.
[23] European Commission (1994) *Strengthening the Mediterranean Policy of the European Union: Establishing a Euro-Mediterranean Partnership*, COM (94) 427 Final, Brussels, 19 October, p. 5.
[24] Barbé, E. (1996), op. cit., p. 25.
[25] See Bulletin of the European Union, EU12-94, pp. 26-7, point I.55; *European Report*, No. 2009, January 21, 1995, Section V, p. 6.
[26] Interview, Brussels, 10 December 1996.
[27] European Commission (1995a) *Euro-Mediterranean Conference*, Doc No. 19/95, Brussels.
[28] Interview, Brussels, 22 November 1996.
[29] Interview, Brussels, 4 November 1997.
[30] Interview, Brussels, 6 November 1997.
[31] See Calleya, S. (2000) 'Regional Dynamics in the Mediterranean' in S. Calleya (ed.) *Regionalism in the Post-Cold War World*, Aldershot: Dartmouth.
[32] For a discussion of this issue, see Xenakis, D. and Chryssochoou, D. N. (2001) *The Emerging Euro-Mediterranean System*, Manchester: Manchester University Press, pp. 105-6.
[33] Interview, Brussels, 23 April 1996.
[34] Youngs, R. (2001) *The European Union and the Promotion of Democracy: Europe's Mediterranean and East Asian Policies*, Oxford: Oxford University Press, p. 79.
[35] Barbé, E. (1996), op. cit. p. 6.
[36] Bulletin of the European Union, EU 6-1995, p. 22, point I.49. It is worth noting that this early draft of the Barcelona Declaration closely followed the broad outline proposed by the Commission in 1994.
[37] *Marchés Tropicaux et Méditerranéens*, December 1, 1995, p. 2624.
[38] Ibid.
[39] Ibid.
[40] Interview, Madrid, 6 November 1996.
[41] Part of the argument made by the Arab group was that if Israel, a state technically still at war with two of the partners, could attend the Barcelona conference, then similar dispensation should be granted to Libya.
[42] *European Report*, No. 2072, October 4 1995, Section V, p. 13.
[43] Manuel Marín, Interview with Ali Wahida (1995) 'Manuel Marin: 'Jeter les bases d'un espace Euro-Méditerranéen', *Arabies*, No. 104, July-August, p. 30.
[44] As well as being blamed for the bombing of Pan Am 103 over Lockerbie in 1988, the Libyans were also accused of bombing of flight UTA 122 (a French airliner) over Niger in 1989. In 1993, the member states adopted a rare common position (Decision 93/614) on Libya, severing ties across a range of economic sectors.
[45] Despite being a strong advocate of normalized relations with Libya, Italy appears not to have raised objections to this stance.

[46] Ministère des Affaires Etrangères (1995) 'Point de presse: Declarations du Porte Parole', *Actualités Françaises*, 27 October, Paris, «http://www.france.diplomatie.fr/cgi/».
[47] I am grateful to Professor Esther Barbé for alerting me to the reaction of the Spanish press.
[48] Barbé, E. (1996) op. cit., p. 6. Gardner, D. and White, D. 'Clashes delay launch of Euro-Med pact', *Financial Times*, 28 November 1995, p. 6.
[49] Pigasse, J. (1995) '15+12: Donnant-donnant', *Jeune Afrique*, Vol. 36, No. 1822, 7-13 December, p. 23.
[50] Interview, Brussels, 26 November 1996; Interview, Brussels, 10 April 1997.
[51] Ibid.
[52] Ibid.
[53] Pigasse, J-P. (1995) 'L'Appel au Sud', *Jeune Afrique*, No. 1821, 30 November-6 December, p. 15.
[54] Khader, B. (1996) 'Euro-Mediterranean Partnership (EMP): The Unaccomplished Tasks', *Institute for Prospective Technological Studies*, Report 25, Seville, http://www.jrc.es/iptsreport/vol25/english/MED1E256.htm.
[55] Antonio Badini, appointed by the Italian government to work on the Barcelona follow up process during the Italian Council Presidency, acquired a reputation as an effective mobilizer of the participants, and was singled out for praise by interviewees from both the EU member states and the partner countries.
[56] European Council (2000) *Common Strategy of the European Council of 19 June 2000 on the Mediterranean Region*, 2000/458/CFSP, Official Journal of the European Communities L183, 22 July, Brussels; See also European Commission (2000) *Reinvigorating the Barcelona Process*, COM (2000) 497 Final, Brussels, 6 September.
[57] European Council (2000) ibid.
[58] Incoming Presidencies were given responsibility for presenting a programme of priorities for the implementation of the CMS to the Council.
[59] See, for instance, French Ambassador Daniel Bernard's evidence to the House of Lords Select Committee on the European Union (2001) *Ninth Report: The Common Mediterranean Strategy*, http://www.parliament.the-stationeryoffice.co.uk/.
[60] A key point of contention here was the potential use of Qualified Majority Voting to take decisions on actions relating to the Middle East Peace Process. The Amsterdam Treaty allowed for QMV in the adoption of Joint Actions, common positions and other decisions that stemmed from Common Strategies. See Spencer, C. (2001) 'The EU and Common Strategies: The Revealing Case of the Mediterranean', *European Foreign Affairs Review*, Vol. 6, No. 1, p. 38.
[61] Ibid., p. 42.
[62] Interview, Brussels, 26 November 1996.
[63] Council Secretariat (1996) 'Euro-Mediterranean Conference, Barcelona, 27-28 November 1995: Thematic Discussions', *Transmission Note*, Euro-Med 3/96, Brussels, 13 February, pp. 2-12.
[64] Interview, Brussels, 25 March 1997.
[65] Interview, Brussels, 11 November 1997.
[66] European Commission (1997) *Second Euro-Mediterranean Ministerial Conference*, Malta, 15-16 April, «http://www.euromed.net».
[67] European Commission (2000) *Fourth Euro-Mediterranean Conference of Foreign Ministers: Presidency's Formal Conclusions*, 16-17 November, http://europa.eu.int/comm/external_relations/euromed/conf/marseilles/conclusions_en.pdf.

⁶⁸ Spencer, C. (1997) 'Building confidence in the Mediterranean', *Mediterranean Politics*, Vol. 2, No.2, p. 41; Peponis, P. (1998) Presentation to Conference, Athens, April 2-3, *Is the Barcelona Process Working: EU Policy in the Eastern Mediterranean*, Brussels: Philip Morris Institute, p. 9.

⁶⁹ European Parliament, Committee on Foreign Affairs, Defence and Security Policy, (1997) *Report on the Joint Report by the Presidency of the Council and the Commission on Mediterranean Policy: Follow up to the Barcelona Conference*, A4-0027/97, Brussels, p. 8.

⁷⁰ Aliboni, R., Said Aly, A. and de Vasconcelos, A. (1997) *EuroMeSCo Working Group on Political and Security Cooperation/Working Group on Arms Control, Confidence Building and Conflict Prevention, Joint Report*, Lisbon, April.

⁷¹ The Baghdad 'mutual assistance' pact of 1955 was a security alliance involving Turkey, Iraq, Britain and Pakistan. Most Arab states, led by Egypt's Gamal Nasser, refused to join, seeing it as a vehicle for western domination.

⁷² Interview, Brussels, 5 December 1996; Interview, Brussels, 13 December 1996.

⁷³ Interview, Brussels, 23 April 1996.

⁷⁴ Chourou, B. (2001) 'The (Ir)relevance of Security Issues in Euro-Mediterranean Relations' in F. Tanner (ed.) *The European Union as a Security Actor in the Mediterranean:ESPD Soft Power and Peacemaking in Euro-Mediterranean Relations*, Zurich: Zurich: Center for Security Studies and Conflict Research, p. 62.

⁷⁵ A useful analysis of this issue is provided by Kadry Said, M. (1999) *Confidence Building Measures: A Pratical Approach*, EuroMeSCo's Working Group on the Euro-Mediterranean Charter for Peace and Stability, October, http://194.235.129.80/euromesco/publi_artigo.asp?cod_artigo=38747.

⁷⁶ For a thorough account of EuroMeSCo's early work on CBMs see Aliboni, R. (1997) 'Policy analysis and public policy in the Euro-Med context: Euromesco as a confidence-building measure', Presentation, *Euro-Med Information and Training Programme for Diplomats*, Malta, 15-17 March, Valletta: Mediterranean Academy for Diplomatic Studies, http://www.diplomacy.edu/euromed/training/documents/aliboni.htm.

⁷⁷ Pargeter, A. (2001) *Italy and the Western Mediterranean*, Working Paper 26/01, ESRC "One Europe or Several?" Programme, Brighton: Sussex European Institute, p. 23.

⁷⁸ Lebanon and Syria decided to channel their communications through the Council Secretariat.

⁷⁹ Spencer, C. (1997) op. cit., p. 43.

⁸⁰ Brauch, H.G. (2000) 'From Confidence to Partnership Building Measures in Europe and the Mediterranean: Conceptual and Political Efforts Revisited' in H.G. Brauch, A. Marquina and A. Biad (eds) *Euro-Mediterranean Partnership for the 21$^{st}$ Century*, Basingstoke: Macmillan, p. 54.

⁸¹ EuroMeSCo (2002) *Working Group I – First Year Report: Security and Common Ground in the Euro-Med Partnership*, Paper 17, June, http://www.euromesco.org/euromesco/publi_artigo.asp?cod_artigo=78885#.

⁸² Biad, A. (2000) 'The Debate on CBMs in the Southern Mediterranean' in H.G. Brauch, A. Marquina and A. Biad (eds) *Euro-Mediterranean Partnership for the 21$^{st}$ Century*, Basingstoke: Macmillan, p. 126.

⁸³ European Commission (2002a) *The Barcelona Process: 2001 Review*, Brussels, p. 14.

⁸⁴ EuroMeSCo (2002) op. cit.

⁸⁵ Khader, B. (1996) *Le Partenariat Euro-Méditerranéen*, Louvain-la-Neuve: CERMAC, pp. 45-54.

[86] Hoekman, B. and Djankov, S. (1996) *Catching Up With Eastern Europe? The European Union's Mediterranean Free Trade Initiative*, World Bank Research Working Paper 1562, Washington DC: World Bank, p. 25; Petri, P. (1997b) *Trade Strategies for the Southern Mediterranean*, OECD Development Centre, Technical Papers No. 127, Paris: OECD, p. 46.
[87] Interview, 4 November 1997.
[88] Marín, M. (1996) *Memo to the Commission from Vice-President Marín: The Barcelona Declaration One Year On*, Brussels, 27 November.
[89] Youngs, R. (2001) op. cit., p. 62.
[90] Interview, Brussels, 5 November 1997.
[91] For useful assessments of the economic dimension of the EMP, see Tovias, A. (1997) 'The Economic Impact of the Euro-Mediterranean Free Trade Area Initiative in Mediterranean Non-Member Countries', *Mediterranean Politics*, Vol. 2, No.1, pp. 31-52; Marks, J. (1998a) 'High Hopes and Low Motives: The New Euro-Mediterranean Partnership Initiative', *Mediterranean Politics*, Vol. 1, No. 1, pp. 1-24; Nienhaus, V. (1999) 'Promoting Development through a Euro-Mediterranean Free Trade Zone?', *European Foreign Affairs Review*, Vol. 4, No. 4, pp. 501-18; Aghrout, A. (2001) 'The Euro-Maghreb Free Trade Area: Challenges and Opportunities', *The European Union Review*, Vol. 5, No. 3, pp. 15-32.
[92] European Commission (1995b) *Barcelona Declaration and Work Programme*, Brussels, p. 8.
[93] Hamdani, S. (1996) *The Barcelona Declaration: A Partnership Looking for Implementation and Improvement*, Workshop, http://www.diplomacy.edu/wshop/abarcel/papers/Hamdani.htm, Malta, p. 2.
[94] Prats, X. (1995) 'Address to Conference' in *Mediterranean Partnerships*, Conference Proceedings, Madrid, 5-6 October, Philip Morris Institute, p. 36.
[95] Joffé, G. (2000) 'Foreign investment and the rule of law' in A. de Vasconcelos and G. Joffé (eds) *Mediterranean Politics, Special Issue on the Barcelona Process: Building a Euro-Mediterranean Regional Community*, Vol. 5, No. 1, p. 34.
[96] European Commission (2000a) *Reinvigorating the Barcelona Process*, COM (2000) 497 Final, Brussels, p. 3.
[97] European Commission (2002b) *Euro-Mediterranean Partnership Regional Strategy Paper 2002-2006 and Regional Indicative Programme 2002-2004*, p. 10, http://europa.eu.int/comm/external_relations/euromed/rsp/.
[98] Barbé, E. (1996), op. cit., p. 7.
[99] Interview, Brussels, 10 December 1996.
[100] Roque, A. (1997) Position paper presented at Civil Forum Euromed, Malta 1997 in *Le Dialogue Interculturel en Méditerranée*, Valletta: Foundation for International Studies, Unversity of Malta, p. 19.
[101] See European Commission (1998c) *Euro-Mediterranean Partnership: Conclusions of the Second Conference of the Ministers of Culture*, http://europa.eu.int/comm/external_relations/euromed/conf/sect/culture2.htm.
[102] See Stavridis, S. (2002) 'The First Two Parliamentary Fora of the Euro-Mediterranean Partnership: An Assessment', *Jean Monnet Working Papers in Comparative and International Politics*, No. 40, May, University of Catania, http://www.fscpo.unict.it/EuroMed/jmwp40.htm.
[103] Youngs, R. (2002) *The European Union and Democracy in the Arab-Muslim World*, Working Paper No. 2, Brussels: Centre for European Policy Studies, p. 15.

[104] Karkutli, N. and Bützler, D. (1999) *MEDA Democracy Evaluation, Final Report: Evaluation of the MEDA Democracy Programme, 1996 – 1998,*
http://www.euromed.net/meda/evaluation/mdp/final-report-meda-96-98-16.htm.
[105] Youngs, R. (2002) op. cit., p. 17.
[106] European Commission (2000b) *The Barcelona Process: Five Years On 1995-2000,* Luxembourg: Office for Official Publications of the European Communities, p. 18.
[107] Ibid., p. 19.
[108] Rhein, E. (1996) *Europe and the Mediterranean: A Newly Emerging Geopolitical Area,* Transcript of a Speech, Brussels, p. 6. I am grateful to a Commission official for providing me with a copy of this document.
[109] European Commission (2000a) op. cit., p.4.
[110] Interview with Dr. Stephen Calleya, Director of the Mediterranean Academy of Diplomatic Studies, Valletta, 19 December 1997.

Chapter 5

# The Politics of the Euro-Mediterranean Partnership: Theory and Practice

**Introduction**

This chapter attempts to conceptually 'unpack' the EU's Mediterranean strategy by employing different theoretical perspectives to explain the development of the EMP. Section 1 considers the characteristics of the Euro-Mediterranean initiative as a policy area, comparing it with the Union's approach to eastern enlargement and setting it in the wider context of Euro-Mediterranean relations. Adapting Theodore Lowi's classic taxonomy of policy types, it takes up the arguments that policy should first be categorized before theory is applied to it and that policy shapes politics.[1] It breaks down the EMP into four more or less discrete categories: distributive, redistributive, constituent and regulatory. Each category is subject to different 'logics' or dynamics that govern how decisions are made and to specific patterns of bargaining and negotiation.[2] The relative influence of actors involved in the policy-making process, both governmental and supranational, also varies with the policy type.[3]

The argument that 'policy matters' is linked in section 2 to an analysis of the impact of intergovernmental politics on the EMP.[4] It contends that the EMP was not simply a product of the self-interested behaviour of the member states, and that negotiating outcomes on specific issues were not effectively pre-determined by the preferences and power of governments as intergovernmentalist theories tend to assume.[5] While member states' economic interests were certainly decisive at given points, policy also developed in ways which cannot be understood by looking at governmental preferences in isolation. Ideas, geo-politics and ideology, factors that are not easily accounted for by rational choice, interest-based theories, must also figure in an explanation of the EMP.

Section 3 engages with the institutionalist claim that institutions have a significant role in determining policy outcomes, and have policy 'preferences' in their own right.[6] The parts played by the EU's institutions in the EMP varied according to their formal, treaty-bound competencies, to the negotiating and decision making procedures that applied on given issues, and to the unique features of the Barcelona process. The focus here is on the roles of the Commission, the European Parliament, the Council Presidency and the Council Secretariat.

## Conceptualising the Euro-Mediterranean Partnership

What were the salient features of the EU's Mediterranean 'challenge' for the way that policy subsequently evolved? First, Mediterranean policy was unequivocally external policy. With the exceptions of Cyprus and Malta (and arguably Turkey), the Mediterranean partners were not eligible for membership of the Union and were not being prepared for future membership. The range of instruments available was therefore restricted to 'accession substitutes', limiting the scope for policy change.[7] The 'templates' of accession substitutes and the rules governing their use are deeply entrenched in the EU's *acquis politique*, laid down in the treaty articles which stipulate the legal bases and decision making procedures for negotiating with non-members. Trade and Association Agreements have been the EU's foremost instruments of foreign economic policy since the Treaty of Rome, leading to what Paul Pierson labels 'accumulated policy constraints' in the handling of its external relationships.[8] There is still sufficient flexibility in the EU's external policy making system to allow innovation – the Barcelona process is an obvious example – and for these standard policy instruments to be incrementally modified, exemplified by the change from Trade and Cooperation agreements to Euro-Mediterranean Agreements. But the history of EU external relations has been consistently conservative and defensive of the status quo. The EMP was, to a considerable extent, 'path dependent'.[9]

To understand the significance of using 'accession substitutes' as the basis for policy, it is worth briefly comparing the EU's relations with the CEECs and the Mediterranean partner countries. Both regions are of fundamental geo-political importance to the EU. Both represented key tests for EU foreign policy in the early 1990s. However, the Union's relationships with the CEECs quickly became an internal issue when the Union decided to offer the Visegrad four membership.[10] Accession presented the Union with a policy challenge of a fundamentally higher order than Association. As Friis observes, the accession process forced the member states 'to embark on a major internal renegotiation' with long-term implications for the Union's existence.[11] Enlargement is a highly politicized process, provoking often bitter and protracted debate among the member states about how the financial burden of integrating economies in transition should be shared. The economic and political costs and benefits associated with enlargement in terms of its impact on individual economic sectors, EU policies and the member governments themselves are usually more or less precisely established before accession actually takes place, providing a clear indication of who stands to gain and who stands to lose from the process.

By contrast, the EMP required comparatively minor internal adjustments and little substantive renegotiation of the existing terms of bilateral agreements between the Union and the partner countries. Since trade with Mediterranean states had long been subject to EU rules, the potential costs of any proposed changes to import quotas were readily available prior to negotiations. Specific issues such as agricultural import quotas, the MEDA budget and the immigration clauses in the Euro-Mediterranean Agreements were highly politicized. But the point here is that the EU's Mediterranean 'strategy' was largely concerned with reorganising the management of its relations with the partner countries. Eastern enlargement aimed to transform the candidates in the short-run and had huge implications for the structure and functioning of the EU's policies and institutions.

A second feature of the Mediterranean challenge was the perceived need for long-term economic, political and social change in the region. The emphasis was on addressing a problem – Mediterranean security – which all the member states accepted, to varying degrees, as a common problem.[12] Bargaining between governments over the Union's strategic objectives in the Mediterranean, though certainly relevant, was not decisive in the early stages of the EMP.[13] While southern member states played a key role in putting Euro-Med on the agenda, the task of defining the problem from a European perspective, setting out the rationale for a Mediterranean strategy and identifying the policy options available to the Union fell to the Commission.[14]

This distinction between problem solving and bargaining in the EU policy process, originally identified by Scharpf, is an important one.[15] Problem solving involves a search for the most efficient and effective solution to a common problem. Rather than simply trying to minimise costs and protect national interests, characteristics of a bargaining approach, member states assess the 'common utility' of policy.[16] Although there is scant evidence that the member states carefully calculated the utility of pursuing the EMP, they undoubtedly saw long-term commercial and political benefits in the initiative. Where bargaining did periodically play a decisive part in shaping the EMP was in negotiations to determine the contents of the policy, such as the Euro-Mediterranean Agreements, the financial aid package and measures which arose out of the Barcelona process.

A third feature of the Mediterranean challenge was that EU policy represented only one level in expanding network of regional and sub-regional governance. Bilateral political and economic relations between individual member states and partner countries had always continued alongside the development of EU Mediterranean policy. At another level were the activities of organisations and forums such as the Arab Maghreb Union, the Middle East and North Africa economic summits, nascent economic integration projects in the Middle East, and a host of NGOs dedicated to functional cooperation in areas such as environmental protection of the Mediterranean Sea.[17] To this list must be added the multilateral financial institutions – the IMF and World Bank – and creditor groups such as the Paris Club which virtually controlled socio-economic development strategies in many of the partner countries.

In policy areas where neither the EU nor the EMP were mandated to act, or where concurrent competencies operated, member governments retained 'privileged bilateral rights' to pursue their own commercial and political objectives and deploy their own set of policy instruments.[18] When Algeria opened up its natural gas industry to foreign investors, the southern EU governments were swift to put together attractive credit packages to support the investment activities of national companies. The Italian government's decision to sign a 'friendship' accord with Libya in July 1998, part of a subtle campaign to bring that notable absentee into the Euro-Mediterranean fold, potentially set it against the UK, France *and* the official EU line.[19] Regardless of the existence of the EMP, traditional, inter-state diplomacy and national foreign economic policies continue to exercise considerable influence over international relations in the region.[20] In signing up to the EMP, the member states were not transferring new foreign policy powers to the EU.

To summarise, devising a strategy to deal with the Mediterranean did not herald sweeping changes to the EU's internal order. Seen in the broader context of international order in the region, the EMP was only one channel for Euro-Mediterranean cooperation, and only one mechanism to promote security and stability, objectives rhetorically shared by many other actors. We would therefore expect the framework of the Mediterranean strategy to have been agreed without a great deal of political controversy, implying a strong role for the Commission and weaker role for governmental interests in policy development. That the EU had agreed on how to approach the Mediterranean security problem mattered far less than the deal it was ultimately prepared to offer the partner countries.

Understanding how flesh was put on the bones of the Mediterranean strategy requires analysis of the policy types which came together in the EMP package, and the negotiating processes associated with each of these types. While the 'path dependency' of the Euro-Mediterranean Agreements limited the potential for the pattern of trade to be significantly changed by bargaining, negotiations within the EU and between the EU and individual partner countries still determined outcomes on all the key issues. Likewise, the funds available for the MEDA budget were largely pre-determined by previous budgetary agreements, but the precise figure was set by negotiation. The Barcelona Declaration was almost entirely the product of intergovernmental negotiations.

As Likke Friis argues, 'any issue area negotiations can *probably* [italics in original] only be understood by conceptualising the various issue area logics which are at play'.[21] The notion of multiple logics is an especially apposite one in the context of the EMP since each of its components was subject to distinct negotiation and decision making procedures. The Euro-Mediterranean Agreements were negotiated on the basis of Articles 300 and 310 of the EU Treaty, giving the Commission responsibility for conducting the negotiations, the Council the duty to conclude the agreement by unanimous endorsement of the member states and the Parliament the right to be consulted during the negotiations and to give its assent. A different logic operated for the Barcelona process, the content of which was prepared by the member states in collaboration with the Commission and the partner countries. The negotiating process was a mixture of standard agenda setting by the Union's Council Presidency, ad hoc consultations between the participating governments, and the drafting of a series of documents leading to the Barcelona Declaration and Work Programme. After the Barcelona conference, the process switched to a typical multilateral format, permitting any participant to propose measures and requiring unanimous agreement for measures to be implemented. The MEDA budget also had its own distinct logic, with the Commission proposing projects, the member states giving their approval in a regulatory committee, and the allocation of funds being open to competitive tendering among private organisations.

One way of making sense of these multiple logics is to break down the EMP into Theodore Lowi's four-fold taxonomy of policy types: distributive, redistributive, constituent and regulatory.[22] The essence of Lowi's argument is that 'policies determine politics'.[23] Each type is subject to different decision making procedures, involves different constellations of actors in the policy-making process and has type-specific costs and benefits associated with it.[24] A corollary of this differentiation is that the degree of politicisation varies according to the policy category and to the individual issue. Many aspects of distributive policy, for instance, may well be treated as 'technical' issues to be managed at the bureaucratic level (by the Commission), while redistributive issues tend to be resolved at the political level (Council).[25]

That said, predicting how politicized a particular issue will be and the likely outcome of negotiations is an uncertain business. As William Wallace argues:

> The art of policy-making is partly a matter of correctly assessing the broadness or narrowness, the political sensitivity or technical complexity, of successive issues. The definition of and redefinition of issues is thus a subjective process, with plenty of room for political intervention and redirection.[26]

The Union had considerable experience of negotiating with the partner countries, and many of the issues at stake in the EMP were familiar from previous negotiating rounds, but neither side entered into the substantive stage of the EMP with a clear idea of the specific problems that would arise. Twenty-seven governments were involved, with an attendantly diverse range of demands, expectations and interests. Negotiations extended to fluid issues such as the changing market situation within the Union, assessments of the individual financial needs of each partner country and the identification of the priorities for cooperation. Moreover, negotiators effectively operated at three levels, searching for agreements that satisfied domestic interests, were mutually acceptable to the EU and to the partner countries and fulfilled the objectives of the partnership strategy.[27] Much, therefore, remained to be settled in the normal course of intergovernmental and institutional politicking.

Distributive politics in the Euro-Mediterranean Partnership centred on sharing the costs of renegotiating trade concessions in the Association Agreements, the allocation of MEDA funds to the partner countries, and the apportioning of public 'goods' such as technical assistance with administrative reform. Two factors militated against a politicisation of the distributive dimension of the EMP. First, trade concessions in the Euro-Mediterranean Agreements were to be negotiated against the background of patterns of imports and exports, a constraint accepted by the Commission, member states and partner countries. Second, there was no suggestion that the existing distribution of financial resources among the partner countries would substantially change.

Nevertheless, it was easy to predict that some distributive issues would prove highly disputatious. Even a cursory glance at the history of EU Mediterranean policy would point to problems over agricultural import quotas. Given the diversity of the partner states' trade with the Union, the range of contentious issues inevitably varied from negotiation to negotiation. Each partner government had a list of products for which they sought substantial new concessions from the Union. Similarly, certain products also presented particular difficulties for individual member states. Finding solutions to the more politicized distributive issues was largely dependent on what the Union was prepared to offer. In other words, outcomes were determined by internal needs, not external demands.

The redistributive politics of the EMP revolved around the question of how the additional funding earmarked for the Mediterranean would affect other priorities for the Union's external spending, principally the European Development Fund (EDF) and aid to the CEECs. Outcomes here were dependent to an even greater extent on negotiations within the EU. The partner governments might have pressed for increased aid, but the decision over resource allocation was the EU's alone. Although Mediterranean policy briefly became highly politicized around the time of the 1995 Cannes Summit, once the funding decision was taken, redistributive politics slipped into the background.

The constituent (or constitutive) aspect of the EMP was to be found in the institutional architecture created to serve the Barcelona process. Constitutive politics refers to a situation 'whereby the member states [in the EMP's case, the 27 participants] adopt a series of decision rules, and in some cases create new institutions, for subsequent policy-making'.[28] The EMP was internally constitutive in that new institutional structures and procedures, such as the Euro-Mediterranean Committee, the Senior Officials Committee and the MEDA budget line, had to be devised. It was externally constitutive in that it gave rise to the Barcelona Declaration and generated a plethora of new multilateral forums. Given the consensual multilateralism of the Barcelona process, it might be expected that the partners would have been more closely involved in designing the EMP's institutional architecture. However, the EU patently had the upper hand in devising the Barcelona framework and European initiatives dominated the agenda of the follow-up process.[29]

The regulatory dimension of the EMP – Lowi's fourth policy type – manifested itself in the legislative changes forced on the Mediterranean partners by the need to adapt their import and export regimes to the requirements of Euro-Mediterranean Agreements (customs duties, tariff systems) and by administrative changes agreed in the context of the Barcelona process. As the Commission's dispute with Israel during 1998 over the abuse of rules of origin showed, this aspect of Mediterranean policy could occasionally become highly politicised. However, such examples were rare, since many of the partners were already in the process of implementing comprehensive economic reforms as part of IMF structural adjustment programmes and moving towards trade liberalisation in the context of WTO agreements.[30]

Pigeon-holing the components of the EMP into these discrete categories does not cover every angle of the policy making process. Several decisions, including MEDA, could be placed in more than one category and there is always a strong element of subjectivity in the definition of such issues.[31] Furthermore, the re-negotiated aspects of the EMP unzipped old issues and created the potential for their politicisation or re-politicisation. But it does offer a neat framework for policy analysis. The next task is to integrate intergovernmental and institutional politics.

**Governments, Interests and the Policy Process**

The preferences (interests) that member states advanced and defended in the Mediterranean policy process clearly mattered. Southern member states in particular demanded 'more' Mediterranean policy. France, Italy, Spain and Greece could each legitimately claim to have real and wide-ranging, if not vital, domestic interests in the elaboration of a more comprehensive EU policy. All the member states had a commercial presence of some sort in the partner countries' markets. Even those states without obvious security interests in the Mediterranean were persuaded that policy change was in the Union's general interest. In narrower terms, governmental preferences were critical in the final stages of negotiations on the Euro-Mediterranean Agreements, in the Cannes budget decision, and in agreeing the measures that would be included and excluded in the implementation of the Barcelona process.

At first sight, the most appropriate theoretical tools for understanding the relationship between governmental preferences, negotiation and outcomes in the formulation and negotiation of the EMP are to be found in interest-based analyses. A strong case exists to use theory that captures the interplay between domestic interests and the behaviour of governments in the EU policy-making process.[32] Diplomats and politicians not only bargain with each other, they must also ensure that any agreement reached is acceptable to their domestic constituencies. An especially relevant example here was the negotiation of Morocco's Euro-Mediterranean Agreement, during which the French, Portuguese and Spanish governments faced vociferous lobbying and protests from farmers and other producers at home over concessions on imports of tomatoes, sardines and oranges. Simultaneously they faced pressure from the Commission, other member states and the Moroccan government to reach an acceptable agreement.

Arguably the most complete and compelling theoretical tool on offer is Andrew Moravcsik's 'liberal-intergovernmentalism', which explains European integration as the product of preference-based negotiations between governments.[33] Moravcsik's central claim is that the EU's 'grand bargains' – treaty negotiations – and resultant policies such as the CAP, EMU and the single market proceed in a causal sequence that sees governments rationally formulating preferences based primarily on dominant domestic economic interests, bargaining with other EU governments to secure the benefits of policy cooperation, then pooling or delegating sovereignty in the EU in order to 'lock in' commitments to cooperation.[34]

Through this intergovernmentalist lens, the EMP might be explained as the product of the member states' need to cooperate in order to maximize the commercial advantages of producers in Mediterranean markets and improve the management of their economic relationships with the partner countries.[35] Qualified trade liberalisation in the Euro-Mediterranean Agreements undoubtedly served the interests of EU manufacturers and suppliers of capital goods. The exclusion of agricultural trade from the free-trade initiative also fits Moravcsik's analysis: 'The greater the competitiveness of third country producers, the greater the pressure for external protection'.[36] Furthermore, much of the work in the second chapter of the Barcelona process was intended to create an economic environment more amenable to trade and investment, with European businesses being the principal beneficiaries.

Yet an intergovernmentalist approach goes only part of the way to accounting for the development of the EMP. First, as section 1 showed, the EMP cannot be regarded as the result of a grand bargain or history-making decision. Intergovernmentalist theory in general tends to be concerned with explaining the motives for inter-state cooperation and the establishment of international institutions rather than with the policy analysis. Mediterranean policy 'existed' well before the EMP, which was more an exercise in policy modification and re-packaging than substantive reform. There is little to indicate that the development of the EMP followed the neat sequence described above.

Second, rational choice theories, of which liberal intergovernmentalism is one, are ill-suited to explaining a policy in which ideas, rhetoric and symbolism often appeared to matter as much, if not more, than concrete interests.[37] Asked to explain his government's interests in relation to the EMP, this official's response was typical:

> It is a good thing to aim at a stable situation in the partner countries, a big advantage to have a stable socio-economic and political environment. So partnership is important. The Mediterranean could threaten the EU.[38]

It is hard to conceive of governments rationally configuring their preferences towards the kind of abstract strategic objectives that underpin the EMP. Regional peace, stability and prosperity are not the stuff of orderly, systematic governmental responses to domestic interests.

Third, the prominence of 'security' as a rationale for the EMP points towards a rather more substantive role for geopolitical factors than Moravcsik's approach appears to favour. His argument is that only where the costs and benefits of cooperation are 'uncertain, balanced, or weak' do 'security externalities' really count.[39] Security interests might be cited as motives *ex post*, but they are almost always secondary to commercial interests.[40] Granted, definitions of the Union's geo-strategic interests in the Mediterranean tended to be ambiguous, but the rise in illegal immigration into southern Europe in the early 1990s, and the violence in Algeria that spilled over into France during 1995 were regarded as very real security problems. The point is not that Moravcsik dismisses security externalities. Rather, it is that his definition of how geopolitics and security influence governmental choices is perhaps too narrow, rooted in Cold War thinking on the subject.

How should governmental preferences be factored into an explanation of the EMP? Clearly, in a manner that acknowledges that the weight of preferences varies with the salience of the issue at stake, with the policy type, with the decision making procedures that apply and with the wider context in which each decision is made. The remainder of this section examines the broader cleavages in the member states' preferences towards the EMP, and assesses the impact of these preferences based on selected evidence from the Euro-Mediterranean Agreement negotiations and the MEDA budget decision.

A key cleavage in intergovernmental bargaining over the EMP was an outgrowth of the 'trade versus aid' debate, a traditional fault-line in the Union's external trade policy.[41] As one official explained:

> This discussion took place in the preparations for Barcelona. We, as others, the UK, the Netherlands, the Scandinavians, took the view that more influence should be given to the framework for private investment and less to public assistance.[42]

The 'trade versus aid' debate set those member states with a liberal, *laissez-faire* prescription for economic development in the Mediterranean region against a group favouring a strategy that balanced trade liberalisation with a substantial aid component. The issue roughly divided the member states across an east-west axis. Northern member states (Denmark, Germany, the UK, Sweden and the Benelux states) firmly positioned themselves in the free-traders camp, while France, Spain and Italy tended to press for higher levels of aid and the maintenance of preferential trading arrangements.

The reasons for this division appear self-evident. Southern member states had more intense economic and security interests in the region than their northern, non-Mediterranean counterparts. It was, therefore, a matter of self-interest for them to persuade their counterparts to increase the EU's budget for the region in order to supplement (and arguably substitute for) their own 'investment' in regional security, in the form of bilateral aid programmes and national defence/security policies. Consistent with this division, France and Spain were the prime movers in pressing for a comprehensive and generous EU Mediterranean policy.

Returning briefly to intergovernmentalist theory, the southern group might have been expected to 'go the extra mile' on trade concessions, since they clearly stood to lose the most if satisfactory agreements were not reached with the partner countries. However, the Mediterranean member states were caught between two stools on this issue. On the one hand, France, Italy and Spain expended much diplomatic effort during their respective Council Presidencies pushing the Union and the partners towards agreement. On the other hand, domestic interests in those countries were openly antagonistic towards Maghrebi importers, restricting their respective governments' room for manoeuvre in the Council.

Here, liberal intergovernmentalism predicts 'side payments' in the form of financial compensation and other support for domestic producers adversely affected by the EMP, and the trading-off of issues in package deals to balance losses with gains. The financial aid awarded to Portugal's sardine canning industry as compensation for concessions on Morocco's sardine import quota is a good example of a financial side-payment. Similarly, Morocco's successful ploy of linking its demands on tomato import quotas to the renegotiation of a fishing agreement with the EU, of which Spanish fishermen were the main beneficiaries, provides a clear example of issue linkage.

By contrast, the preferences of the northern member states on import concessions ought to have been both more disposed to liberalisation and less intense than those of their southern counterparts. Yet both German and Dutch negotiators came under similarly concerted pressure from domestic producers (flower-growers) to stand their ground on quotas. This ever-present tension between ideological orientation and domestic political expediency lies at the heart of the often schizophrenic character of EU trade policy.[43] It also appears to confirm a basic assumption of Moravcsik's theory: that governments will favour agreements whose net effect is to boost exports except where politically powerful, non-competitive producers stand to lose.[44] The broader pattern of negotiation in the EMP – liberalisation on non-sensitive issues, continued protection on sensitive issues – also corroborates this assumption.

Nevertheless, there were instances of governmental concessions on politicized issues without obvious side-payments and issue linkage. The reason offered by one official for his government's eventual decision to compromise on import quotas suggested ideological motives:

> We conceded more than we intended on [this product]. As usually in the final phase of negotiations, in the end it is excluded for us to block negotiations with any country. It is about our positive attitude to European integration. In the end, at least on this issue we got agreement.[45]

In a similar vein, another official argued that:

> We do have agricultural interests as well, but [we] made it clear during the negotiations with Egypt and we are making it clear with Jordan that the development of trade and the Euro-Mediterranean Partnership must be the priority.[46]

Hence, the Union's long-term strategic objectives, the 'greater good' of European integration and the imperative of concluding the agreements sometimes outweighed intense domestic pressures.

A second broad cleavage divided the member states into two camps according to their preference for deepening the EU's relationship with Central and Eastern Europe or the Mediterranean, a division which at times harmed the internal cohesion of the Community.[47] Again, however, competition for resources between east and south was not a zero-sum game, and membership of either 'camp' was not exclusive. France, under Edouard Balladur's premiership, sought to be an influential player in both directions, sponsoring the EU's stability pact initiative in Central and Eastern Europe while at the same time calling for the Union to devote more resources to the Mediterranean. Germany is a major trading partner of the Mediterranean partners, particularly Algeria and Egypt, and is also one of the top three aid donors to the region among the member states. The fact that preferences on this issue were mutable was to play a crucial part in bargaining on the MEDA budget.

The MEDA budget – a product of distributive, redistributive *and* constitutive decisions – was fought over tooth and nail by the member states. The decision was made against a background of several constraints that actually reduced the leverage of the member governments. First, any changes in funding had to comply with the EU's total projected budget agreed at the Edinburgh European Council in 1992 (for the period 1993-9). Second, the Mediterranean faced stiff competition for funds from other regions, including the Central and Eastern European countries and Latin America. Third, the responsibility for deciding how much of the budget to bid for lay with the Commission, which ran the Union's foreign aid programmes. Fourth, the Mediterranean was not the EU's number one external budgetary priority at that time. A row over increased contributions to the European Development Fund for the Lomé countries topped the agenda, followed by pre-accession measures for the CEECs.

The key players in the MEDA deal were the Commission, France, Germany and Spain. Both the French and Spanish governments supported Commissioner Manuel Marín's proposal of 5.5 billion ECUs, although the Spanish expressed concern that budgetary provisions for Latin America should not be adversely affected by any increase.[48] The German government, by contrast, argued that since most of the Mediterranean partners were not potential members of the EU, the existing balance in the distribution of resources, skewed in favour of the CEECs, should be preserved.[49] Meanwhile, Finance Minister Theo Waigel was pressuring Chancellor Kohl to negotiate a reduction in Germany's overall contribution to the EU budget.[50] Ministers were left to thrash out a deal at the Luxembourg General Affairs Council and subsequently at the Cannes European Council in June 1995.

The final deal in Cannes reduced the Commission's indicative figure to 4.7 billion ECUs (1995-1999). A proportionate reduction from 7.1 billion ECUs to 6.7 billion ECUs was agreed in the financial provision for the CEECs. Both regions lost out as a result of a compromise negotiated between the French, German and Spanish governments which increased contributions to the European Development Fund for Lomé at the expense of other areas.[51] However, vigorous diplomacy by the Spanish delegation at Cannes convinced their German colleagues to accept that the original ratio of funds proposed by the Commission for the east and south should be retained.[52]

Up to a point, the function of governmental preferences in the EMP does conform to intergovernmentalist theory. Negotiators from the member states clearly had to reconcile domestic interests with the need to reach agreement with the partner countries. Preferences varied according to the issue on the table and to its salience to governments, with predictably hard bargaining over agricultural quotas and finances. Outcomes on the most politicised issues were decided at a political level involving compromises and trade-offs. But intergovernmentalist theory can offer only a snapshot of the policy process, explaining specific decision points at which governmental preferences were necessarily crucial. Agreements with third countries have to be concluded by the member states in the Council (Article 300), while decisions about allocating funds from the EU budget also primarily rest with the national governments. To fully capture the dynamic nature of the process that led to the EMP, institutional politics cannot be ignored.

## EU Institutions and the Euro-Mediterranean Partnership

The influence of the EU's institutions in policy-making is a matter for vigorous theoretical debate. Broadly speaking, intergovernmentalists see only marginal influence for the institutions, whose primary function is to act as guarantors for agreements between states.[53] Even in daily decision making, the activities of the Commission, Parliament and the European Court of Justice are argued to 'stem primarily from the desire to lock-in credible national commitments'.[54] Institutionalists argue that institutions are political actors in their own right, capable of exercising supranational autonomy in policy-making and pursuing their own preferences.[55] This section explores the notion that 'institutions matter', assessing the parts played by the Commission, European Parliament and two of the Council's multiple institutions – the Presidency and Council Secretariat – in the negotiation of the EMP.

### The Commission

The Commission was heavily involved in all aspects of the Euro-Med Partnership, from the kernel of the initiative right through to its implementation. In new institutionalist terms, it developed an 'endogenous institutional impetus for policy change that exceed[ed] mere institutional mediation'.[56] As the institutional memory bank of EU Mediterranean policy, it was in a strong position to push for policy change. As the EU's negotiator on the Euro-Mediterranean Agreements, its creativity in assembling mutually acceptable deals was essential. Its responsibility for coordinating the three chapters of the Barcelona Declaration had the potential to make it the institutional engine room of the Barcelona process.

The Commission's agenda setting role in EU policy-making is now well-established in the literature, although studies tend to limit themselves to EU internal policies.[57] The institution has proved adept at maximising both its own competencies and those of the EU, habitually pushing for 'more Europe'.[58] Its formal right of initiation (Article 211), and the freedom it has to stimulate policy development in the EU's institutional structure, have made it an essential source of policy ideas and policy change.

In the case of Mediterranean policy, DG1B had little difficulty getting the backing of the member states for the partnership strategy. The Mediterranean challenge was already high on the EU's foreign policy agenda, having been put there by the French, Italian and Spanish governments. What the Commission did was simply react to the already 'informed demand' for policy change.[59] A sterner test for the Commission was to translate proposals into deliverable actions. The earliest EMP documents showed that some of the lessons of the past had been learned. Its 1995 paper, for instance, excluded agricultural trade from the proposals for a free-trade area.[60] Although the Commission was fully cognisant of the economic significance of agricultural trade liberalisation to the Mediterranean partners, it also recognised that protecting EU producers and preserving the integrity of the CAP system were judged to be higher priorities.[61] Furthermore, the partnership paper shifted the onus of responsibility for reform to the Mediterranean third countries themselves. In doing so, the Commission developed a strategy that could be sold to member governments of all ideological persuasions; there was something in it for everyone. Free-traders could point to the self-help elements, while the interventionists could point to the call for a more focused and comprehensive programme of assistance.

Evidence of 'conceptual innovation' and 'purposeful opportunism' were also discernible in the Commission's proposals.[62] By reasoning that an integrated, 'multidimensional' strategy – encompassing 'linked actions in the economic, social and political spheres' – was required, the Commission put the case for changing EU Mediterranean policy from a simple framework for managing trade and channelling aid to a more comprehensive policy framework based on a detailed programme for cooperation with the partner countries.[63] In doing so, it staked a strong claim to expand its own competencies. On everything from support for private sector development to 'democratisation' projects, DG1B would be responsible for selecting projects, allocating funds and overseeing their implementation.

How, then, did the Commission fare in the negotiation of the EMP? Its most important task was to persuade the member states to accept a doubling of the aid budget for the Mediterranean. By preparing a thorough case for the increase based on its informational resources, it gave the member governments little cause to question the logic of its figures. An official described the process thus:

> [The Commission] did various calculations based on what countries had absorbed out of the financial protocols, World Bank analyses of their needs for the future and comparison of US and World Bank aid...also on how much headroom there was on chapter 4 of the [Edinburgh] financial perspective.[64]

Linking its plans to the activities of the multilateral financial institutions reassured the more sceptical member states such as Germany and the UK that the Union would not simply be pouring money into an empty hole.[65]

That said, Commissioner Manuel Marín had first to convince his counterparts in the Commission that the proposed level of funding was appropriate. He initially requested 6.3 billion ECUs, but was faced down by Commissioners

Hans Van den Broek, responsible for the CEECs, and Erkki Liikanen, responsible for the EU budget.[66] Even so, Marín eventually got a lot more money than he expected and the Commission's political commitment to the partnership when his colleagues unanimously approved a figure of 5.5 billion ECUs to be put to the Council.[67] This figure represented 70 per cent of the amount awarded to the CEECs and was a step towards the rebalancing of resources sought by the southern member states and Marín.

Yet despite the Commission's strong case, the member governments still reduced the MEDA budget by 1.6 billion ECUs. Criticised as derisory by several of the Mediterranean partners, the Cannes deal raised more questions about the strength of the Union's commitment to economic development in the region than it answered.[68] Indeed, a more substantial reduction might even have jeopardized the entire EMP project. The handling of the Cannes decision was a good example of the limits on the power of the Commission to secure its preferences on redistributive issues. Even with the backing of France, Italy and Spain, the final outcome was beyond its control.

Distributive issues proved equally vexatious for the Commission, with disputes over trade concessions regularly being taken out of its control and pushed up to the political level. The Euro-Mediterranean Agreements saw the Commission's negotiating flexibility more restricted than ever by its mandates from the Council. One official summed up the problem in the following terms:

> The Commission had little margin for negotiation on agriculture because of the traditional flows line. By playing with the schedules, [it] sometimes can take more favourable years as the basis to calculate traditional flows. But the ministers don't see the concessions in a broader context. They ask for a free trade area as a precursor for south-south trade and then fail to conclude an agreement because no one can agree whether [they] should accept 18,000 or 30,000 tonnes.[69]

Only where non-contentious issues, such as dismantling tariffs on industrial products, were at stake was the Commission able to conduct the negotiations as 'technical' issues, consulting the Council only on an informal basis when it proposed concessions that exceeded traditional trade flows. That all but the negotiations with Tunisia were stalled for long periods attested to the restraining effect of politicisation on the Commission's power to offer the partners significantly improved access to the EU's market.

On the face of it, the constitutive aspects of the Barcelona process were more positive for the Commission. As coordinator of the Barcelona process, DG1B was guaranteed a major initiating role across the three chapters and *de facto* control of its implementation. Although it relied to a great extent on the 'Barcelona spirit' to keep the process moving, its status as the only EU representative on the two main steering committees gave it a comparative advantage over the member states in setting the agenda and articulating the EU's interests.

The MEDA Regulation also represented a qualified success for the Commission, since the region-wide, multi-annual basis of the instrument increased the scope to link the objectives of the Mediterranean strategy with the financial aid programme.[70] However, the member states put in place a number of safeguards that kept the Commission on a fairly tight rein. In line with the general trend in comitology during the 1990s, Article 11 of the MEDA regulation made the Commission's proposals for projects subject to a 3A (regulatory committee) which requires a qualified majority vote in the Council for *approval*, rather than a 2A (management committee) in the draft regulation, which requires the Council to muster a qualified majority to *overturn* Commission proposals.[71] In the Commission's draft regulation, it had argued for the latter procedure to apply.[72] This institutional configuration ensured that the national governments closely monitored both the technical side of the proposed projects and their political context.

To summarise, most of the Commission's key demands on the EMP were met by the member states at the formative stage with few questions raised about the objectives and content of the strategy. The Commission was assisted in this respect by the functional basis of its strategy and the absence of obviously high costs to the member states, which helped keep politicisation to a minimum. Nevertheless, the nature of the EU policy process gives governments 'another bite at the cherry' when it comes to taking decisions on distributive and redistributive issues. The Commission's attitude towards agricultural trade concessions, on which it closely adhered to the Council's negotiating mandate, and its 'softly softly' approach to proposing measures in the Barcelona process, were indicative of its wariness about pushing the member states too hard. It is arguably this continuous tension between the Commission and the states that limits the Union's capacity for truly forward-thinking, transformative strategic action.

*The European Parliament*

It is difficult to point to any clear instance of the European Parliament directly influencing the development of the EMP. This unstartling finding simply reflects the continued weakness of the EP in policy initiation and its limited range of powers in external policy making. While its views on how Mediterranean policy should evolve were usually somewhat more far-sighted and strategic than the EU's end product, they were rarely heeded. In the formulation of the EMP initiative, the Parliament backed the Commission's call for substantive policy reform and passed resolutions emphasising the 'extension of regional cooperation' and the need for genuinely 'binding decisions' in the fields of security, economic cooperation, human rights, democracy and social development.[73] Its subsequent criticisms of the EMP betrayed its frustration at the result.

Still, the EP was able to make a mark on the EMP at certain points in the policy process. Its input derived both from the powers ascribed to it in EU Treaties and its informal position in the EU's institutional framework. First, its power of assent on agreements concluded between the EU and third countries (Article 300) endowed it with a *de jure* veto. Second, its right to question the Commission and the Council enabled it to raise awkward questions about issues that the EMP was failing to address. Third, as the democratic arm of the Union, the EP naturally gravitated towards the socio-cultural aspects of the Barcelona programme. The democratic void left in the Barcelona Declaration prompted it to launch its own initiatives to stimulate similar parliamentary participation in the EMP and to give some semblance of representative legitimacy to the third chapter, which was conspicuously failing to engage 'civil society' in the process. A civil servant in the Parliament's Division for Relations with Parliamentary Assemblies was designated to establish contacts with parliaments in the partner states and organise a standing forum.[74] The result was the Euro-Mediterranean Parliamentary Forum.

The EP has never withheld its assent to a full Association or Cooperation Agreement with a Mediterranean third country. It has relied instead on the threat of non-ratification as a means to highlight its concerns and extract concessions from governments. Even that tactic has been judiciously used. The Euro-Mediterranean Agreements with Morocco, Tunisia, and the interim agreement with the Palestinian Authority all safely passed through the EP.[75] Non-ratification is a rather blunt instrument and the Parliament judged it, in the EMP context, to be counter-productive. This statement on the agreement with Morocco illustrates the point:

> Where improvements need to be made, experience shows that this is better achieved through friendly dialogue than verbal assault.[76]

Since the EU's strategy assumes that socio-cultural transformation, democratisation and improvements in the human rights situation in the region will follow economic development, blocking measures intended to foster the latter was justifiably deemed to be self-defeating.

When entire agreements are not at stake, the EP has tended to exercise its power of assent more freely, employing a combination of delayed votes and outright rejection to impose its preferences. Several times during the 1980s the Parliament blocked financial protocols and protocols to Association Agreements with Mediterranean third countries. In 1987, it delayed its vote on an additional protocol to Turkey's association agreement for over a year in protest at the state's treatment of its Kurdish population. In the same year it temporarily blocked three protocols to the EU-Israel association agreement over the obstruction of Palestinian exports from the occupied territories. Similarly gestures were made in 1992, when the Parliament refused to approve the fourth financial protocols with Morocco and Syria over the human rights situation in the two countries. By the time the Barcelona process began, the EP had acquired a reputation among the Mediterranean partners for the politicisation of issues that they preferred to keep off the table in their negotiations with the EU.

One episode in particular demonstrated where the Parliament's strengths lay. During the ratification process of the Customs Union agreement with Turkey in 1995, the EP engaged in a high profile campaign to force action from the Turkish government on human rights, particularly over its treatment of the country's Kurdish population. In the nine months between the EU-Turkey Association Council's decision to go ahead with the Customs Union and the EP's vote, 20 per cent of its members undertook missions to Turkey to secure guarantees from the Çiller government on a number of human rights issues. Over the same period, parliamentarians were subjected to intense pressure from, among others, the USA, EU member governments, European and Turkish businesses and the United Nations to give their assent. Pauline Green, leader of the Socialist group in the Parliament, complained of 'excessive and counterproductive pressure'.[77] The Parliament finally approved the agreement in December 1995 with a majority of two to one.[78] Despite failing to carry through its threat to withhold its assent, it could legitimately claim to have achieved its objectives. The Turkish government was forced to remove a series of 'anti-terrorist' clauses from the constitution and to release several political prisoners associated with the Kurdish cause. The whole episode served to establish the EP as the human rights watchdog of the EMP, a role that gained in significance as the Barcelona process developed.

The introduction of MEDA represented a retrogressive step as far as the Parliament's input into the financial aid dimension of the Euro-Mediterranean initiative was concerned. Whereas the bilateral financial protocols were subject to Article 300, requiring the EP to approve the budget for each individual partner country, the MEDA regulation entitled the Parliament only to be 'kept regularly informed' of the programme's implementation.[79] Out of 22 amendments to the Regulation tabled by the EP, the Commission accepted only 6 outright, and 5 with modifications.[80] Amendments designed to increase the reporting requirements on allocations to individual projects, to increase the regularity with which the Commission had to report to the Parliament, and to give it the right to demand a suspension of aid in the event of human rights violations all failed to find their way into the Regulation. Its call for an inter-institutional agreement on the MEDA budget also met with rejection.

Given no say in the individual projects to be funded by MEDA, the Parliament threatened to block future budgetary appropriations unless money was explicitly set aside for 'civil society' projects.[81] It received some nominal compensation when the Commission and Council met its demand for a separate budget line to promote the activities of non-governmental organisations in the region.[82] The new budget line – MEDA Democracy – was initially allocated just 10 million ECUs, transferred out of the MEDA budget.

The Parliament's powers of questioning and debate took on more significance than usual in view of the disappointing outcome on the constitutive elements of the EMP. According to procedural convention, the Parliament debates commercial agreements with the Commission and Council before negotiations commence, and is kept informed by both institutions of progress which includes the possibility of receiving confidential briefings about the negotiating mandates.[83] In practice, the application of this convention in the EMP meant that the EP's potential reaction had to be taken into account prior to the opening of negotiations on the Euro-Mediterranean Agreements. The Parliament's propensity for making life awkward for the Commission ensured that DG1B officials exceeded the formal requirement to keep the Parliament informed during the negotiations. In an appearance before MEPs during the ratification of the Moroccan accord, for instance, Commissioner Marín promised to deliver an annual assessment of Morocco's action on human rights in the context of the agreement.[84] Similar undertakings were given for the agreements with the other Mediterranean partners. Through suasion rather than outright sanction, the Parliament thus ensured that its agenda was taken into account in the EMP.[85]

In sum, there was little in the EMP to increase the EP's influence in EU Mediterranean policy. But as long as the Commission considered the views of the Parliament and provided it with a steady supply of detailed information on which to base its resolutions, it stood a reasonable chance of having some of its concerns heard and addressed. Faced with a process dominated by 27 governments, its most effective tactic was to raise the kind of awkward questions, especially on human rights, that the same governments deliberately avoided.

## The Council

The Council's primary function in the EMP was as the venue for intergovernmental bargaining between the member states. Meetings of the two Barcelona coordinating committees took place in the Council, while COREPER and the various Mediterranean-related Council working groups met regularly to discuss issues ranging from the Euro-Mediterranean Agreements to the Middle East Peace Process.[86] However, in their own right, both the Presidency and the Council Secretariat made important contributions to the policy process and to the management of the Barcelona process.

## The Presidency

It was no coincidence that 1995 was the EU's 'Year of the Mediterranean'. The successive Council Presidencies of France, Spain and Italy from January 1995 to June 1996 were guaranteed to keep the EMP moving. As managers of the Council's business, it is standard practice, particularly during the Presidencies of the bigger member states, to 'impose a particular topic' on the EU during their terms in office.[87] The EMP was high on the Council's agenda throughout the period leading up to the Barcelona Conference.

The best illustration of the importance attached to the Presidency by the member states arose in the debate over the EU's presence in the Barcelona coordinating committees. The Troika represented the member states on both committees and enjoyed a *de facto* right of initiative alongside the Commission. At the start of 1996 an attempt was made to change the formula for the Union's representation on the Committees to allow all the member states to participate in meetings.[88] However, revision of the procedures was ruled out, perhaps for fear of setting of a precedent that might further complicate the Union's representation in international negotiations. Instead, an informal practice was introduced that allowed member states not represented on the Troika to address meetings through the Presidency.[89]

The composition of the Troika was also a salient factor in sustaining the early momentum of the Barcelona process. French, German and Spanish officials all expressed concern that the initial collective enthusiasm for the process might be lost as the Presidency passed to Italy, absorbed by another round of national elections during the first half of 1996, then to a succession of smaller, non-Mediterranean member states with inevitably fewer civil servants dedicated to the task. Initially, such fears proved groundless. The Presidencies of Ireland, Luxembourg and the Netherlands were also judged to have performed effectively. All three were keen to avoid accusations that they were any less capable of dealing with the EMP than the southern member states.[90]

When the breakdown of the Middle East Peace Process caused the implementation of the Barcelona process to stall in mid-1996, the Presidency found itself performing the role of political mediator between the partner countries. This role obliged the Presidency to resolve disputes and defuse diplomatic stand-offs among the participants. For instance, during its hectic six-month tenure in 1997, the Dutch Presidency persuaded the Palestinian leader Yasser Arafat and Israeli Foreign Minister David Levy to sit down for bilateral talks at the Malta Conference and oversaw talks between the Greek and Turkish government over sovereignty in the Aegean.

That it was left to the Presidency to perform this crucial function was indicative of the limits to the Commission's political role in the Barcelona process. Low politics and functional cooperation were left to DG1B. High politics remained the preserve of the governments.

*The Council Secretariat*

The Secretariat's primary task is to provide 'administrative backup' to the working groups, COREPER and meetings of the Council.[91] However, it is actually more than just a facilitator of the Council's business, and frequently acts as a broker of compromise and agreement among the member states. In the EMP, it played a key role in drafting the Barcelona Declaration and in preparing texts on the Union's position in follow-up meetings. The importance of the Working Groups and the ministerial committees in various guises in the implementation of Barcelona Declaration made the Secretariat, as the coordinator of their activities, an indispensable part of the process.

The Secretariat's main assets in the EMP were its expertise, its neutrality and the regularity of its contacts with the member states' Permanent Representations and national officials. The handful of staff assigned to Mediterranean policy acted, like their counterparts in the Commission, as an institutional memory bank for the policy area. Having responsibility for keeping records of the Euro-Med Committee and Senior Officials Committee meetings – Secretariat officials sat on both – made these officials an essential source of information for member governments and particularly for the Council Presidencies when they took over. Their awareness of the political sensitivities of both the member states and many of the partner countries also equipped them to judge what the participants in the Barcelona process would be prepared to accept. Its neutrality made the Secretariat an important middleman between the participants and the Presidency. As one official explained, the Secretariat is regularly:

> approached by states who don't want to go to the Presidency directly. They want to filter through the Secretariat who subtly assesses their difficulties and tries to provide a solution.[92]

This practice allowed governments to test the water before putting an initiative to the Council or to the Barcelona coordinating committees.

The degree of influence possessed by the Secretariat waxed and waned with changes in the Council Presidency. When smaller states – such as Ireland and Luxembourg – were in the chair, it tended to be more influential, a consequence of the considerable organisational and political resources demanded by the EMP. Preparing texts on issues such as the Middle East Peace Process and Mediterranean security cooperation required a level of expertise and experience not always available to member states with small foreign ministries and modest diplomatic resources. During these periods, the Secretariat became an ally of the Presidency, helping smaller states 'prove that they can run [EU business] efficiently and well even in areas without strong interest'.[93] Conversely, the drafting of texts and the planning of Council activity tended to be concentrated more in national capitals when the larger member states held the Presidency.

The role of the Council in the EMP should be seen as both complementary and supplementary to that of the Commission. Individual member states used the Presidency to keep Mediterranean policy at the top of the EU's foreign policy agenda during 1995. Emphasis then shifted to the Presidency as co-coordinator alongside the Commission, with the former arranging schedules of follow-up meetings and the latter undertaking the technical legwork. When political problems arose, Presidential mediation came into its own. The Council Secretariat essentially provided continuity between Presidencies and assistance to the smaller member states. Neither body in any sense gained new competencies from the EMP, but both were an integral part of its institutional architecture.

## Conclusions

Only when the EMP is set alongside core 'external' policies such as eastern enlargement and the Union's trade relationship with the USA does its comparatively low political salience become apparent. The Union's Mediterranean strategy was chiefly concerned with improving the management of existing relationships with the partner countries over the longer term rather than embarking on the kind of grand renegotiation and reformation demanded by accession. As a result, the politics of agreeing the strategy were never likely to provoke the in-fighting among the EU's institutions and member states that frequently accompanies the Union's 'history-making' decisions. Problem solving, as opposed to bargaining, characterised the passage of the EMP from proposed strategy to concrete policy.

Conceptualising the EMP along the lines of Lowi's taxonomy suggests that this relatively low level of overall politicisation did not translate into straightforward decision making on the individual policy components of the EMP. The distributive decisions to which clearly identifiable costs were attached – such as the MEDA budget and import quota concessions – became significantly politicised. Politicisation occurred partly as a consequence of the restrictions imposed on the Union by its limited financial resource and partly as a consequence of the 'path dependency' of Mediterranean policy instruments which left little scope for flexibility on the Union's part. When pressed to change its position on distributive and redistributive issues, the member states and Commission frequently engaged in highly visible internal rows which damaged its credibility with the partner countries.

Intergovernmental politics clearly mattered at key stages in the negotiation of the EMP. A central claim of intergovernmentalist theories – that domestic interests determine governmental preferences and the behaviour of governments in international negotiations – was certainly borne out by the hard bargaining over trade concessions. Furthermore, differing preferences among the member states on issues such as trade-aid and the uneasy peace on the east versus south debate were never far from the surface, evidenced by the deal struck in Cannes.

But the EMP cannot be explained by intergovernmentalist theory alone. First, the undoubted importance of geo-politics and security as underlying rationales for the Union's Mediterranean strategy are not easily accounted for by theories that are predicated on the rational calculation of economic self-interest by governments. Converging perceptions among the member states that Mediterranean security presented a challenge to the whole of western Europe demonstrated a collective impetus for increased policy responsibilities to be delegated to the EU and for the EU to be utilised as the lynchpin of a multilateral framework for Euro-Mediterranean relations.

The institutional politics of the EMP provide a good indication of how far Mediterranean policy has been 'Europeanised'. Policy change was led by the Commission which both defined the Union's strategic objectives and prescribed solutions. Its persuasive case for the partnership strategy went largely unopposed, and many of its preferences, at least on the appropriate framework for policy, were willingly accepted by the member states. When governmental preferences reasserted themselves over substantive distributive, redistributive and constituent political issues, the limits of the Commission's autonomy became clear. The Parliament remains a bit player in EU foreign policy, denied any meaningful role in the design of strategic actions, and caught between its power to obstruct the conclusion of agreements and the danger of damaging the Union's relations with third countries. The Council remains at the sharp end of the policy process, with its multiple institutions empowered to determine the Union's foreign policy priorities and to dictate policy outcomes.

It was testament to the EU's maturing as an international actor that a comprehensive external policy initiative like the EMP was formulated at the supranational level, producing action based on 'the institutional assets and international agency of the EC'.[94] With the Euro-Mediterranean venture, Mediterranean policy became more than just a disparate collection of external relationships. The Union defined a set of objectives in response to identifiable European interests, some clearly collective, others reflecting the specific preferences of the Mediterranean member states. However, when it came to the implementation process, the deficiencies of EU strategic action surfaced. Strategies still tend to be subjected to the perennial tension between the Commission's broader, long-term objectives and the short-term political interests of the member states. That the collective interest is routinely overridden by strong national interests shows how far the EU still has to go as a foreign policy actor.

## Notes

[1] Lowi, T. (1971) 'Four Systems of Policy, Politics and Choice', *Public Administration Review*, Vol. 32, No. 4, pp. 298-310; Lowi, T. (1964) 'American Business, Public Policy, Case Studies and Political Theory', *World Politics*, Vol. 16, No. 4, pp. 677-715.

[2] Wallace, W. (1983) 'Less than a Federation, More than A Regime: The Community as a Political System' in H. Wallace, W. Wallace and C.Webb (eds) *Policy Making in the European Community*, 2$^{nd}$ Edition, Chichester: John Wiley and Sons, pp. 403-36.

[3] Pollack, M. (1994) 'Creeping Competence: The Expanding Agenda of the European Community', *Journal of Public Policy*, Vol. 14, No. 2, p. 95.

[4] Webb, C. (1983) 'Theoretical Perspectives and Problems' in H. Wallace, W. Wallace and C. Webb (eds), Ibid., esp. pp 1-41. A version of this approach is applied in an external policy context to the EU's relationship with the CEECs in Friis, L. (1997) *When Europe Negotiates: From Europe Agreements to Eastern Enlargement*, Copenhagen: Institute of Political Science, esp. p. 6.

[5] Moravcsik, A. (1993) 'Preferences and Power in the European Community: A Liberal Intergovernmentalist Approach', *Journal of Common Market Studies*, Vol. 31, No. 4, pp 473-524; Moravcsik, A. (1997) 'Taking Preferences Seriously: A Liberal Theory of International Politics', *International Organization*, Vol. 51, No. 4, Autumn, pp. 513-53.

[6] March, J. and Olsen, J.P. (1989) *Rediscovering Institutions*, New York: Free Press, p. 5.

[7] Friis, L. (1997) op. cit., p. 48.

[8] Pierson, P. (1998) 'The Path to European Integration: A Historical-Institutionalist Analysis' in W. Sandholtz and A. Stone Sweet (eds) *European Integration and Supranational Governance*, Oxford: Oxford University Press, pp. 46-7.

[9] Krasner, S. (1984) 'Approaches to the State', *Comparative Politics*, Vol. 16, No. 2, p. 225; Guy Peters, B. (1998) 'The New Institutionalism and Administrative Reform: Examining Alternative Models', *Estudios Working Papers 1998/113*, Madrid: Instituto Juan March de Estudios e Investigacíones, p. 19; Peterson, J. and Bomberg, E. (1999) *Decision-making in the European Union*, Basingstoke: Macmillan, p. 19.

[10] For accounts of how the Union initially dealt with the CEECs as an external policy issue, see Bideleux, R. (1996) 'Bringing the East Back In' in R. Bideleux and R. Taylor (eds) *European Integration and Disintegration*, London: Routledge, pp. 225-52; Kramer, H.

(1993) 'The European Community's Response to the "New Eastern Europe"', *Journal of Common Market Studies*, Vol. 31, No. 2, pp. 213-44.

[11] Friis, L. (1997) op. cit., p. 52.

[12] As Fritz Scharpf has argued, governments in the EU have increasingly found themselves faced with internal and external policy problems which they are unable to solve 'alone'. See Scharpf, F. (1999) *Governing in Europe: Effective and Democratic?*, Oxford: Oxford University Press.

[13] This apparent consensus over the Euro-Mediterranean Agreements and the Barcelona process as the main tools of the Union's Mediterranean strategy contrasts with the relative lack of consensus over how to deal with the CEECs post 1989. See Sedelmeier, U. and Wallace, H. (1996) 'Policies towards Central and Eastern Europe' in H. Wallace and W. Wallace (eds) *Policy-Making in the European Union*, Oxford: Oxford University Press, p. 366; Friis, L. (1998) 'The End of the Beginning' of Eastern Enlargement – Luxembourg Summit and Agenda-setting', *European Integration Online Papers (EioP)*, Vol. 2, No. 7, http://eiop.or.at/eiop/texte/1998-007a.htm, p. 2.

[14] For discussion of how the Mediterranean and CEECs competed for position on the EU's political agenda, see Barbé, E. (1998) 'Balancing Europe's Eastern and Southern Dimensions' in J. Zielonka (ed.) *Paradoxes of European Foreign Policy*, The Hague: Kluwer Law International, p 117-29. For an institutionalist analysis of agenda setting in the EU, see Guy Peters, B. (1996) 'Agenda-setting in the European Union' in J. J. Richardson (ed.) *European Union: Power and Policy-making*, London: Routledge, pp. 61-76.

[15] Scharpf, F. (1988) 'The Joint-Decision Trap: Lessons from German Federalism and European Integration', *Public Administration*, Vol. 66, No. 3, pp. 239-78. The drawback with applying Scharpf's dichotomy is that it is grounded in rational choice theory, seeking to explain how the negotiation of policy in the EU has been hostage to the 'joint decision trap': sub-optimal outcomes produced by inter-governmental bargaining. This assumption relies on establishing what is sub-optimal in a given case. Since the EMP is designed to achieve objectives over the long term, it is impossible to accurately assess its optimality.

[16] Ibid, pp. 258-9.

[17] For empirical and theoretical analyses of regional institution building in the Mediterranean, see De Vasconcelos, A. (1993) 'Disintegration and Integration in the Mediterranean', *The International Spectator*, Vol. 28, No. 3, pp. 67-78; Chatelus, M. (1996) 'Economic Cooperation among Southern Mediterranean Countries' in R. Aliboni, G. Joffé and T. Niblock (eds) *Security Challenges in the Mediterranean*, London: Frank Cass, pp. 83-113; Chatelus, M. and Petit, P. (1997b) 'Le partenariat euro-méditerranéen: Un projet régional en quête de cohérence', *Monde Arabe: Maghreb Machrek*, Special Issue, December, pp. 3-7.

[18] Flaesch-Mougin, C. (1990) 'Competing Frameworks: The Dialogue and its Legal Bases' in G. Edwards and E. Regelsberger (eds) *Europe's Global Links: The European Community and Inter-regional Cooperation*, London: Pinter, p. 37.

[19] See BBC News Online Network (1998) 'World Europe: Italy and Libya Sign Pact', http://news.bbc.co.uk/hi/english/world/europe/newsid%5F129000/129464.stm. The accord included an apology for Italy's colonial past in Libya and an agreement to establish a joint company to deal with a number of related issues, such as mine clearing and the search for deportees of both states. In a press conference, Italian Deputy Foreign Minister Rino Serri described the two countries' 'strong common interests on the level of trade, the economy,

tourism, energy, oil and gas' and their 'prospects for security and development', an agenda strikingly similar to the priorities of the Barcelona process.

[20] A good measure of the comparative importance of the bilateral and EU levels is given by the total financial aid channelled through *national* development assistance programmes and trade credit packages which exceeded the total multilateral financial aid provided by the EU. French overseas development assistance to the Middle East and North Africa, for instance, averaged around 450 million ECUs per annum, while the cumulated total for all the EU member states stood at around 1 billion ECUs per annum. OECD (1997) (Development Assistance Committee) *Development Cooperation*, Paris: OECD, p. A67-8.

[21] Friis, L. (1997) op. cit., p.78.

[22] This taxonomy is based on Lowi, T. (1964) op. cit.; See also Lowi, T. (1971) op. cit. Lowi tentatively employs the same taxonomy in a study of non-crisis foreign policy-making in Lowi, T. (1967) 'Making Democracy Safe for the World: National Politics and Foreign Policy' in J. Rosenau (ed.) *Domestic Sources of Foreign Policy*, New York: The Free Press, pp. 295-331. For analysis of its application to the EU see Wallace, W. (1983) op. cit.; Pollack, M. (1994) op. cit.; Wallace, W. (1996) 'Government without Statehood: The Unstable Equilibrium' in H. Wallace and W. Wallace (eds) *Policy-Making in the European Union*, Oxford: Oxford University Press, esp. pp. 446-450; Friis, L. (1997) op. cit., esp. pp. 69-88.

[23] Lowi, T. (1971) op. cit., p. 299.

[24] Lowi's work does not deal at length with the definition of 'actors' in the policy process, though the inference is that the actors are governments. For a thorough, game theoretic, discussion of the definition of actors in policy-making, see Scharpf, F.W. (1997) *Games Real Actors Play: Actor-Centred Institutionalism in Policy Research*, Boulder: Westview, esp. pp. 43-96.

[25] This approach to policy research confronts one of the most fundamental questions of politics: the allocation of scarce resources. See Lasswell, H.D. (1950) *Politics: Who Gets What, When, How?*, New York: Peter Smith, p. 2.

[26] Wallace, W. (1983) op. cit., p. 415.

[27] Friis, L. (1997), op. cit., pp. 33-5.

[28] Pollack, M. (1994) op. cit., p. 113; Armstrong, K. and Bulmer, S. (1998) *The Governance of the Single European Market*, Manchester: Manchester University Press.

[29] Some measures were 'co-sponsored' by an EU member state and a partner country but the majority emanated from the Commission and from member states holding the Council Presidency.

[30] Legislation and agreements connected with the Euro-Mediterranean free-trade area could not contravene WTO rules.

[31] Wallace, W. (1983), op. cit., p. 415.

[32] Putnam, R.D. (1988) 'Diplomacy and Domestic Politics', *International Organization*, Vol. 42, No. 3, pp. 427-61.

[33] Moravcsik, A. (1991) 'Negotiating the Single European Act: National Interests and Conventional Statecraft in the European Community', *International Organization*, Vol. 45, No. 1, pp. 19-56; Moravcsik, A. (1993), op. cit., pp 473-524; Moravcsik, A. (1998) *The Choice for Europe: Social Purpose and State Power from Messina to Maastricht*, London: UCL Press.

[34] Moravcsik, A. (1998), op. cit., pp. 18-24.

[35] This distillation of Moravcsik's arguments does not attempt to do justice to the sophistication of his analysis. However, it does apply the basic logic of liberal intergovernmentalism.

36 Moravcsik, A. (1998) op. cit., p. 39.
37 Wallace, H. (1996), op. cit., p. 25.
38 Interview, Brussels, 4 November 1997.
39 Moravcsik (1998) op. cit., p. 477. Moravcsik concedes that *'major* changes in geopolitical situation should trigger shifts in European policy'. (p. 34) (Emphasis added).
40 Ibid., p. 474.
41 Shlaim, A. (1976) 'The Community and the Mediterranean Basin' in K. Twitchett (ed.) *Europe and the World: The External Relations of the Common Market*, London: Europa Publications, p. 19; Peterson, J. and Bomberg, E. (1999) *Decision Making in the European Union*, London: Macmillan, pp. 104-5.
42 Interview, Brussels, 5 December 1996.
43 Peterson, J. and Bomberg, E. (1999), op. cit., p. 119.
44 Moravcsik, A. (1998).
45 Interview, Brussels, 26 April 1996.
46 Interview, Brussels, 11 April 1997.
47 Aliboni, R. (1992b) 'The Mediterranean Dimension' in W. Wallace (ed.) *The Dynamics of European Integration*, London: Pinter, 2nd Edition, p. 164.
48 Interview, Brussels, 25 April 1996. By early 1995, the proposed figure had been reduced to 5.16 billion ECUs, a consequence of Norway's 'no' vote on membership which reduced the Union's projected budgetary contributions.
49 Interview, Brussels, 5 December 1996.
50 In a search for a compromise to the EDF problem, the prudent Finance Minister Theo Waigel was eventually overruled by Chancellor Kohl who accepted in return a decrease in EU aid to both the CEECs and the Mediterranean. The German government may well have realised that it would be in a much stronger position to negotiate reductions in the budget during its Presidency in 1999, when the next financial perspective was to be set. *Le Monde*, 26 May 1995, p.2; *Le Monde*, 26 June 1995, p. 2.
51 Barber, L. 'Euro-clouds on the Riviera', *Financial Times*, 29 June 1995, p. 15.
52 Interview, Brussels, 25 April 1996; Interview, Brussels, 11 April 1997.
53 Moravcsik, A. (1998), op. cit., p. 73; Puchala, D.J. (1999) 'Institutionalism, Intergovernmentalism and European Integration', *Journal of Common Market Studies*, Vol. 37, No. 2, p. 319.
54 Moravcsik, A. (1999) 'A New Statecraft? Supranational Entrepreneurs and International Cooperation', *International Organization*, Vol. 53, No. 2, p. 302.
55 Pollack, M. (1998) 'The Engines of Integration? Supranational Autonomy and Influence in the European Union' in W. Sandholtz and A. Stone Sweet (eds) *European Integration and Supranational Governance*, Oxford: Oxford University Press, p. 219; Hix, S. (1994) 'The Study of the European Community: The Challenge to Comparative Politics', *West European Politics*, Vol. 17, pp. 1-30.
56 Bulmer, S. (1998) 'New Institutionalism and the Governance of the Single European Market', *Journal of European Public Policy*, Vol. 5, No. 3, p. 370. See also March, J. G. and Olsen J.P. (1989) op. cit.; Bulmer, S. (1994) 'The Governance of the European Union: A New Institutionalist Approach', *Journal of Public Policy*, Vol. 13, No. 4, pp. 351-80.
57 Cram, L. (1994), 'The European Commission as a Multi-Organisation: Social Policy and IT Policy in the EU', *Journal of European Public Policy*, Vol. 2, No. 1, pp. 195-217; Guy Peters, B. (1994) 'Agenda Setting in the European Community', *Journal of European Public Policy*, Vol. 1, No. 1, pp. 9-26; Guy Peters, B. (1997) op. cit., p. 61; Nugent, N. (1995) 'The Leadership Capacity of the European Commission', *Journal of European Public Policy*, Vol. 2, No. 4, pp. 603-23; Pollack, M.A. (1997) 'Delegation, Agency and

Agenda Setting in the European Community', *International Organization*, Vol. 51, No. 1, pp. 99-134.
[58] Pollack, M. (1998), op. cit., p. 219.
[59] Smyrl, M. (1998) 'When (and How) Do the Commission's Preferences Matter?', *Journal of Common Market Studies*, Vol. 36, No. 1, p. 90.
[60] European Commission (1995d) *Strengthening the Mediterranean Policy of the European Union: Proposals for a Euro-Mediterranean Partnership*, COM (95) 72, 8 March, Brussels.
[61] A European Ambassador in North Africa summed up the Union's position thus: 'This is a problem whose only resolution can come from scrapping the Common Agricultural Policy, and that's not going to happen'. Quoted in Marks, J. (1995) 'Looking for a new deal from the EU', *Middle East Economic Digest*, Vol. 39, no. 20, 19 May, p. 3.
[62] Cram, L. (1994), op. cit., p. 197.
[63] European Commission (1995d) op. cit., p. 2.
[64] Interview, Brussels, 13 December 1996.
[65] The Commission's insistence that the distribution of MEDA funds would be tightly controlled should be seen in the context of its experience with the 'MED' programmes. The programmes, which began in 1992, provided funds for NGOs in the EU and the partner countries (universities, research bodies, regional authorities, media organisations) to set up joint projects. The programmes were suspended in 1995 after several instances of 'bad management' came to light. Committee of Independent Experts (1999) *First Report on Allegations regarding Fraud, Mismanagement and Nepotism in the European Commission*, Brussels, 15 March, http://www.europarl.eu.int/experts/en/3.htm.
[66] *European Report*, No. 1983, 12 October 1994, Sect. V, p. 7.
[67] Interview, Brussels, 13 December 1996.
[68] In a debate in the European Parliament (3 March 1998), Ambassadors to the EU from several partner countries criticised both the level of MEDA funding available and the persistence of the donor/beneficiary structure in the EMP. European Parliament (1998) (Delegations for Cooperation with the Maghreb, Machrek and Gulf Countries), *Hearing on the Euro-Mediterranean Partnership*, March.
[69] Interview, Brussels, 16 October 1998.
[70] Under the bilateral financial protocol system, the distribution of funds to each partner country was driven more by the short term needs of the individual governments and by the ad hoc allocation of financial support to specific projects than by any coherent strategy.
[71] European Commission (1995e) *Proposal for a Council Regulation on Financial and Technical Measures to Support the Reform of Economic and Social Structures in Mediterranean Non-member Countries and Territories*, COM (95) 204, Brussels, July.
[72] Ibid., p. 5.
[73] Köhler, M. (1994) *Towards a Comprehensive Policy Framework for Relations Between the European Union and the Mediterranean Basin*, Working Paper W-10, Directorate General for Research (DGIV), European Parliament, Brussels, November, p. 20.
[74] Interview, European Parliament, Brussels, 14 October 1998.
[75] In Morocco's case, the EP's Foreign Affairs committee professed itself satisfied that the agreement contained a sufficiently strong human rights dimension. Recital 3 states: 'Considering the importance which the Parties attach to the Principles of the United Nations Charter, particularly the observance of human rights, democratic principles and economic freedom, which form the very basis of the Association'. However, several MEPs on the Committee expressed reservations about the Western Sahara conflict and the general human rights situation in the country. European Parliament (1996) (Committee on Foreign Affairs,

Security and Defence Policy) *Report on the Conclusion of a Euro-Mediterranean Agreement*, A4-0173/96, Brussels.
[76] Ibid., p. 6.
[77] *Financial Times*, 13 December 1995, p. 2.
[78] European Parliament (1995a) *EC-Turkey Relations – Human Rights in Turkey*, Doc. No. PE195.288, Brussels, December.
[79] European Commission (1995) op. cit.
[80] Data obtained by comparison of European Parliament report and Council Regulation. European Parliament (1996c) *Report on the Proposal for a Council Regulation on Financial and Technical Cooperation Measures to Accompany the Reform of Economic and Social Structures in the Framework of the Euro-Mediterranean Partnership (MEDA)*, A4-0198/96, Brussels; Council Regulation (EC) *Financial and Technical Measures to Accompany (MEDA) the reform of economic and social structures in the framework of the Euro-Mediterranean Partnership*, No. 1488/96, Official Journal OJ L 189, Brussels, 30 July 1996.
[81] I am grateful Dr Annette Junnemans of the Universität Gesamhochschule, Kassel, Germany for alerting me to the Parliament's demand. Dr Junnemans had been involved in a number of civil society projects linked to the Barcelona process.
[82] European Parliament (1995b) *Report on the Mediterranean Policy of the European Union with a View to the Barcelona Conference*, A4-232/95, Brussels, 3 October, p. 20.
[83] This convention is known as the Luns-Westerterp procedure, named after the two Dutch foreign ministers that established it during the 1970s. For an explanation, see Corbett, R., Jacobs, F. and Shackleton, M. (1995) *The European Parliament*, 3rd edition, London: Cartermill, pp. 214-5.
[84] *European Report*, No. 2138, 8 June 1996, Sect. V., p. 14.
[85] Whether or not the Parliament could claim any responsibility for the inclusion of human rights clauses in the agreements themselves is a moot point. The practice of including a human rights clause in the preambles of agreements with third countries was established well before the Euro-Mediterranean accords.
[86] The three principal working groups involved were the Maghreb/Machrek working group, the South East Europe working group, the Middle East Peace Process working group and the Gulf working group. Many of the national officials interviewed during the research period sat on one or more of these groups.
[87] Hayes-Renshaw, F. and Wallace, H. (1997) *The Council of Ministers*, Basingstoke: Macmillan, p. 140.
[88] Interview, Brussels, 10 April 1997.
[89] Interview, Brussels, 5 December 1996.
[90] Interview, Brussels, 4 November 1997.
[91] Hayes Renshaw, F. and Wallace, H. (1997) op. cit., p. 148.
[92] Interview, Brussels, 10 April 1997.
[93] Interview, Brussels, 10 April 1997.
[94] Smith, M. (1998) 'Does the Flag Follow Trade? "Politicisation" and the Emergence of a European Foreign Policy' in J. Peterson and H. Sjursen (eds) *A Common Foreign Policy for Europe? Competing Visions of the CFSP*, London: Routledge, p. 92.

Chapter 6

# Influence Without Power? The EU and the Middle East Peace Process

*The Europeans will be unable to achieve anything in the Middle East in a million years.* Henry Kissinger (1974)[1]

*The US has power but Europe has influence.* Miguel Moratinos (1997)[2]

**Introduction**

The EU's role in the Arab-Israeli conflict has long been a benchmark of its status as an international political actor. Yet in an area of vital strategic interest to the Union, it has struggled to make its political influence felt. A combination of a lack of cohesion among the member states on the issue and the weakness of the EU's foreign policy machinery have left it playing second and third fiddle to the US and other mediators. The USA continues to be the dominant external political force in the Middle East and has appeared to be the only actor capable of forcing the Palestinian Authority and Israeli governments to engage in dialogue.[3] However, during the 1990s the EU carved out distinct roles for itself as the major financial underwriter of the Peace Process and projected itself as an 'honest broker' in diplomatic efforts to bring the protagonists together. This chapter considers the development of the Union's role in the Peace Process and examines the utility of the Euro-Mediterranean partnership in strengthening its economic and political influence in the region.

Section 1 briefly examines European reactions to the US-sponsored Madrid conference between Israel and the Palestinians. At that critical juncture, the EU missed, or was denied, an opportunity to assume a more important role in the Peace Process. Section 2 focuses on the period after the introduction of the CFSP and the realisation on the part of the EU that its strengths lay in low-profile diplomacy and the provision of financial support to the Palestinian Authority rather than in high-profile political initiatives. Section 3 begins by showing how the fortunes of the Barcelona process ebbed and flowed with developments in the Middle East. It moves on to assess how the Union fared in using the Euro-Mediterranean Association Agreements to influence the behaviour of the Palestinians and Israelis.

## Launching the Middle East Peace Process

The EU had strong grounds for expecting that its growing economic and political weight would enable it claim a significant role in the Middle East Peace Process. With the end of the Cold War, balancing independent EU foreign policy action against harmonious relations with the USA had become less imperative. European calls for a 'comprehensive' solution to conflicts in the Middle East assumed new resonance in view of the involvement of so many of the region's states in the Gulf crisis.[4] Moreover, as Leon Hadar observes, the crisis 'showed President Bush that the US needed European support and, perhaps more importantly, European money'.[5] Inside the Union, renewed interest in political integration, inspired by the Delors Commission and the Franco-German alliance, generated political momentum behind the creation of a more coherent and cohesive common foreign policy. Moves to complete the Single Market cemented the Union's position as the world's largest economic entity and promised to bring it even greater influence in the global economy.

However, it soon became clear that Israel and the USA had little appetite for the EU to play a political role in the Peace Process. The extent of the Union's marginalization was revealed when it could only secure observer status as the USA and Russia co-sponsored the launch of the crucial Israeli-Palestinian 'bilateral track' in Madrid in November 1991.[6] European leaders reacted by playing down the Union's exclusion from the top table. French Foreign Office Minister Roland Dumas, for instance, claimed that his government had actively contributed to the preparation of the Madrid conference and that US leadership was essential to keep Israel at the negotiating table.[7] Despite the positive spin, Madrid was undoubtedly a setback to the Union's ambitions since the bilateral negotiations covered the key political issues in the Peace Process: territorial control, sovereignty, borders, security arrangements and the rights of the Palestinians.[8]

Instead, the EU had to settle for a leading role in the Multilateral Working Groups set up to channel international financial aid to the region and coordinate projects in the economic, infrastructural, social and environmental spheres.[9] It acted as co-organizer of the Environment, Refugee and Water working groups.[10] More significantly, it was made 'gavel holder' of the Regional Economic Development Working Group (REDWG), allowing it to direct international financial assistance to the Palestinian territories.[11] REDWG work was divided into 10 areas, with 'shepherd' states responsible for coordinating projects in each area:

| | |
|---|---|
| France - communications and transport | Spain - agriculture |
| UK - financial markets | EC - energy and 'regional networks' |
| Germany - trade | |

**Figure 6.1 EU Member States' Roles in the Regional Economic Development Working Group**

In addition to its responsibilities for individual project areas, the Community also provided crucial logistical support. A secretariat and executive secretary for the Monitoring Committee set up to oversee EU funded projects were funded by the EU.

The Union also became an active contributor to the Arms Control and Regional Security working group (ACRS), another rolling multilateral forum established by the Madrid conference. Again, individual member states were entrusted with leading discussions in certain areas. The Netherlands, for instance, chaired talks on a regional crisis communication network. Participation in the ACRS was potentially significant in two respects. First, it offered the Union a means to contribute to the handling of issues such as arms control and non-proliferation, confidence-building measures and regional security structures. It was thus a 'back door' into the politico-security aspects of the Peace Process. Second, it gave the Europeans hands on experience of the security problems that would arise as the Washington agreement was implemented. This experience proved valuable in the Barcelona process and influenced the wording of the Barcelona Declaration.

As Joel Peters argues, the multilateral track was based on a 'functionalist-liberalist conception of cooperation' where the enmeshing of the region's states through multi-sectoral cooperation would enable them to set aside their political differences.[12] This methodology was ideally suited to the Union's external policy strengths – trade and aid – and to its own experience with regional economic and political integration. The multilateral working groups provided a mutually reinforcing institutional link between its emergent Mediterranean partnership strategy and the Peace Process. The Commission was quick to recognise the opportunity, arguing that:

> On the economic front the time is now right for the EC, together with the international community and especially the Gulf countries, to embark on an ambitious cooperation programme which would embrace the economic development of the West Bank and Gaza, bearing in mind the need also for international efforts in favour of the region as a whole.[13]

The economic development of the occupied territories and support for the economic integration between the Arab countries became the guiding principles of the EU's contribution to the Peace Process.

Nevertheless, the importance of the multilateral track should not be overstated. Madrid served as a powerful reminder that the US was the only external power capable of acting as a mediator. While the post-Madrid decisions did at least open a window of opportunity for the EU to gain influence over the longer-term in the Middle East, the multilaterals were designed to capitalise on any peace dividend. The prospect of such positive developments in international relations in the region proved illusory in the face of the inexorable, and arguably inevitable, breakdown of the Madrid process.

## Between Banker and Broker: Defining a European Role

The signature of the Oslo Declaration of Principles and Washington Agreements in September and October 1993 injected new dynamism into the flagging Israeli-Palestinian negotiations. Even the USA had proved powerless to bring together Rabin's government and Arafat's beleaguered and conciliatory PLO. It was left to Norway, not a member of the EU, to act as a secret intermediary and restart the talks. Between March and September 1993, a series of discussions, initially between academics and researchers, led to the historic mutual recognition agreement by the Palestinian and Israeli authorities and set a timetable for the withdrawal of Israeli forces from the West Bank and Gaza.

Immediately after the Washington meeting, the REDWG was convened in order to discuss a World Bank report, co-financed by the EU, US and Norway, about economic rebuilding in the region. As one commentary put it, 'the Israel-PLO agreement will only survive if it results in a quick and sustainable improvement in the standard of living of the people of the Occupied Territories'.[14] At the Washington donors' conference (October 1, 1993), EU heads of government pledged 500 million ECUs from the Community budget to be channelled to the region from 1994-98 through the Commission (50 million ECUs per annum in grants) and the European Investment Bank (250 million ECUs per annum in loans), the largest single pledge of aid.[15] A new body – the Ad Hoc Liaison Committee (AHLC) – chaired by Norway, was mandated to promote and coordinate aid from individual donors to the Palestinian people. Much of the real work of the AHLC was done in advance of informal meetings of the major participants, with the EU, United States and World Bank (as well as the Palestinian Authority and Israel) taking the key decisions among themselves.

The Washington conference firmly established the EU as the biggest contributor to the Palestinian state-in-waiting. With other funding streams available for the Mediterranean, the Union appeared to have an impressive array of financial incentives at its disposal to influence the behaviour of both the Arabs and the Israelis.[16] Increased political influence was not an automatic corollary of this role as banker. That depended on the multiplier effect of aid, including anticipated dividends such as increased inward investment, the stabilisation of the business environment and the normalization of relations at both the governmental and societal levels.[17] But the Union's largesse had simultaneously made it indispensable to the economic dimension of the Peace Process and raised its profile in the Middle East. For many inside the Union, the time was right to explicitly seek a more visible and substantive political input into the Peace Process. In an exchange with the Belgian Council Presidency, one MEP complained that:

> you have not explained what the European Community or European Union specifically intends to do to encourage the Peace Process. I have the impression that Norway has done a great deal more in real terms that the European Union and I am rather sad about that.[18]

### Table 6.1 Donor Pledges - October 1993, November 1996 (Million ECUs)

| Donor | Grants | Loans | Total |
|---|---|---|---|
| EU (Budget+EIB) | 250 | 250 | 500 |
| USA | 315 | 105 | 420 |
| Japan | 215 | 0 | 215 |
| Saudi Arabia | 168 | 0 | 168 |
| Norway | 126 | 0 | 126 |
| Netherlands | 101 | 0 | 101 |
| Germany | 78 | 0 | 78 |
| Italy | 67 | 0 | 67 |
| Sweden | 58 | 0 | 58 |
| France | 54 | 0 | 54 |
| Denmark | 43 | 0 | 43 |
| Spain | 43 | 0 | 43 |
| Canada | 28 | 0 | 28 |
| World Bank/IDA | 0 | 176 | 176 |
| Israel | 21 | 42 | 63 |
| Other donors | 297 | 239 | 537 |
| Total | 1864 | 858 | 2667 |

The Union's move to capitalise on its economic leverage initially centred on pillar II. Just as the Middle East had been a priority for European Political Cooperation, so it seemed that the CFSP would devote an equally large percentage of the EU's diplomatic resources to the region. At the Brussels European Council of December 1993, the first after the ratification of the Maastricht Treaty, a list of possible initiatives was set out by the Heads of Government identifying priority areas for EU initiatives. The principal themes of the framework were as follows:

- Participation in international supporting arrangements.
- Strengthening the democratic process through, *inter alia*, assisting with the preparation and monitoring of elections in the Palestinian territories.
- Building regional cooperation, chiefly through participation in the REDWG and Arms Control and Regional Security Working Group.
- Support for Palestinian institution-building through the mobilisation and implementation of EU aid programmes for the occupied territories.
- Providing aid to other parties to the bilateral negotiations (Syria, Lebanon).
- Assuring follow-up to action underway on confidence-building measures submitted to the regional parties.
- Using the EU's influence to encourage full support on all sides for the Peace Process.[19]

**Figure 6.2 Proposed EU Initiatives in the Peace Process**

To follow up the Brussels initiative, the Commission was instructed to prepare the ground for CFSP Joint Actions. A Commission communication had already set out the broad parameters for EU policy post-Washington.[20] Consistent with Europe's call for a 'global' settlement, the paper emphasised the Union's specific role in promoting regional cooperation and stressed the need to involve Israel in 'a balanced triangular relationship' with Europe and the Mashreq countries.[21] Pillar I would be the major source for the Union's long-term contribution to the Peace Process, while its political objectives would be set in pillar II.

Any immediate prospect of an emboldened EU having a significant political impact on the Peace Process was quickly stymied by the collapse of the Oslo agreement. The stalemate ostensibly resulted from disputes over the speed and scale of the hand-over of the Occupied Territories. A far more serious problem was the irreconcilable Israeli policy of withdrawing troops while simultaneously expanding Jewish settlements. The massacre in January 1994 of dozens of Palestinians in a Mosque in Hebron by an Israeli settler exposed the fragility of the process and called into question the ability of the two sides to guarantee the security of their respective populations. The EU's reaction to events in Hebron was confined to a short statement by the Council condemning the massacre and calling for 'the authorities [Israeli] to take full responsibility for protecting the inhabitants of the occupied territories'.[22]

Eventually, a Joint Action (94/276, 19 April 1994) on the Peace Process was adopted by the Council. The political element of the Joint Action took the form of funding (10 million ECUs) for the establishment of the Palestinian police force, and a programme of assistance for elections in the occupied territories, including the provision of electoral observers. As Esther Barbé and Fernando Izquierdo argue, the ambit of the Joint Action confirmed the low key approach adopted by the Union.[23] A promise to issue *démarches* to the Arab states over their economic boycott of Israel, and to the Israelis over their settlement policy was indicative of the EU's continuing nervousness about making overtly political interventions.

It was at this stage that long standing differences among the member states resurfaced and undermined the Union's tentative steps towards a more clearly defined position on the Peace Process. The election of Jacques Chirac as French President in May 1995 heralded a new interventionism in the country's foreign policy. From the outset, Chirac demanded a greater say for Europe in the Peace Process commensurate with its financial contributions. But the new President's European vocation masked an even stronger desire to reassert France's 'special' status in the region. France's position as the biggest individual donor to the Palestinian authority lent his vision some credibility. Chirac used the final days of the French Council Presidency to arrange a series of high profile meetings with Middle Eastern leaders, including Yasser Arafat. In a press interview following a diplomatic visit to Cairo, Foreign Minister Hervé de Charette, stated that 'the situation in the region requires that Europe in general, and France in particular, take account of their traditional links and historical interests' and promised 'a bigger French presence'.[24]

French activism was taken a step further when de Charette travelled in quick succession to Beirut, Jerusalem and Damascus to negotiate a cease fire after the Israeli shelling of Southern Lebanon in April 1996. France's part in securing the ceasefire won it a seat as co-chair of the monitoring committee alongside the USA. In contrast to Chirac's diplomatic efforts, the collective response of the EU to the Lebanon crisis could best be described as tardy. The Troika, led by Italian Foreign Minister Susanna Agnelli, arrived in the region behind the French team. One of the major shortcomings of EU foreign policy – the inability of the organisation to speak with one voice – and the obvious tension between the two European delegations attracted widespread media coverage.

Further evidence of internal discord within the Union came with its lengthy silence after the election of Binyamin Netanyahu's Likud coalition in May 1996. Despite the obvious implications for the Peace Process and political relations with Israel, no statement was issued on what the Union expected from the new government *vis-à-vis* the Oslo process.[25] Only after a summer of violence precipitated by Israel's failure to adhere to the Oslo accords and the USA's reluctance to put pressure on Netanyahu did the EU finally respond with a diplomatically worded CFSP statement and a decision to despatch Irish Foreign Minister Dick Spring to the Middle East for talks with Netanyahu and Arafat.[26] In a sudden flurry of activity, the Troika also held talks with Arafat and Israeli Foreign Minister David Levy, but was unable to offer more than consoling words to the Palestinians and was rebuffed by the Israelis. The Union's efforts were met with an extraordinary warning from US Secretary of State Warren Christopher. In a letter to each of the 15 member governments, Christopher exhorted the Union to refrain from interfering in the Peace Process at such a 'delicate moment'.[27]

The outcome of the Union's experience during this tense period was the decision to appoint a Special Envoy, Miguel Moratinos, to represent the EU in the Peace Process. The appointment of Moratinos was a shrewd move by the EU. A former Spanish Ambassador to Israel, the Special Envoy had considerable inside knowledge of regional politics and the respect of the core protagonists.[28] Furthermore, Moratinos had been instrumental in preparing the Barcelona conference as part of Spanish Prime Minister Felipe Gonzalez's diplomatic team, so was aware of the limits of EU diplomacy in a multilateral context. Another factor in Moratinos' favour was his nationality. It is difficult to see how either side would have tolerated a diplomat from one of the big three member states – France, Germany and the UK.[29]

The Special Envoy's appointment and mandate, the subject of another CFSP Joint Action, were confirmed in only one hour by Foreign Ministers in October 1996. The alacrity of the decision was an indication of the strength of support for the initiative among the member states.[30] Having scored a minor diplomatic success with Carl Bildt as EU Special Envoy to the Yugoslavian conflict, the lessons learned from that experience were applied in the Joint Action.[31]

- To establish and maintain contacts with all the parties involved.
- To observe the negotiations, offer the EU's advice and its 'good offices'.
- Contribute to implementing international agreements and 'engage with them diplomatically' in the event of non-compliance.
- To promote, by engaging with signatories, compliance with norms of human rights, democracy and the rule of law.
- To report to Council bodies about the best way of pursuing EU initiatives and ongoing Peace Process-related business.
- To monitor actions which might affect permanent status negotiations (i.e. actions in the occupied territories).[32]

**Figure 6.3 EU Special Envoy's Mandate**

The initiative appeared to be carefully judged and realistic: to project the political presence of the EU by offering its good offices rather than by attempting major diplomatic offensives. As Moratinos himself put it:

> My role is complementary to the US. It has to be so. My role is not about competing for influence but in striving to help the Middle East Peace Process.[33]

The fact that a civil servant rather than a politician was appointed also appeased those member states which remained wary about a higher profile EU presence in the region. Similarly, the Israeli government would have been less likely to work with an obviously political figure. Any kind of direct European pressure on Netanyahu would have further weakened the EU's position.[34] At first, the Israeli government had been sceptical, with David Levy arguing that 'the [Israeli-Palestinian] negotiations must be direct and without any external pressure'.[35] But Moratinos' patient, neutral approach gradually won him the approval of Netanyahu's government and the US administration.

The early signs for the Special Envoy were good as his work behind the scenes facilitated dialogue between the Israelis, Palestinians and other Arab countries. One of his most significant early achievements was to bring Arafat and Levy together in Brussels for a relaunch of the peace talks after the crisis over new Israeli settlements in East Jerusalem. He was also instrumental in brokering the deal over Hebron, securing the commitment of the Palestinians while the USA took care of Israel.[36]

For the Palestinians, and the Arab side in general, the impact of the EU's Joint Action was less satisfactory. One official lamented that:

> Moratinos would have been more effective if there was an effective mandate, an effective initiative. He needed something to offer in the framework of an initiative. It is a good thing for the Arabs to underline the importance attached to a European role, but he must have a clear position. He must be able to use all the resources at Europe's disposal.[37]

Another diplomat expressed similar sentiments, arguing that:

> A clearer mandate is necessary. At the moment, his role is presenting the European Union's position and going back to Brussels.[38]

These reactions to the Special Envoy's arrival in the region highlighted the differences in expectations about the EU's involvement in the Peace Process. His presence was plainly more important to the Palestinians than the Israelis. Arab states would continue to vigorously press for the Union to back the Palestinians in the same way that the US government backed Israel.

By late 1997, the EU had accumulated sufficient political capital to enable it to present a 'code of conduct' to the Israelis and Palestinians.[39] True to form, Moratinos went to great lengths to clear the code with both parties before making it public. The code incorporated a number of confidence building measures drawn from the Barcelona process. Its key principles were firstly, that the Israeli government should respect the commitments made by its predecessor. Secondly, the code called for the Palestinians to do more to combat terrorism. Significantly, it received a cautious welcome from the Israeli government, which praised the envoy 'for establishing excellent relations with both sides'.[40] Moratinos had thus become the conduit for a more substantive political input from the Union.

European diplomacy in the Peace Process took a new twist in March 1998 with the visit of UK Foreign Minister and President of the Council, Robin Cook, to Egypt, Israel and Jordan. In advance of the trip, EU Foreign Ministers made it clear that Israeli settlement policy was their main concern. It was also a subject on which Cook had resolved to push Netanyahu as far possible, a task he spectacularly accomplished. Cook chose to ignore Israeli warnings and met Palestinians at the disputed Har Homa/Jabal Abu Ghneim settlement in East Jerusalem, a visit that provoked violent demonstrations by Israeli settlers.[41] On the same visit, the Foreign Secretary used a meeting with Netanyahu to ask for an explanation of Israel's continued refusal to open the airport in Gaza, whose construction was funded by the Union. Cook's actions signalled the EU's displeasure with Netanyahu's policies and earned much needed political capital from Arab states. It also heightened the sense that the Union had become the key ally of the Palestinians.

The latitude enjoyed by the British Foreign Secretary bore testament to a stronger degree of cohesion among the member states on the EU's involvement in the Peace Process. Before his trip, Cook had been careful to draw attention to the backing he had received from all the EU Foreign Ministers at an informal meeting in Edinburgh.[42] As French Foreign Minister Hubert Vedrine optimistically commented:

> It is one of the things that have struck me since I took on this position. Coherence in the analysis, the diagnosis of the objectives is stronger and stronger within the European Union.[43]

Behind the scenes, European diplomatic activism was working to persuade Arafat to accept a US proposal for an Israeli withdrawal from an additional 13 per cent of the West Bank, a crucial issue if progress were to be made towards final status talks. On the ground, European funding to develop the Palestinian Authority's capacity to combat terrorism went some way to addressing Israeli concerns about security, also a key issue in the bilateral negotiations.[44] For a brief period the Union appeared to be having a modicum of success in using its economic clout to support its political objectives for the Peace Process.

However, regardless of the modest headway made by Moratinos and the Union's European diplomatic forays of 1997 and 1998, interventions by the Europeans clearly had no lasting effect on an increasingly defiant Israeli government. A meeting of the US, Israeli and Palestinian representatives in London during May 1998 – partly facilitated by the EU's diplomatic pressure on the Palestinians – failed to secure Netanyahu's agreement to further Israeli redeployments from the West Bank. As the Peace Process teetered on the brink, it was left to the Clinton Administration to force the Israelis and Palestinians to re-engage.

The diplomacy that led to the Wye River Memorandum of October 1998 required intensive mediation by US officials. The accord, signed in Washington, included a pledge by Israel to go ahead with the 13 per cent withdrawal from the West Bank and guarantees on security from the Palestinian side.[45] Despite the groundwork laid by the London summit, the Union's pressure on Arafat and its critical financial backing for the Palestinian Authority, the EU took no part in the Washington talks. Shortly after the Wye River agreement, Moratinos revealed his exasperation with the Union's continued exclusion from the sharp end of the Peace Process, stating that:

> We do not want to do only cheque-book diplomacy. The EU wants to be a player, not only a payer'.[46]

Yet the Washington Donors' Conference of November 30 1998 left the EU in precisely that position. The conference saw 3.2 billion ECUs pledged over the 5 years to 2003. This figure included 400 million ECUs from the EU's budget, with the member states offering a similar amount. By the end of 1998, the EU accounted for 53 per cent of total financial assistance to the Palestinians.

Nonetheless, neither the USA nor the EU were able to prevent a further deterioration of Israeli-Palestinian relations. Last-ditch diplomatic action was required to prevent the Palestinians unilaterally declaring statehood ahead of the Israeli elections of May 1999. The Clinton Administration announced that final status talks would commence after the elections. Meanwhile, the EU's Berlin Declaration of March 1999 explicitly recognised the Palestinian's right to statehood and suggested that the EU member states might still support a unilateral declaration if a negotiated solution proved impossible within a year. When the 'deadline' was reached, the Palestinians claimed to have received signals from the EU, specifically from French officials, that it was prepared to 'accept the Palestinian state without connecting it to the peace solution'.[47] But an attempt at final status negotiations at Camp David in July 2000 broke up without agreement. The onset of a new intifada in September 2000 and Sharon's subsequent election victory left the Peace Process in tatters.

The EU's political role in the Peace Process was always destined to be subordinate to that of the USA. Internal divisions among its member states, its lack of political credibility with Israel and US reservations about EU interference combined to keep it firmly in the back seat. The REDWG ground to a halt in 1996, leaving the EU in the chair of a forum that no longer met. The brokering role performed by Moratinos did represent a moderate, if low visibility, success for the Union. Its principle and highest profile function in the Peace Process as underwriter of an embryonic Palestinian state was essential, even if it consistently failed to convert its economic influence into political power. Nevertheless, while the USA remained the only external force capable of mediating at the highest level, European ambitions in the Middle East would continue to be frustrated.

## The Euro-Mediterranean Partnership and the Middle East Peace Process

*The Barcelona Process*

From the outset, the EU made a determined bid to keep clear blue water between the Barcelona process and the Peace Process. In a joint report on the implementation of the EMP, the Commission and Council Presidency claimed that:

> Strong efforts have been made to ensure respect for the principle that, while the Barcelona Process can exert a positive influence on the Middle East Peace Process, it should not replace other activities and initiatives undertaken in the interest of peace, stability and prosperity in the region.[48]

Officially, the primary function of the EMP was to provide the institutional basis for low-key, functional cooperation between Arabs and Israelis. The Barcelona process would 'step in' if or when peace finally broke out in the region. According to Eberhard Rhein:

> The Euro-Med partnership should be seen as a catalytic factor helping to, *inter alia*, allow Israelis and Arabs to work together in a wider context, with Europe as a sort of *'chaperone'* between the two.[49]

Some within the EU pursued a more ambitious line, seeing Barcelona as a response to its exclusion from the political track of the Peace Process.[50] But there was no serious suggestion that the EMP could or should emulate the Oslo process.

When an already fragile Peace Process began to break up in 1996, the Barcelona process initially appeared to withstand the rising tension between the Arab participants and Israel. The low key, functional method appeared to be bearing fruit, particularly at the administrative level where diplomats involved in the two central follow-up committees continued to attend meetings. Similarly, the programme of sectoral conferences, meetings and seminars proceeded with little obvious disruption. Most notably, a meeting of the Senior Officials Committee went ahead in July 1996 despite the Israeli bombing of southern Lebanon. Commissioner Marín was not alone in proclaiming the durability of the process to be a major achievement in its own right.[51] Reflecting on the turmoil of 1996, one official stated that:

> We should be happy that we still have the Barcelona process running after this year. Just being able to meet is a confidence building measure in its own right.[52]

Behind the scenes, though, cracks were appearing in the façade. First, the Israeli, Lebanese and Syrian representatives on the two steering committees refused to address each other directly at meetings, opting instead to read out prepared statements on the situation in the Middle East. Meetings frequently started with condemnation of one side by the other and their productiveness was adversely affected. Second, at a meeting of the Arab League in September 1996, Foreign Ministers from the Arab partner countries discussed a proposal to withdraw from the Barcelona framework if the Israelis reneged on the Oslo agreements.[53] That they eventually decided not to owed more to the lack of alternatives than to any optimism about the prospects for the EMP. Third, progress in the political and security basket – a barometer for the Barcelona process – virtually ground to a halt. The *impasse* between the Arab and Israeli governments rendered impossible any progress on confidence building measures.

A defining moment for the Barcelona process arrived with Israel's decision to go ahead with the construction of Israeli settlements in East Jerusalem, a decision which effectively halted the bilateral track of the Peace Process.[54] The ensuing row occurred only weeks before the second ministerial conference in Malta, meant to inject new momentum into the EMP. Dutch Foreign Minister Hans van Mierlo was forced to embark on an exhaustive tour of the Middle East simply to persuade the Arab and Israeli Foreign Ministers to travel to Valletta.[55] Work on a conference declaration had to be put to one side as van Mierlo's team searched for a form of words acceptable to both sides. The Arab governments pressed for a passage condemning the settlements to be included in the final declaration, while the Israeli government flatly rejected any references to the issue and to the Middle East in general.[56] It took a meeting between Israeli Foreign Minister David Levy and Yasser Arafat, brokered by van Mierlo, to prevent an acrimonious break-up of the gathering.[57] Nevertheless, the participants still left Malta without agreement on the Barcelona process and several more weeks of discussions were required to produce a sterile text which simply summarised progress and identified future priorities.

The Malta debacle put an end to any pretence that the Barcelona process could be insulated from the Peace Process. As Commissioner Manuel Marín admitted:

The fundamental aim of peace and stability in the Mediterranean cannot be achieved without a permanent and just solution to the Middle East conflict. Although the Peace Process and the Euro-Mediterranean partnership are two distinct and separate processes, eventually the latter cannot fully succeed without the success of the former.[58]

For many of the participants, the very essence of the 'Barcelona spirit' was the novelty of having Israel, Lebanon and Syria engaged together in dialogue in a multilateral forum, something that had not been achieved in the multilateral track of the Peace Process. The health of the EMP was therefore always inextricably linked to the state of the Peace Process. An Arab diplomat was unequivocal about this linkage:

There is no way that this process will succeed without progress on the Peace Process. How can we talk about economic cooperation while we have a government [in Israel] that is reneging on all its previous international commitments?[59]

The Arab partner countries perceived the Barcelona process as a means to draw the EU further into the Peace Process and as a potential counter-weight to US-led diplomacy. Their commitment to the EMP was inevitably dampened when it became clear that the EU did not share the same vision of the process.

From the outset, Israel's lukewarm attitude towards the Barcelona process reflected its traditional suspicion of European interference in the Middle East. Indeed, after the Likud coalition's election victory in May 1996, the Israelis became distinctly more critical of EU initiatives. Netanyahu's government continued to regard the USA as the only acceptable external mediator, perceiving the Union to be overtly supportive of Palestinian demands and generally 'pro-Arab'.[60] One diplomat summed up the Israeli position thus:

The Barcelona process is not going to replace the Middle East Peace Process. Barcelona is for the future. Strategically, the US is much more 'present' than any of the European countries.[61]

Israel had another reason to play down the significance of Barcelona. The non-implementation of the Oslo accords and the economic blockade on the Palestinian territories could be argued to represent a violation of both the spirit and letter of the Barcelona Declaration. The Israeli government was therefore keen to prevent the process becoming another platform from which the Arab states could mount attacks on its policies.

The negative spillover from developments in the Middle East penetrated throughout the Barcelona process. The Arab group began selectively refusing to meet Israeli representatives on Arab soil, effectively ending the diplomatically important practice of holding meetings in all the countries participating in the Barcelona process.[62] Under pressure from the other Arab governments, the Moroccan government decided to cancel a high profile Conference of Industry Ministers due to be held in Marrakesh, blaming Israel's 'continued obstruction of the Peace Process'.[63] An ad-hoc Foreign Ministers' meeting, scheduled to be held in an Arab country in June 1998, had to be switched to Palermo by the UK Council Presidency. Ironically, the point of the meeting was for the participants to make a political statement about the necessity of keeping the Barcelona process separate from the Peace Process.[64] Syria's demands that the meeting specifically address Israel's policies subsequently threatened to turn Palermo into a repeat of Malta, an embarrassing outcome both the new UK government and the Italian hosts desperately wanted to avoid.[65] In the end, the Palermo meeting did the minimum necessary to ensure the survival of the Barcelona process, avoiding further controversy over the Peace Process and focusing instead on the commercial and financial priorities for the EMP.[66] When the Euro-Mediterranean Foreign Ministers gathered again in Stuttgart in April 1999, they did so without the Israeli government and the Palestinian Authority.

The text of the EU's 2000 'Common Strategy on the Mediterranean Region' represented the first formal acknowledgement that the Barcelona process could not be isolated from the Middle East Peace Process. However, the Union was careful to avoid any reference to progress in the EMP being conditional upon a settlement in the Middle East. It emphasised the benefits that the Euro-Mediterranean initiative might bring to a 'post-conflict' Middle East, and suggested that the Stability Charter should be a 'deciding factor in the post-conflict process'.[67] To ensure consistency across the Union's activities in pillars I and II, implementation of the Common Strategy would require, *inter alia*, coordination between the CFSP High Representative, the Special Envoy, the Commission and individual member states. The document contained few proposals for specific measures linking the Barcelona framework to the Peace Process, though it referred to 'synergies' between the two. The implication was that Euro-Mediterranean initiatives – on the management of the region's water resources, for instance – would be relevant to the multilateral track. What the Common Strategy deliberately steered clear of was any indication that the EMP might directly contribute to the immediate need for bridge-building between the Israelis and Arab states.

There are several conclusions to be drawn from the way the relationship between the Barcelona process and the Peace Process evolved. First, the multilateral strand of the EMP turned out to be contingent upon the situation in the Middle East rather than complementary to it. Incremental confidence building and functional economic cooperation had little more than symbolic value without forward movement in the Peace Process.[68] Second, the EU found itself unable to desensitize the Barcelona process. Part of the blame lay at the Union's own feet, since it devoted too much attention to the Political and Security Partnership where the specific measures on the table were clearly highly politicised. But the problem also stemmed from the inter-governmental nature of the process. It relied on consensus among parties that were, in many respects, in conflict. Third, the inseparability of the two processes called into question the wisdom of the EU's decision to apply the partnership concept to the Mediterranean region as a whole. The all-pervasive influence of the Middle East situation meant conflict resolution and regional integration in other sub-regional strategic arenas (Cyprus, Greece-

Turkey, the Maghreb) was neglected, prompting calls for regional sub-groups (Western Mediterranean, South East Europe) to be created within the Barcelona framework.[69] It was difficult to avoid the conclusion that the Barcelona process was a creature of the uniquely favourable political conditions at the end of 1995. Once the Peace Process broke down, the EMP was left floundering.

*The Euro-Mediterranean Agreements*

In contrast to the ailing Barcelona process, the bilateral strand of the EMP proved to be a quietly fruitful channel for the EU to strengthen its role in the Middle East. The starting point was the conclusion of an Interim Agreement with the Palestinian Authority, a natural complement to the Union's substantial financial investment in the nascent Palestinian state. Although the accord merely formalised existing trade concessions, containing none of the political and social provisions of the other Euro-Mediterranean Agreements, it nevertheless represented another important step towards the recognition of Palestinian aspirations to statehood. A measure of the agreement's political significance came from Israel's reaction to it: Netanyahu's government described it as 'almost a barrier to the Peace Process'.[70]

Agreements signed in Brussels were one thing. Following them through in the Occupied Territories was another. Increasingly frequent border closures and restrictions on the movement of Palestinian people and goods by the Israeli authorities greatly reduced the trade creating potential of the accord, delayed the construction of donor-funded projects, and impeded the operation of completed projects.[71] Imports of EU-funded infrastructural equipment destined for Gaza were routinely held in Israeli depots for 'security reasons', after which the Palestinians were presented with large bills for storage costs.[72] Agricultural produce frequently sat rotting in customs warehouses for months, with Union representatives unable to intervene.[73] As an Arab official put it, 'the EU ought to be asking ask how much it loses in Palestine of the money it provided because of the Israeli blockade'.[74]

The Commission's exasperation with the situation in the Palestinian territories was palpable. In a blunt statement to the European Parliament, the Desk Officer for Palestine argued that:

> Unless there is safe passage between the West Bank and Gaza, an open port and airport, customs controls and free movement, we may as well not have signed the agreement.[75]

But the options open to the EU were limited, constrained both by the terms of a 1994 Agreement on bilateral relations between the Israelis and Palestinians and by its inability to put effective political pressure on Israel to lift the physical barriers to the movement of goods and people.[76]

It was undoubtedly this combination of frustration and impotence that prompted a shift in the Union's approach towards the end of 1997. The 'demand' for EU action was clearly expressed by Yasser Arafat:

Seventy per cent of the economy of Israel is with European countries and this card has not been used until now. Why not? You only have to wave this economic card and they will listen to you directly. At least wave it.[77]

Seizing the opportunity presented by Moratinos' groundwork and the hardening of the member states' attitudes towards the Netanyahu government, the Commission chose to raise the political stakes through the Euro-Mediterranean Agreements.[78] The decision to focus on trade formed part of an EU strategy that targeted three specific issues:

- Improving Palestinian access to external markets.
- Unblocking the Israeli restrictions on free-movement, particularly access to Gaza airport and port.
- Promoting and funding new projects such as border-based industrial zones.[79]

This episode signalled the increased determination of the EU to use Community policy instruments as the basis to exert a greater political impact on Israel's policies in the Occupied Territories.

More overt signs of the Union toughening its approach towards Israel came with two trade disputes in 1997. First, the practice of labelling exports produced in the Occupied Territories as Israeli was challenged by the Union. This issue rumbled on for more than three years, with the EU insisting on the right of its customs officials to verify the origin of goods.[80] The second dispute over orange juice imports arose in October 1997.[81] It centred on claims that Israel had been re-exporting Brazilian orange juice to the EU under its own duty free quota.[82] Despite a blunt written warning from Commissioner Manuel Marín to Israeli Foreign Minister David Levy, the Israeli government failed to address many of the Commission's concerns.[83] Consistent with established procedures, it was earmarked by DG1B as a 'technical' issue and passed to the Commission's trade policy and legal experts. The Israeli authorities were subsequently given an official admonishment detailing the nature of the complaint and threatening EU importers of the product with fines.[84] The row was defused at a special meeting of the EU-Israel Cooperation Committee on November 28 when Israeli customs officials gave an undertaking to tighten controls on orange juice traders.[85] Nevertheless, the official warning provoked accusations from Israel that the Union was using the case to make a political point about the situation in Israel.[86]

Both the disputes – ostensibly of a technical-legal nature – were politicized to an extent not previously seen in EU-Israeli trade relations. The orange juice case was only the first salvo in an increasingly bitter war of words over Israel's application of the rules of origin clauses in its Euro-Mediterranean Agreement with the EU. The Commission's patience with Israel was pushed to the limit as other instances of products from the Occupied Territories being exported to the EU under the Israeli flag came to light. Finally, in May 1998, the Commission officially notified Israel that the terms of the agreement were being violated, and that products originating from the occupied territories might be excluded from the EU-Israel free trade area, a threat backed by the Council.[87] Marín was defiant: 'We gave peace a chance. But now we are acting.'[88] Netanyahu's retort was equally confrontational:

> Be careful with the use of ultimatums and dictates of any kind. That is the one thing that doesn't go well in Israel and with me.[89]

It was a measure of the EU's new-found assertiveness that, in spite of Netanyahu's attempt to play the 'anti-Israel' card, Israeli officials were forced to sit down with the Commission to discuss ways of lifting the restrictions on Palestinian trade.[90] Economic policy instruments were being used to send a political message about the EU's stance on the status of the Occupied Territories.

To what extent did the Union's handling of the Euro-Mediterranean Agreements increase its influence over the behaviour of the Israelis and Palestinians? How did the use of these policy instruments impact upon the Peace Process? Roy Ginsberg's comprehensive analysis of the EU's political impact on the Peace Process predictably confirms that it had a more significant effect on the Palestinians than the Israelis.[91] The Palestinian's heavy dependence on exports of goods into the European Union made the signature of the interim Euro-Mediterranean Agreement an important piece of the jigsaw at a time when the Peace Process still had momentum. However, beyond the powerful symbolism of concluding a formal accord, the Agreement could not appreciably boost export revenues for the Occupied Territories without a change in the obstructive policies of the Israeli government. Instead, it was the near total dependence of the Palestinian Authority on European financial aid to function which provided the Union with a more direct and sustained means to influence the situation in the Occupied Territories. The primary function of Union policy instruments was to ensure that the Palestinian Authority and the Palestinian economy would survive in the short term. That undoubtedly translated into a political impact on the Peace Process since the collapse of Arafat's already fragile government would have resulted in a dangerous vacuum.

The Israeli economy was also heavily dependent on trade with the EU. Successive Israeli governments pushed hard for an upgraded trade agreement during the 1990s. Initial reluctance on the Union's part to negotiate a new agreement ended with the signing of the Oslo accords. Once the negotiations were completed, the only 'use' of the new agreement to score political points against the Israeli government was the lengthy delay in the ratification process by the Belgian and French parliaments. The economic impact of the delay was minimal. That the Union stopped short of non-ratification was indicative of its cautious approach to deploying its policy instruments to influence the Israelis. Subtle threats to withdraw cooperation occasionally emanated from various sources within the Union. The Commission's tactics on the trade disputes displayed the potential to make life awkward for the Israeli authorities through the singling out of specific issues. But the bottom line was that only the USA possessed the combination of economic and political power necessary to consistently and positively influence the behaviour of Israeli governments.

## Conclusions

It is evident that the EU was forced to settle for a limited and sporadic capacity to influence the Middle East Peace Process. The ability to effect decisive changes in the behaviour of the main protagonists – the exercise of effective power – proved largely beyond it. On the occasions when the Union flexed its muscles with the government of Israel, the impact was temporary and did not lead to significant and sustained changes to Israeli behaviour in the Occupied Territories. The EU showed itself to be much better equipped to exercise 'soft power', using economic and financial instruments to ensure the viability of the nascent Palestinian economy and contribute to the stabilisation of the new Palestinian institutions. Yet the difficult questions which began to be raised about the returns from Europe's huge investment cast doubt on the wisdom of backing Arafat's government to such a significant extent.

The inherent limitations of the EU's foreign policy machinery have been a determining factor in its handling of the Middle East Peace Process. A complex mix of historical experiences, contemporary commercial and political interests, and domestic pressures has shaped member states policies towards the Middle East. Even when national governments have set aside their differences to generate strong political statements, EU foreign policy does not regularly turn to the traditional tools of power politics – coercion, sanctions and threats – to go one step further. The defects of the CFSP in this regard are transparent. A mechanism based on unanimous decision-making reduces the likelihood of the member states habitually coalescing around agreed positions, particularly on the highly sensitive issues associated with the Arab-Israeli conflict. The problems that have beset EU foreign policy making have been recognised as serious barriers to its ability to project itself as a political force in the region.[92] As one senior official from a partner country put it:

> The EU's role is to balance the role of the USA which in our opinion is dictated by the powerful Israeli lobby. Until now, the Americans have not put enough pressure on the Israelis who have not respected the Oslo accords. Unfortunately, an EU role is not yet possible, not just because the US and Israel don't want it, but because there is no CFSP.[93]

Joint Actions to send electoral observers to the Occupied Territories and to support the Palestinian police force did not amount to decisive political interventions. The appointment of a Special Envoy might have raised the Union's profile, but it was consistent with the propensity of the member states to appoint representatives in the absence of agreement on collective strategies.

However, there were two positive aspects to the EU's experience in the Middle East Peace Process. First, the Union's increased willingness to utilise pillar I policy instruments could only improve the appearance of coherence and strategic consistency in EU external policies. Second, there was a fine strategic thread running through much of what the EU did in relation to the Middle East after the Madrid Conference. Building outwards from the Euro-Mediterranean Partnership, the Union linked together its Mediterranean policy, its role as the key financial donor to the Peace Process and the new generation of Association Agreements to make itself economically indispensable to the long-term future of the Middle East. Though the prospects of peace seem ever more distant, the Union may one day be ideally placed to reap the benefits.

## Notes

[1] Cited in Ifestos, P. (1987) *European Political Cooperation: Towards a framework of supranational diplomacy*, Aldershot: Avebury, p. 369.
[2] Turner, M. (1997) 'Code aims to aid Middle East talks', *European Voice*, 2-8 October, p. 6.
[3] Roberson, B.A. (1998) 'Introduction' in B.A. Roberson (ed.) *The Middle East and Europe: The Power Deficit*, London: Routledge, p. 11.
[4] Most of the states in the region were drawn into the conflict. Jordan, the PLO and Syria backed Iraq, a decision that cost them the financial support of their wealthy Arab neighbours. Turkey was used as a base by NATO to police Iraq's northern border. Israel was subject to several Iraqi Scud missile attacks during the military conflict but was dissuaded from retaliation by severe US pressure.
[5] Hadar, L.T. (1991) 'The United States, Europe and the Middle East', *World Policy Journal*, Vol. 8, No. 3, p. 427.
[6] Hooper, J. 'Conference Table Built on a Political Minefield', *The Guardian*, 30 October 1991, p. 9.
[7] Dumas, R. (1991) 'Interview à Europe 1', *Déclarations de politique étrangère depuis 1990*, Paris: Ministère des Affaires Etrangères, 14 November, http://www.diplomatie.fr/cgi/nph-bwcgis/BASIS/epic/www/doc/SF.
[8] Ginsberg, R. (2001) *The European Union in International Politics: Baptism of Fire*, Oxford and Lanham: Rowman and Littlefield, p. 150.
[9] The multilateral talks were designed to run in parallel to the bilateral negotiations.
[10] Hollis, R. (1995) *After Madrid: The EU and the Peace Process*, Palestinian Academic Society for the Study of International Affairs, Seminar, March, http://www.passia.org/.
[11] Muscheidt, B. (1995) The European Union and the Peace Process Since Madrid', Palestinian Academic Society for the Study of International Affairs, Seminar, March, «http://www.passia.org/».
[12] Peters, J. (1997) *Europe and the Middle East Peace Process: Emerging from the sidelines*, Centre for Euro-Mediterranean Studies, University of Reading, http://www.rdg.ac.uk/EIS/GSEIS/EMC/pubs.html, May, pp. 5-6.
[13] European Commission (1993) 'EC Support to the Middle East Peace Process', *Communication from the Commission to the Council and the European Parliament*, COM (93) 458, 29 September, p. 1.

[14] O'Sullivan, E. (1995) 'Cementing Peace with Prosperity', *Middle East Economic Digest: Middle East Business Weekly*, Vol. 37, No. 38, p. 4.
[15] European Commission (1993b) op. cit., p. 2. By the end of 1997, the EU had committed 444 million ECUs in grants from the EU budget, 100 million ECUs in EIB loans, and 156 million ECUs made available by the EU to the UNRWA under the standard budget support programme. The priority areas were: education (130 million ECUs); health care (33 million ECUs); humanitarian assistance (36 million ECUs) and contributions to the UNRWA (156 million ECUs).
[16] EU aid to the Palestinians removed some of the cost to the Israelis of paying for security in the occupied territories. It enabled the Israeli government to reduce the number of Palestinians employed in Israel on the assumption that donors would pick up the bill through business projects.
[17] For an evaluation of the utility of aid, see Beck, M. (1997) 'Can Financial Aid Promote Regional Peace Agreements? The Case of the Arab-Israeli Conflict', *Mediterranean Politics*, Vol. 2, No. 2, p. 66.
[18] Langer, B. (1993) 93/451, Question No H-1095/93 on the Israel/Palestine Peace Process, *European Political Cooperation: Documentation Bulletin*, Brussels, p. 538.
[19] European Council (1993) 93/506 'Conclusions of the European Council meeting in Brussels' (10-11 December 1993), *European Political Cooperation: Documentation Bulletin*, p. 590.
[20] European Commission (1993a) *Future Relations and Cooperation between the Community and the Middle East*, COM (93) 375 Final, Brussels, 8 September, p. 4.
[21] Ibid., p. 4.
[22] Press Statement by the Greek Council Presidency (1994) 'Statement on events in Hebron', *European Political Cooperation: Documentation Bulletin*, No. 9, p. 131.
[23] Barbé, E. and Izquierdo, F. (1997) 'Present and Future of Joint Actions for the Mediterranean Region' in M. Holland (ed.) *Common Foreign and Security Policy: The Record and Reforms*, London and Washington: Pinter, p. 130.
[24] De Charette, H. (1995) 'Interview with the Minister of Foreign Affairs in "Al-Ahram Weekly"', *Official Documentation: Ministry of Foreign Affairs*, Paris: Ministry of Foreign Affairs, 26 July.
[25] By contrast, the Arab states were quick to react collectively, discussing Netanyahu's election victory and the possibility of a common position on it at the Cairo Summit in June 1996.
[26] Council of Ministers (1996a) *Declaration by the Presidency on Behalf of the European Union on the Middle East Peace Process*, PESC/96/83, October 1, Rapid Database, http://europa.eu.int/rapid/cgi.
[27] Fisk, R. 'US Warns Europe on Middle East Meddling', *The Independent*, 22 October 1996, p. 12.
[28] Without exception, all the officials interviewed mentioned Moratinos' reputation and experience in the region as a reason for the good working relationships he managed to establish with all the major players in the Peace Process.
[29] This argument is especially valid for the Israeli government. Scepticism about European interference in the Peace Process was a useful way of strengthening its nationalist credentials.
[30] Interview, Brussels, 5 November 1997.
[31] Interview, Brussels, 11 November 1997.

[32] Council of Ministers (1996b) *1958th Council Meeting: General Affairs*, Luxembourg: 28-29 October, http://europa.eu.int/rapid.
[33] Quoted in Dempsey, J. (1997) 'EU envoy builds a Mideast role', *Financial Times*, 7 February, p. 4.
[34] Interview with Professor Bichara Khader, University of Louvain-la-neuve, Belgium, 21 April 1997. Bichara Khader was a member of EuroMeSCo.
[35] Cited in Awwad, E. (1997) 'Paix menacée au Proche-Orient', *Défense Nationale*, 53, January, p. 102.
[36] Interview, Brussels, 5 November 1997.
[37] Interview, Brussels, 6 November 1997.
[38] Interview, Brussels, 4 November 1997.
[39] Turner, M. 'Code aims to aid Middle East talks', *European Voice*, 2-8 October 1997, p. 6.
[40] Halevy, E. (1997) *Exchange of Views on the Middle East Peace Process and relations between the EU and Israel*, European Parliament: Delegation for Relations with Israel, Brussels, 18 March. Halevy was Israeli Ambassador to the EU at the time.
[41] It was the start of construction on this site that brought the Peace Process to a halt. Perhaps surprisingly, Cook's action seemed to be backed by Moratinos, despite the latter's greater sensitivity to Israeli concerns.
[42] *Agence Europe*, 16/17 March 1998, p. 4.
[43] Vedrine, H. (1998) 'Réunion Informelle des Ministres des Affaires Etrangères de l'Union européenne', *Point de Presse du Ministre des Affaires Etrangères*, Edinburgh 14 March, http:// www.diplomatie.fr/cgi/nph-bwcgis/BASIS.
[44] Ginsberg, R. (2001) op. cit., p. 167.
[45] The Wye agreement also provided for the release of Palestinian prisoners and the reopening of discussions about a direct link between the West Bank and Gaza. Discussions on the status of Jerusalem, the issue of Israeli settlements and the return of Palestinian refugees were all postponed.
[46] Quoted in Ciricai, F. (1998) *Jordan, EU working closely to ensure being "associated" with final status talks*, http://www.jordanembassyus.org/121098003.htm, 10 December. The phrase 'player, not only a payer' was originally used by Luxembourg's Prime Minister Jean Claude Juncker.
[47] Hazboun, I. (2000) 'EU to "recognise Palestine"', *The Guardian* (Internet Edition), 21 June.
[48] European Commission, (1996) *Joint Report from the Presidency and Commission: Mediterranean Policy – Follow Up to Barcelona*, Brussels, 3 December, p.3.
[49] Rhein, E. (1996) 'The Future of Economic Cooperation in the Middle East', *Transcript of Speech*, London, 23 April, p. 6.
[50] European Parliament (1996d) (Committee on Foreign Affairs, Security and Defence Policy), *Report on the Middle East Peace Process*, Doc. No. A4-0351/96, 4 November, p. 12; See also Ginsberg, R. (2001) op. cit., p. 108.
[51] *International Herald Tribune*, November 27 1996, p. 11.
[52] Interview, Brussels, 12 December 1996.
[53] Interview, Brussels, 14 October 1998. The threat was issued at a meeting of Arab League foreign ministers in September 1996.
[54] The EU expressed its disquiet over the settlement issue at a meeting between Ambassadors representing the Troika and Israeli foreign ministry officials in February 1997. The Israelis noted the Union's concerns, but responded with a list of reasons why the

construction project was permitted under the Oslo agreements. Israeli Mission to the European Communities (1997) *Note d'Information*, 25 February, Brussels.
⁵⁵ Turner, M. (1997) 'Euro-Med Still Makes Progress Despite Tension', *European Voice*, 3-9 April, p. 8. On 31 March 1997, the Arab League took a decision to freeze the 'normalization' of relations with Israel.
⁵⁶ Interview, Brussels, 13 November 1997.
⁵⁷ The presence of US mediator George Ross as an observer in Malta went largely unnoticed. However, immediately after the meeting Ross flew to Israel for talks with Netanyahu, and travelled on to Gaza to meet Arafat. One official claimed that the EU's intervention in Malta had 'got the US back on the bike'. Interview, Brussels, 20 April 1997.
⁵⁸ Marín, M. (1997) *The European Union's Mediterranean Policy*, Address to the Nobel Institute, Oslo, May 23, http://europa.eu.int/rapid.
⁵⁹ Interview, Brussels, 5 December 1996.
⁶⁰ In a 1997 poll conducted by Tel Aviv University, 60 per cent of Israelis polled thought Europeans were more supportive of the Palestinians, while only 31 per cent considered Europeans to be neutral. By contrast, 20 per cent thought the US was more supportive of the Palestinians, while 50 per cent felt that the USA was neutral. For a brief summary of the poll, see The Tami Steinmetz Center for Peace Research, Tel Aviv University (1997) *Israeli-Palestinian People to People Peace Index*, http://spirit.tau.ac.il/code/instit.html.
⁶¹ Interview, Brussels, 6 December 1996.
⁶² Syria in particular became an increasingly regular absentee from lists of participants.
⁶³ Turner, M. (1997) 'Morocco Decision Frustrates EU', *European Voice*, 30 October-5 November, p. 9. European diplomats complained that months had been spent preparing the meeting and that the Arab group had given little advanced warning of its decision.
⁶⁴ The idea of holding a 'mid-term review' of the Barcelona process was agreed at the Malta meeting. *Agence Europe*, 16/17 February 1998, p. 5.
⁶⁵ *Agence Europe*, 28 February 1998, p. 6; *Financial Times*, 4 June 1998, p. 6.
⁶⁶ Prior to the Palermo meeting, the Arab participants discussed whether to hold the Barcelona process hostage to the peace process. Again they chose a more moderate line, opting to 'use Arab-European cooperation to strengthen the Arab position in the dormant negotiations with Israel.' Given that funding for the EMP was to be re-examined under a year later during the German Council Presidency, the Arab group had to find a balance between criticism and optimism. Egyptian State Information Service (1998) *Letter from Cairo*, No. 202, June 11-13, Internet Edition, http://www.uk.sis.gov.eg/public/letter/html/frame202.htm.
⁶⁷ European Council (2000) *Common Strategy of the European Council of 19 June 2000 on the Mediterranean Region*, 2000/458/CFSP, Official Journal of the European Communities L183, 22 July, Brussels. Point 5.
⁶⁸ The same applied to the multilateral working groups which had also ceased to function.
⁶⁹ Aliboni, R., Said Aly, A. and de Vasconcelos, A. (1997) *Euromesco Working Group on Political and Security Cooperation/Working Group on Arms Control, Confidence Building and Conflict Prevention: Joint Report*, Lisbon, April, p. 35.
⁷⁰ Palestinian Delegate General to the European Union, *Exchange of Views on the EU-Palestine cooperation agreement*, European Parliament: Delegation for Relations with the Palestine Legislative Council, Brussels, 18 March 1997.
⁷¹ Economic indicators unequivocally show that the Palestinian people were worse off by 1998 than they had been before the start of the peace process. GNP per capita fell by 35 per cent between 1993 and 1996. Annual 'closure days' rose from around 5 per cent in

1993 to 37 per cent in 1996. Annual trade lost as a result of the closures were estimated at 275 million ECUs. European Commission (1998a) *The Role of the European Union in the Peace Process and its Future Assistance to the Middle East*, COM (97) 715 Final. For a thorough account of the problems facing the Palestinian economy, see Diwan, I. and Shaban, R.A. (1997) *Development Under Adversity: The Palestinian Economy in Transition*, Palestinian Economic Forum, http://www.palecon.org/wbdocs.
72 Farmers were particularly badly hit by the closure policy. Land converted for high value flower, fruit and vegetable production for the European market had to be re-converted to low-value production for local markets.
73 Interview, Brussels, 11 November 1997.
74 Interview, Brussels, 14 October 1998.
75 Evans, G. (Commission representative with responsibility for relations with the Palestinian Authority) Address to European Parliament's Delegation for Relations with the Palestinian Territories, 18 March 1997.
76 The 1994 Paris Interim Protocol on Economic Relations established a customs union between the autonomous Palestinian Territories and Israel. Two features of the agreement in particular restricted the Palestinians' freedom to trade with the outside world. First, the list of products covered by the agreement was provided by Israel, giving the Palestinians little control over the quantity and type of products they were allowed to import and export. Second, the agreement meant that a sizeable proportion of the tax revenue from Palestinian trade actually finished up in the Israeli government's hands. In 1997, 50 per cent of revenues were collected by Israel. For a useful commentary on the Paris Protocol, see Huleileh, S., Bashkin, G. and Al-Qaq, Z. (1999) *Guidelines for Final Status Economic Negotiations Between Israel and Palestine*, Jerusalem: Israel/Palestine Centre for Research and Information.
77 Arafat, Y. (1997) cited in Ash, T. 'Arafat urges action from Europe', *Middle East Economic Digest*, 25 July, p. 5.
78 European Commission (1998) op. cit., p. 8.
79 Fouet, S. (1998) *The Middle-East Peace Process: de jure – de facto realities. What is the Role of Europe?*, Presentation to Summer School on The Mediterranean and the New International Order, University of Catania, 5-12 July. Sylvie Fouet worked with Moratinos' team on the problem of infrastructural links between the Palestinian territories.
80 Ginsberg, R. (2001) op. cit., p. 122. The Union adopted a rather softer line on this issue after the election of Ehud Barak as Israeli Prime Minister in 1999.
81 As early as 1995, the Commission's anti-fraud unit (UCLAF) drew attention to possible fraud involving orange juice imports. Given the sensitivity of the Peace Process at that stage, and ongoing negotiation of the Euro-Mediterranean agreement with Israel, no action was taken. *European Report* (1997) No. 2264, November 1, Section V, p. 4.
82 The scale of the alleged fraud was substantial. The Israeli press suggested that the amount involved could be up to 25 billion ECUs, though the Commission believed that figure to be exaggerated. The EU's Court of Auditors found that Israeli exports of orange juice to the EU were equivalent to three times its total domestic production capacity. Ibid.
83 *Financial Times*, 13 November 1997, p. 6.
84 *Official Journal of the European Union*, C 97/31, January 1997.
85 Had the issue not been resolved in the Cooperation Committee, then it would have come up before the Foreign Ministers in the Council. Israeli Foreign Minister David Levy and Council President Jacques Poos discussed the matter prior to the Cooperation Committee.

[86] Both the Israeli government and the Israeli Federation of Chambers of Commerce discussed possible retaliation measures, claiming that exporters would be seriously harmed by the Commission's decision. FICC (1997) 'EU and Israel Agree to End Origin of Orange Juice Dispute', *Newsletter*, Vol. 9, No. 9, http://www.chamber.org.il/docs/nl1297.html; *The Jerusalem Post*, 13 November 1997, Internet Edition, http://www.jpost.com/com/Archive/13.Nov.1997/Business/Article-2.html.

[87] European Commission (1998b) 'EU-Israel: Implementation of the interim agreement in the framework of a strengthened regional cooperation', *Press Release* IP/98/426, Strasbourg, 13 May; General Affairs Council (1998) *2111th Council Meeting*, Luxembourg, 29 June.

[88] Quoted in *Financial Times*, 27 May 1998, p. 7.

[89] Quoted in Harries, D. and Gilbert, N. (1998) 'Netanyahu blasts EU boycott', *The Jerusalem Post: Internet Edition*, May 20, http://www.jpost.com/com/Archive/20.May.1998/News/Article-0.html.

[90] Lemaître, P. (1998) 'La Communauté européenne accuse Nétanyahou de politiser le débat commercial', *Le Monde*, 19 May, p. 3.

[91] Ginsberg, R. (2001) op. cit., p. 105.

[92] Marín, M. (1997) 'The European Union's Mediterranean Policy', *Address at the Nobel Institute*, Oslo, 23 May, http://europa.eu.int/rapid/cgi/.

[93] Interview, Palestinian Delegate General to the European Union, Brussels, 6 November 1997.

Chapter 7

# The EU and the Algeria Crisis

*We don't know what is going on and we're not sure the state even knows. It is not clear who is being targeted and why.* European Diplomat.[1]

*Whoever fails to export stability to Algeria today will import instability in the form of big movements of refugees tomorrow.* Klaus Kinkel, German Foreign Minister.[2]

**Introduction**

The response of the EU and its member states to the Algerian crisis of the 1990s might best be described as janus faced. The Union failed to censure the military for halting the electoral process in 1992 and made little concerted effort to press for negotiations between the regime and the opposition parties. Moreover, Algeria was welcomed into the Barcelona process, despite the fact that the military's annulment of the national elections in 1992 violated fundamental principles of both the Barcelona Declaration and the EU's own treaties. The same period saw a substantial increase in European economic aid to Algeria. European companies, with financial backing from national governments and support from the EU's budget, also significantly expanded their investments in Algeria's lucrative natural gas sector. Yet the deals were signed with a regime that stood accused of complicity in the murder of citizens it was supposed to protect. Confronted with a crisis in a state which was of considerable strategic importance to the Union, the EU's performance was both an indictment of its feeble collective diplomacy and another example of the weakness of the Euro-Mediterranean Partnership. In a situation in which the EU, rather than the USA or other external forces, looked best placed to exert a strong political impact, its inaction says much about the organisation's behaviour as an international actor.

Above all, the EU's handling of its relations with Algeria demonstrated the constraints imposed on its foreign policy when one member state, in this case France, 'captures' policy and dominates decision making. Franco-Algerian relations played a crucial part in determining the EU's position on the Algerian crisis. As Yahia Zoubir and Youcef Bouandel argue:

> France has the most complex interests in the region; it also hosts the largest immigrant community from the Maghreb. Therefore, France's policy has to be studied separately.[3]

Once part of Metropolitan France, Algeria has become since the 1960s as much a domestic as a foreign policy issue for successive French governments. The presence of one million immigrants of Algerian origin, and over three million Muslims, on French soil, coupled with the intertwined recent histories of the two states, set France apart from its partners in the Union.[4] Respect among the other member states for the notion that Algeria remained a French *chasse gardée* has certainly constrained, and perhaps even defined EU-Algerian relations during the 1990s. In short, as Hugh Roberts contends, in determining EU policy, 'power lies with France'.[5]

The first section of this chapter analyses the origins of the Algerian crisis and the Community's irresolute response to it. Section two considers the EU's collective reaction, and the reaction of individual member governments, to the cancellation of the Algerian national elections and the spiralling violence that followed. Section three examines EU policy and diplomacy as the situation in Algeria degenerated into a *de facto* civil war, one which spilled over onto European soil. The fourth section focuses on Algeria's negotiation of a Euro-Mediterranean Agreement with the EU and its participation in the Barcelona process.

**Algeria's Breakdown and the EU's Initial Response**

The breakdown of order in Algeria began with the mass demonstrations and riots of 1988.[6] A series of strikes orchestrated by the *Union Générale de Travailleurs Algériens (UGTA)*, a banned socialist party, and left-wing elements of the ruling *FLN* showed the full extent of the opposition to President Benjedid Chadli's programme of accelerated economic liberalisation.[7] In September 1988, the state became almost bankrupt after several years of declining oil revenues following the 1985/6 price crash. Debt servicing to foreign creditors accounted for 97 per cent of export earnings, while 80 per cent of state owned companies, Algeria's biggest employers, were in the red.[8] Rising unemployment, swingeing cuts in welfare spending and a sudden hike in the price of basic foodstuff sparked violent demonstrations in October 1988.[9] As many as 500 people were killed as the army and police brutally crushed the protests.[10] The riots released years of pent-up frustration with one-party domination by the *FLN* and with a socio-economic structure that entrenched huge disparities in wealth.[11] Significantly, the aftermath of 'Black October' also saw the emergence of the *Front Islamique du Salut (FIS)* as a political force.[12]

The European Community's reaction to the 1988 riots was low key, with no statement issued through EPC. Speaking for the member states, the Spanish Council Presidency told MEPs that:

> The Twelve have been following closely the recent developments in Algeria. Individual partners have expressed their opinion publicly or to the Algerian authorities.[13]

Existing EC-Algeria cooperation programmes – attached to a Cooperation Agreement and financial protocols – continued uninterrupted. In addition, the Commission granted the Algerian government emergency economic assistance in the form of food aid worth 10.7 million ECUs.[14] However, the Community's political approach was to sit back and watch the situation develop. The announcement by President Chadli of constitutional changes, further economic reforms and moves towards political pluralism soon after the riots seemed to vindicate this 'wait and see' approach. It was left to the European Parliament to speak to the implications for democracy and human rights. It condemned the Algerian government's repression of the protesters, although it too commended Chadli's proposals for reform.[15]

The member states' individual political responses were similarly low-key, but there were substantial increases in bilateral financial assistance to Algeria, particularly from the Mediterranean group. Jean-Jacques Queyranne, spokesman of the French Socialist Party, argued that any solution should come 'from within the Algerian government'.[16] At the same time, the Socialists pushed for extra economic aid to the Algerian government. Chadli's reforms, which responded to the increased use of political conditionality by the French government, were welcomed by President Mitterrand. By November 1988, the French government had agreed to a near tripling of its annual financial credits to Algeria.[17] In January 1989, Spain's Ministry of Trade announced a mixed trade credit package worth 970 million ECUs to boost trade and allow the purchase of much needed industrial and capital goods by the Algerian government. Similarly, Italy offered Algeria a 3 year export credit and aid package worth 196 million ECUs. The point here is that the level of assistance granted by the member states dwarfed direct aid from the Community. Bilateral relations between member states and the Algerian authorities were to remain the dominant level at which the EU dealt with Algeria throughout the 1990s.

There were powerful ulterior motives for the Community to throw its weight behind Chadli. As a leading article in *Le Monde* argued:

> To help Algeria on the road to democracy and prosperity (which in the long term will hardly mean more than providing enough food, at least for the masses) will be expensive. To let the Algerians sink into chaos and fundamentalism will cost more.[18]

Islam rose to prominence after the 1988 riots as the voice of disaffected youth and the poorest segments of Algerian society.[19] The harsh climate of economic austerity provided fertile ground for a movement whose greatest appeal was to the country's burgeoning population of young, unemployed people. Leaders of the Islamic movement accused Chadli's government of trying to pacify the population by filling shelves in shops rather than addressing Algeria's deep social cleavages.[20] But financial aid from western Europe, usually targeted at the energy sector and other big businesses, did not attack the root of the problems. Indeed, Algeria's external debt continued to rise, pushing the government inexorably towards a potentially unpopular rescheduling agreement with the IMF.[21]

The Algerian economy was highly dependent on trade with the Community, with the latter absorbing around 70 per cent of Algeria's exports and supplying around 63 per cent of its imports. Access to European markets was essential for Algerian exporters and to the government's attempt to diversify away from the hydrocarbon sector. Table 7.1 (below) shows the evolution of trade between Algeria and the Community during the 1980s. Algeria was the only country in the southern and eastern Mediterranean with which the Community ran a trade deficit. However, when account is taken of the fact that oil and natural gas provided 95% per cent of Algeria's Community-derived export revenues, the asymmetry of the commercial relationship becomes apparent.[22] Moreover, Algeria accounted for only 0.3 per cent of the Community's external trade, making it relatively unimportant in the broader commercial context (outside the hydrocarbon sector).

**Table 7.1 Trade between the EC and Algeria (Million ECUs)**

|  | 1980 | 1982 | 1983 | 1984 |
|---|---|---|---|---|
| Imports | 4028 | 8246 | 7732 | 9309 |
| Exports | 4754 | 5334 | 6147 | 7032 |
| Balance | 726 | -2912 | -1585 | -2277 |

|  | 1985 | 1986 | 1987 | 1988 |
|---|---|---|---|---|
| Imports | 10289 | 6875 | 5383 | 4793 |
| Exports | 7145 | 5257 | 3884 | 3693 |
| Balance | -3144 | -1618 | -1499 | -1100 |

*Source*: European Commission (1989) 'EEC-Algeria Cooperation Council', *Rapid Database*, Memo 89/33, http://europa.eu.int/rapid.

When the dominance of the energy sector is taken into account, it becomes clear that the Community's quiet response to Black October was also laced with a heavy dose of economic self-interest. Algerian gas was taking a rapidly growing portion of the European market, especially in France, Italy and Spain.[23] At the end of the 1980s, it accounted for nearly a third of the French market and was projected to capture over 50 per cent of the Italian market and 70 per cent of the Spanish market by the mid-1990s. Much of it was to be supplied through a transnational pipeline running from Algeria through Morocco and into Spain.[24] Given the physical vulnerability of the pipeline and past experiences with the renationalization of western energy companies operating in Algeria, political stability was seen as an essential prerequisite of guaranteed supplies.[25] Revenues had sharply contracted after 1986 as world market prices fell and the dollar's value appreciated, driving Sonatrach to seek new partners and new markets.[26] As

Chadli's economic liberalisation project subsumed Sonatrach, new gas supply contracts were signed with European, Japanese and US companies, and existing contracts were renegotiated and upgraded. The political significance of these deals was evident. The French government, for instance, linked its credit package to the resolution of a long-standing dispute over prices for the supply of gas.[27] Similarly, both Spain and Italy negotiated new price and supply deals with Sonatrach shortly after concluding their new financial agreements with Algeria.[28]

Chadli's 'fast track to democracy' gathered momentum with the introduction of a new constitution in November 1989.[29] In contrast to the more cautious reforms underway in the other Maghreb countries, the new pluralist constitution notionally promised to open up politics to the full spectrum of parties and ideologies, including the nascent Islamic movement. By way of encouragement, Community and national leaders made a number of official visits to Algeria during 1989. Commenting on a visit by President François Mitterrand, a leading article in *Le Monde* claimed that:

> The French authorities believe that Chadli is the best placed to be able to change Algerian society and that he has the best chance of attaining it if he is able to steer through political reforms and relaunch the economy.[30]

The European Commission shared this view, sending Commissioner Abel Matutes to Algeria to agree a schedule for the distribution of Community aid. Four agreements were subsequently signed under the third financial protocol, giving Algeria 26 million ECUs for food management, energy and management training projects.

Ultimately, however, the reform process could not mask the regime's growing unpopularity. For many of the opposition parties, the changes did not go far enough. The separation of the Presidential from the executive and legislative branches of government gave Chadli – who had been re-elected in December 1988 – nominal neutrality but he used his role as 'arbiter' to try and ensure the survival of the *FLN* regime. With the floor open for opposition politicians to exploit the government's poor performance, the old order quickly came under sustained attack over its record on corruption, public morality, secularism and the continued influence of France in Algeria.[31] The big winner in this febrile political environment was the growing Islamic movement which proved highly adept at mobilising popular support by offering itself as a substitute provider of social services and as a radical alternative to the *FLN*-state. As Hugh Roberts argues, 'Chadli actually facilitated the development of the *FIS*', the movement whose electoral appeal was to prove his undoing.[32]

## Europe's Silence: The End of the Democratic Experiment

Chadli's grip on power in Algeria continued to loosen during 1990 and 1991 as the *FIS* and other opposition movements capitalised on the country's worsening socio-economic situation and the opportunity to publicly criticise the *FLN*. Notice was served of the *FIS'* electoral strength in the communal elections of June 1990 when those standing under its banner secured a 54 per cent share of the vote. Despite changes to the electoral system, the postponements of polls and widespread gerrymandering, Chadli's government was unable to counter the momentum building behind the *FIS* as national elections approached.[33] In the first round (December 1991), the *FIS* won 47.3 per cent of the vote and 43.7 per cent of the parliamentary seats.[34] Overall, the Islamic 'opposition' took a 55 per cent share and secured a resounding endorsement for their anti-establishment platforms.[35]

In France, the results were greeted with a mixture of alarm and quiet resignation. Many politicians took an apocalyptic view of the crisis, warning of the potential for mass immigration if Algerians sought to escape the fundamentalist state that was expected to replace the old order. But former Foreign Minister Roland Dumas appeared less perturbed, arguing that there was 'no more to fear now than before or in future', and that Islam was 'a reality' in the region.[36] The official line was that the choice of the Algerian people should be respected. Behind the scenes, though, France and the rest of the EU had misjudged the strength of the *FIS* at the national level and Chadli's ability to bargain with its leaders. This uncertainty was exemplified by the taciturn attitudes of Mitterrand and the French Foreign Ministry in the run up to the second ballot.[37]

The situation took a dramatic and decisive turn when, in January 1992, the army removed Chadli and cancelled the elections.[38] Chadli had offered to share power in secret negotiations with the *FIS* but hard-line elements in the army were totally opposed to any concessions to the Islamists.[39] In effect, a military coup ended the democratic experiment and left a politically unstable state facing the EU across the Mediterranean. Again, opinion in France wavered between the hawkish pronouncements of the right and the apparent pragmatism of the left. The Gaullist Charles Pasqua argued that French cooperation with Algeria should be reviewed and even abrogated. A number of Socialists, including President Mitterrand, expressed disquiet at the cessation of the democratic process and urged its resumption.[40]

It was at this stage that the EU settled on what amounted to a 'non-decision' on Algeria. The EU member states made a vaguely worded call for a return to 'normal institutional life' and 'dialogue' between the regime and opposition, but avoided aligning the Union with either camp.[41] The notion of a 'non-decision' does not imply that the crisis was ignored. Rather, as Michael Clarke argues, 'it describes a failure to confront a choice, or even to recognise that one exists'.[42] That the Union initially decided to do nothing owed much to France's 'relational' power over its European partners *vis-à-vis* Algeria.[43] From the outset, the French government, like the regime itself, ruled out external intervention by the Union. Unwilling (or unable) to challenge this position, the other member governments were forced to follow the French lead.

However, by February 1992, the Union's position had subtly shifted, though it still stopped short of a political decision on the elections. A statement issued in the EPC framework put the ball in the regime's court:

> The Community and its member states strongly urge the Algerian authorities to pursue their publicly announced commitments, namely, the social and economic reforms, the restructuring of public administration and the protection of fundamental freedoms. The Community and its member states are willing to cooperate with the Algerian authorities in the economic recovery of their country, bearing in mind that compliance with the aforementioned principles will be important in the context of bilateral relations.[44]

Essentially, the Union gave the regime time to bed itself in by promising that financial aid to Algeria would not be disrupted.[45] This non-decision (on the suspension of aid) was not without logic. The Islamists' campaign of violence alienated the *FIS* from many of its supporters, reducing the likelihood that any re-run of the elections would produce a similar result.[46] Yet the Union made little effort to justify its silence. Nor did it give the regime a time limit for the resumption of the democratic process. In evading such decisions, the Union may have missed the best opportunity to set a precedent for international peace-making initiatives. As Barbara Smith argues:

> There were still some possible courses of action outsiders could recommend to the Algerian government. And, at the time, the regime was so divided over what policy to adopt toward dissident Islamic political groups that it is at least possible that some of Algeria's leaders could have been persuaded to listen.[47]

It is easy to criticise the EU's inaction as the crisis unfolded. It is rather more difficult, even with the benefit of hindsight, to suggest what policy options were available and credible. Three factors combined to discourage external involvement. First, the political situation was extremely fluid. It was neither clear what form a *FIS* government might take nor whether the wider Algerian public would accept the imposition of Islamic order by a *FIS* administration. As Claire Spencer argues:

> At no stage had a clear and unequivocal statement been made by the *FIS* leadership that it would respect the form of democracy laid down in the 1989 Constitution. A victory for the *FIS* would possibly have created an Islamic state governed by some variant of the Charia code on the Community's doorstep, a development it was anxious to prevent.[48]

Second, the *Haut Comité d'Etat*, installed by the military as a quasi civilian government after the coup, was quick to ward off external interference in what it viewed as a purely internal problem. Indeed, it drew attention to the fact that the *FIS* leadership itself had approved of France's choice not to intervene. Given the reservations about a *FIS* victory, this message gave the Union a convenient excuse to stand back. Third, European investments in the gas sector may well have been jeopardised if the *FIS* had come to power. While the *FIS* would have found it hard to maintain high levels of public spending without the revenue from oil and gas sales, the investment climate for foreign capital would certainly have been judged to be less stable. Abdelkader Hachani, provisional leader of the *FIS*, described the regime's new legislation on foreign investments in the sector as 'a transaction of shame'.[49]

In light of the constraints outlined above, the Union's 'non-decision' was not surprising. Yet Europe's political impotence markedly contrasted with the apparent regularity of decisions being taken on the economic front. In line with the overall increase in financial resources for the Mediterranean non-member states, Algeria had seen its allocation of financial aid rise under the fourth financial protocol (Table 7.2).

**Table 7.2 EC-Algeria Financial Protocols (Million ECUs)**

| Financial Protocol | Duration | EIB Loans | Budget | Total |
|---|---|---|---|---|
| 01 | 1976-1981 | 70 | 44 | 114 |
| 02 | 1981-1986 | 107 | 44 | 151 |
| 03 | 1986-1991 | 183 | 56 | 239 |
| 04* | 1992-1996 | 280 | 70** | 350 |

\* Among the 8 Mediterranean non-member countries benefiting from the fourth financial protocol, Algeria's share of resources amounted to 17 per cent.
\*\* Amount includes 18 million ECUs in venture capital.

*Source*: Khader, B. (1997) *Le Partenariat Euro-Méditerranéen après la conference de Barcelone*, Paris: L'Harmattan, p. 36.

No direct connection was made by the Community between the disbursement of resources and the annulment of the elections. Indeed, the Commission reportedly expressed surprise at rumours that financial aid might be frozen.[50] In 1991, the member states had agreed to set aside 300 million ECUs to support structural adjustment programmes in the Mediterranean non-member countries, including Algeria. As a supplement to this programme of macro-economic aid, the Community had also offered Chadli's government a medium-term loan of 400 million ECUs prior to the cancellation of the elections. Even after the events of January 1992, the only new conditions attached to the loan related to the negotiation of a reform programme between Algeria and the IMF, not to the resumption of the democratisation process.[51]

This decoupling of the Community's economic relations with Algeria from the political crisis reveals much about EU external policy-making. First, it lends further weight to the argument that pillar I policy instruments hold the key to the EU's ability to exert external impact. A collective political initiative from the EU might have been desirable in the context of its foreign policy ambitions, but would have had little effect on a regime that had already warned off the international community from attempting to intervene in the Algerian crisis. However, there can be no doubt about the highly politicised nature of EU and bilateral aid from the member states and its importance to the regime's survival. With an external debt of 24 billion ECUs in 1992, the goodwill of western creditors and their willingness to underpin the regime's faltering macro-economic reform programme and income from oil and gas exports were crucial to the financial liquidity of the Algerian state.[52]

Second, an approach based on economic support and technical cooperation was in line with the Union's strategy of dealing with functional issues rather than the big political questions. Cooperation in the energy field was a particularly salient example. As Janne Haaland Matlary argues, 'energy is a prime instrument for such linkage politics'.[53] After talks between Commissioners Abel Matutes (DG1), Carlos Cardoso e Cunha (DG17 energy) and the Algerian government in March 1992, the Union agreed to look at Algeria's proposals in the context of the budgetary allocation for regional cooperation in the Mediterranean.[54] Of even greater financial significance were the new contracts being signed by Sonatrach with multinational oil companies. The Community's assistance was sought in establishing a conducive climate for investment, but the rest was left to private capital.

Third, the Union's decision to offer economic support without political interference represented another instance of an external policy position being defined by the lowest common denominator. The French government's assumption that 'Islam would be "soluble" in the face of economic progress' effectively became the Union's strategy.[55] As a 'mediator' between Algeria and the EU, the French government clearly exerted pressure on its European partners to meet the regime's financial needs.[56] The decision to provide increased balance of payments assistance at the Luxembourg European Council in 1991, for instance, was a French initiative.[57] Only as the crisis worsened did divisions within the EU begin to surface and its political position come under fire.

## The Descent into Violence and the EU's First Initiative

The assassination of President Mohamed Boudiaf in June 1992 seemed to stiffen the resolve of the EU to take an 'arms length' approach. Commission President Jacques Delors stated that:

> The Commission is sure that the Algerian people and the nation's leaders will survive this new crisis with reason and determination. In these tragic hours, it plans to remind them of its solidarity and expresses the hope that Algeria will return to a period of peace in which democratic freedoms and pluralism are respected.[58]

President Mitterrand expressed the hope that 'Algeria [would] be able to overcome this severe test', and pledged that the Algerian people could 'count on the friendship of France'.[59] The resort to violence by armed elements of the Islamic opposition, principally the *Groupe Islamique Armé (GIA)*, may have made it easier for the EU to exonerate its position, as an identifiable 'enemy' of the state and ordinary people had showed its hand. Furthermore, the decision by the regime (May 1993) to break diplomatic relations with Iran signalled the military's desire to be at the forefront of the struggle against radical Islam, underlining its self-proclaimed status as a bulwark against fundamentalism. As it became ever more difficult to identify the perpetrators of violence, an 'arms length' approach increasingly appeared to be the safest option.

A new and more dangerous phase was entered late in 1993 when armed Islamic groups began to target foreign residents in Algeria. In September, two French surveyors were kidnapped and murdered, the first such attack on foreigners. Until then, the safety of European citizens working in Algeria had not given undue cause for concern. In October, the audacious kidnapping of three employees of the French Consulate in Algiers galvanised the EU into another EPC statement urging the Algerian authorities to 'take every possible measure for a rapid return to a climate that will ensure their safety'.[60]

French citizens working in Algeria were inevitably prime targets.[61] When the kidnappers eventually released the Consulate staff, they issued a warning giving French expatriates one month to leave Algeria. Other foreign nationals were also warned to leave. Foreign minister Alain Juppé responded by offering his government's assistance.[62] Nevertheless by the end of 1994, only 2000 French citizens were left in the country.[63] Other member states paid more heed to the warnings, however, and advised their citizens not to travel to Algeria unless for exceptional reasons.

The deliberate targeting of French nationals prompted the Balladur government to adopt a harder line and temporarily put the administration's hawks in the ascendancy. Alain Juppé, questioned about how France intended to help Algeria combat fundamentalism, set out three objectives:

- To halt 'terrorist activities' on French soil.
- To prevent the production of 'hostile' literature, essentially pro-*FIS/GIA* literature.
- To increase France's annual bilateral financial aid to Algeria to around 960 million ECUs.[64]

Implementation of these objectives was swift. In a sweeping police operation across France, 88 Islamic activists were arrested and Islamic propaganda was seized. This action drew an angry response from both sides in Algeria. Prime Minister Rheda Malek insisted that the rights of Algerians living on European soil should be respected.[65] Raba Kebir, a leading figure in the *FIS*, demanded the release of those arrested and called on France to cease its backing of *'le pouvoir'*.[66]

A key player in defining the Balladur administration's policy on Algeria was Interior Minister Charles Pasqua. As Spencer observes, 'in contrast to the policies of its less engaged neighbours, France's reactions to events in Algeria [were] led as much by the Interior as the Foreign and Defence Ministries'.[67] Pasqua's name appeared atop a restrictive and much criticised 1993 law on immigration, and it was largely his decision to clamp down on the activities of Islamists within France. Relations with the Algerian and wider Muslim communities in France were seriously damaged by the new measures.[68] Part of the rationale for the so-called *loi Pasqua* was an emotive appeal for the 'preservation of the essential values of French society', a thinly disguised reference to a perceived Islamic threat to the secular basis of the French state.[69] Algeria's generals formed an unspoken alliance with Pasqua, who became associated with the *eradicateur* faction in the regime.[70] The *GIA* viewed France's actions as a declaration of war and responded by stepping up its campaign of violence.[71] Other action by the Balladur government took the form of pressure on the London and Paris international creditors clubs to obtain a debt rescheduling agreement for Algeria. It successfully secured increased aid from the World Bank and western governments, though the Algerian regime continued to reject another debt rescheduling agreement with the IMF.

While many of France's EU partners shared its concern about an Islamic 'domino effect' in North Africa, they were averse to restricting the activities of the exiled Algerian opposition on their own territories. The presence and freedom of speech of opposition activists were regarded as civil liberties matters on which the host states were reluctant to compromise. Germany and the UK, for instance, both attracted criticism from the Algerian and French governments for allowing *FIS* leaders to operate on their soil. Both governments also kept an open mind about dialogue with the *FIS*.[72] Such divisions among the member governments undoubtedly prolonged the tendency for 'non-decisions'. Since no consensus could be reached on a political line, the subject of Algeria was rarely broached.

The hijacking of an Air France flight in Algiers during Christmas 1994 brought the Algerian crisis onto French soil, into the media spotlight and subsequently into the Presidential election campaign. The hijackers – who described themselves as *FIS* representatives rather than *GIA* activists – timed their action and chose their target to achieve the maximum effect. Air France aircraft were among the last symbols of France's presence in Algeria. Despite a much lauded rescue operation by France's *Groupe d'Intervention de la Gendarmerie Nationale*, the episode highlighted the vulnerability of French citizens both in Algeria and in France, leading Balladur and Pasqua to clamp down even harder on the activities of Islamic groups. The hijacking also opened a rift between the French government and the regime, which was criticised by Balladur for having delayed giving permission for the aircraft to leave Algiers.[73]

In the absence of governmental action, it was left to NGOs to maintain a critical watch on the deteriorating human rights situation in Algeria. Human rights organisations, particularly Amnesty International, continually reproached the regime and armed Islamic groups, and berated the international community for failing to deal with the crisis.[74] The most promising peace-making initiative was brokered by a small, Christian NGO based in Rome, the Sant'Egidio Community. In the so-called 'Rome platform' of early 1995, the majority of Algeria's opposition parties, including the *FIS*, agreed on a set of principles and mutual guarantees designed to allow the democratic process to be resumed. Critically, though, neither President Liamine Zeroual's representatives nor representatives of the *GIA* attended. Moreover, the document explicitly ruled out external intervention, stating that the parties were 'opposed to any interference in the internal affairs of Algeria'.[75] As Dominique Moisi argued, 'if the army doesn't feel the need to compromise, then what happened in Rome will be just talk'.[76] The regime immediately rejected the Rome Platform.

Italy was the first member state publicly to break rank over EU policy on the Algerian crisis.[77] As Rich and Joseph argue, 'the Italian government [was] torn between its need to safeguard hydrocarbon imports and concern over the potential security risks posed by any deepening of the conflict'.[78] In January 1997, an under-secretary in the Italian Foreign Ministry, Pierre Fassino, hinted that Italy was about to launch a peace initiative and called for the EU's backing. Foreign Minister Lamberto Dini quickly disavowed Fassino's proposal, ruling out any independent mediating role for Italy.[79] But he too called for the EU to pursue a negotiated settlement, arguing that the Union should 'emerge from a condition of passivity and lack of interest and help Algeria, though without interfering, to overcome the current crisis'.[80] However, in a trilateral meeting with the French and Spanish governments shortly after, the Italians were persuaded by France to put their proposal on ice.[81]

At the end of 1997, the EU finally started to take a tougher line with the regime. When Foreign Minister Ahmed Attaf came to Luxembourg in November and accused Belgium, France, Germany, Italy and the UK of harbouring terrorists and of giving them logistical support on the pretext of their being asylum seekers, he received a rebuke from Luxembourg's Foreign Minister Jacques Poos. Poos defended the Union's right to consider exiled members of the Islamic opposition as asylum seekers and warned the Algerian government that it should not just treat the crisis as an issue of terrorism but should do more to protect its own citizens.[82] At the same time, Poos called for greater openness on the part of the regime about the conflict in Algeria and for restrictions on the media to be lifted.

In the end, European governments were forced to act by the sheer scale of the violence. An upsurge in violence during the winter of 1997-8 to unprecedented levels – 1500 deaths during Ramadan alone – received sustained press coverage. A new EU initiative, launched by UK Foreign Minister Robin Cook after strong pressure from German Foreign Minister Klaus Kinkel, was a first test for the British Labour government's new 'ethical' foreign policy. A succession of extended press reports in the UK and a direct appeal to the European Parliament by the *FIS* convinced the Foreign Office that something had to be done.[83] After discussing an initiative with its partners in Brussels, the UK announced that the EU would send a team to Algeria.

Initially, a delegation comprising of regional directors from the foreign ministries of the UK, Luxembourg and Austria was rejected by Foreign Minister Attaf as 'inappropriate'.[84] The fact that the EU had to concede on both the composition of the delegation and the subjects it would be permitted to discuss was indicative of the regime's sensitivity about external intervention and of the EU's own failure to define the purpose of its mission. Attaf argued that the delegation should primarily focus on the fight against terrorism.[85] The EU, however, aimed to raise the issue of human rights with the regime, calling for a UN *rapporteur* to be allowed to investigate the situation. It was another example of a superficially activist but reliably hesitant EU passing the buck.

Following prickly negotiations with the regime, the EU was forced to upgrade the status of its delegation to junior ministerial level. Meetings were held with both ministers and representatives of the opposition and press and were a limited success for the Union in raising its diplomatic profile. However, in substantive terms the mission merely underlined the regime's intransigence in the face of external pressure. Attaf was persuaded to accept the idea of an ad hoc political 'dialogue' with the EU, but in practice this commitment meant nothing more than periodic meetings where the Union could maintain the impression that it was taking action. The mission failed to make much headway on the subject of mediation, although an invitation was extended to Attaf to meet with Robin Cook in London at the end of the year. The regime flatly refused a request to allow the UN to conduct an inquiry into human rights in the country.

The reaction of the *FIS* leadership to the Troika's visit revealed a shift away from outright rejection of external intervention. In a letter to Robin Cook, Anwar Haddam, President of the exiled *FIS* members, made a number of demands of the EU:

> It is our hope, at a time where there is a lack of political freedom in Algeria, to see the European Union, under the leadership of the government of Her Majesty, open the doors of its countries to *FIS* representatives to freely express the suffering and the aspirations of the Algerian people. It is our deep hope and strong request to the European countries to immediately put an end to the activities of those who had claimed responsibility for these horrible massacres and crimes committed against civilians in Algeria, and to bring them to justice. It is also our hope to see the EU monitor different Algerian embassies and their suspicious activities. Finally, we hope to see an end to any military or financial aid to the regime in place.[86]

In a partial *volte face*, however, the Algerian authorities finally agreed to allow a UN team into the country in July to undertake an 'information gathering' mission.[87] The so-called 'Eminent Persons Committee', led by former Portuguese President Mario Soares, was requested not to meet the *FIS*, and was only allowed entry on condition that its report would not be binding on the UN.[88] Its report balanced encouragement for political liberalisation with criticism of both sides for a campaign of violence which had claimed an estimated 120,000 lives by 1999. However, the committee's report was short on recommendations for the international community. It made only vague calls for the west to offer 'cooperation and support' for political, economic and social reforms, and the fight against terrorism.[89] Keeping diplomatic channels to the regime open was all the outside world could realistically achieve.

## Algeria and the Euro-Mediterranean Partnership

The subtle change of approach heralded by the diplomatic initiatives of 1998 was not a precursor to the EU methodically deploying its policy instruments to exert political pressure on the Algerian authorities. Discussion of the situation in Algeria was never likely to feature on the agenda of the Barcelona process given the difficulties in taking forward the human rights and democratisation elements of the first and third chapters. The temporary suspension of the negotiation of Algeria's Euro-Mediterranean Association Agreement signalled to the regime that the political climate in the country was problematic for the Union, but it was not accompanied by explicit conditions for a resumption of the talks. The funding by the MEDA programme of a small number of projects – including assistance with training on human rights and legal reform – did represent something of a concession by the Algerians.[90] However, these decisions and measures were also in keeping with the low key, cautious approach which continued to be the principal characteristic of EU action on the crisis.

Why was the Euro-Mediterranean Partnership so ineffectual? First, any attempt to attach strong political conditions to the opening of negotiations on an Association Agreement may well have been futile given the low-level of non-hydrocarbon trade between the EU and Algeria. The regime did not 'need' a trade liberalisation agreement to anywhere near the same extent as other Mediterranean partner countries. Agricultural trade with the EU presented 'no special difficulties' for Algerian producers, accounting for only 1 per cent of export revenues, while imports of oil and gas products were not regulated by the agreement.[91] From the EU's perspective, it could ill afford to jeopardise the rapidly expanding European investments in the country's energy industry. A formal Agreement would help to create greater certainty for investors by promoting administrative and legal changes.

Exploratory discussions on the Association Agreement began in March 1997, several years behind schedule. The delay had been a deliberate move by the Commission, which chose to wait until the election of Liamine Zeroual as President in 1995 and parliamentary elections in 1997 had taken place in order to give some semblance of legitimacy to its negotiations with the regime. The Commission was also concerned that securing the passage of the agreement through the European Parliament might be difficult before the Algerian people had been given a chance to pass judgement on the regime.[92] When the polls were approved, albeit with reservations, by international observers, the Commission began to negotiate.

A second problem – the practical difficulty of dealing with a regime which was strongly resistant to external 'interference' – emerged once the negotiations had opened. Algeria entered the talks seemingly determined to stick to its guns on key issues. Areas of contention already flagged up by Algerian negotiators prior to the EU mission, including the negative impact of free trade on the manufacturing and agricultural sectors and the question of provisions on the free movement of people became major sticking points. The government claimed that the dismantling of tariff barriers and the removal of duties on the scale required by the EU would cause substantial damage to an economy which was heavily reliant on subsidies and other forms of state protection.[93] It also argued that the idea of 'partnership' was meaningless without allowing for the free movement of people and better protection of Algerian immigrants in EU countries. The EU member states viewed Algeria's insistence on a stronger justice and home affairs component in the agreement as an attempt to secure assistance for its counter-terrorism operations.[94] The Commission justified its decision to halt negotiations at the end of 1997 on the grounds that the two sides could not resolve a dispute about the terms of liberalisation in the oil and gas sectors.[95] In equal measure, the regime's unwillingness to give ground on political reform made progress virtually impossible.

Talks on the Agreement reopened at the start of 2000 after the election of Abdelaziz Bouteflika as President. Despite the lack of opposition candidates after the withdrawal of the other six candidates on the eve of the poll, Bouteflika's 'victory' gave the Union the cover it needed by bringing a measure of stability to the political situation in Algeria. This period offered the Union a short-lived opportunity space to overcome a third problem in the Euro-Med Partnership: the member states' inability to agree amongst themselves on how to engage with the regime. Northern governments, particularly the Scandinavians, maintained a sceptical attitude about Bouteflika's government. They were critical, for instance, of his failures to reduce the army's political role and to negotiate with the *FIS* leadership. By contrast, France, Spain and Italy took a more positive view of developments. Taking a lead from France, the 'southern' group favoured a supportive approach based on generous transitional periods for economic liberalisation, the opening of new commercial channels and guarded backing for democratisation projects.[96] Both camps could agree that, in the aftermath of Bouteflika's election, a swift conclusion of an Association Agreement without the imposition of new conditions was important. However, internal differences in the Union ruled out the possibility of moving beyond that lowest common denominator position to one which ratcheted up the pressure on the Algerian government.

The fourth problem for the EMP centred on the operation of the Barcelona machinery. With 27 governments involved in the process, different interpretations of the aims and objectives of the Declaration were inevitable. Foreign Minister Attaf, for instance, sought to exploit provisions on the fight against terrorism in the Barcelona Declaration to enlist the assistance of the Mediterranean partners and to use as a stick to beat those EU member states which played host to opposition leaders.[97] The government even tabled its own version of a Mediterranean Stability Charter, again with a heavy emphasis on counter-terrorism measures.[98] For its part, the EU persisted with the line that the Barcelona process should not interfere in the domestic politics of a signatory state. Despite the Declaration's rhetoric on human rights and civil society, and the Union's formal commitments to promote democracy, Algeria was regarded as a 'normal' participant in the EMP. Indeed, it even emerged as the *de facto* leader of the Arab group.[99]

Nevertheless, the Barcelona process appeared to offer some new opportunities to influence the Algerian authorities. Its 'low profile' multilateral format helped to smooth relations between the French and Algerian governments by offering them an alternative avenue for diplomatic engagement.[100] France consequently adopted a rather more constructive position in the European context which, on paper, partially cleared the way for the Union to broaden the scope of its policy. The implementation of measures under each of the EMP's three chapters also had a potentially positive impact. By tying together support for economic reform, tentative cooperation in the political and security spheres and projects which scratched at the surface of civil society, the Union at least began to work from a more coherent script. What it could not do was utilise the EMP to force more substantive political reform on Bouteflika.

## Conclusions

Faced with a highly unstable 'neighbour' and a domestic crisis which clearly had a negative impact on the Europe, the EU's neglect of Algeria became a serious threat to the credibility of its Mediterranean policy. Instead of leading by example, the Union stood back and watched human rights abuses occur on a breathtaking scale. When European governments did finally launch a tentative diplomatic initiative in 1998, the mission manifestly lacked purpose. It is difficult to avoid concluding that the Union was simply not suited to dealing with the kind of complex civil conflict that beset Algeria.

Three problems were particularly conspicuous. First, the EU's relations with Algeria during the 1990s were largely determined by French policy. Indeed, it was France's analysis of the source of the conflict (Islam versus democracy) and the most appropriate means to resolve it (to back the regime with qualified support for elections and a return to a tenuous form of political pluralism) that prevailed in Brussels. As an Algerian human rights lawyer argues:

> The EU has failed by giving a free rein to France in leading EU policy on Algeria. The flagrant failure of the French approach and that of the regime which they support has been amply demonstrated over the last three years. It does EU credibility in North Africa and the Arab world no good for the EU to continue to allow the French a virtual monopoly in EU foreign policy on this matter.[101]

This capture of a policy issue by a single member state exemplifies the weakness of the Union's foreign policy-making process. Where intergovernmentalism prevails, the interests, perceptions and positions of one state can define the EU's position or exclude the possibility of a political position altogether. Since the CFSP operates on the basis of unanimity, it was inevitable that no Common Position or Joint Action on Algeria would be adopted by the Union.

Second, the opposition of the regime and Algerian political parties to external interference in the conflict provided the Union with a convenient, but poor, excuse for its non-decision.[102] The 1990s saw the Union devote an increasing volume of financial and political resources to so-called 'good governance' – respect for universal human rights, fundamental freedoms and the democratic process. Justifying its silence on the grounds that the conflict was Algeria's problem called into question the Union's commitment to stick to these principles. Similarly, the Euro-Mediterranean Partnership, which was also intended to encourage 'good governance' in all the Mediterranean partner countries, has proven impotent when conflicts have arisen either between or within partner countries.

Third, pillar I policy instruments proved equally ineffective as a means to influence the behaviour of the Algerian regime. The Euro-Mediterranean Agreement had comparatively little economic value to Algeria, the key to using trade policy as a tool of suasion. Nor were serious questions raised about the continued provision of financial assistance from the MEDA budget which, in any case, was greatly exceeded by bilateral aid and trade credits from the member states. Indeed, almost the reverse applied, with the regime having sought to use the Agreement for its own ends.

The 'election' of regime representatives is certainly no substitute for genuinely competitive elections. As population growth continues to outstrip the capacity of the Algerian economy to provide a sufficient number of new jobs, the likelihood of a social explosion increases. World Bank estimates suggest that a 5 per cent annual economic growth outside the hydrocarbon sector would be needed simply to keep up with the flow of young people entering the job market.[103] Trade credits, macro-economic restructuring and IMF austerity programmes mean little to the burgeoning number of jobless, disenfranchised people of Algeria. The EU's response to these challenges will be a test of its commitment to work for a more stable, secure and prosperous Mediterranean region.

## Notes

[1] Quoted in *Financial Times*, August 30 1997, p. 2.
[2] Quoted in *International Herald Tribune*, 21 January 1998, p. 3.
[3] Zoubir, Y.H. and Bouandel, Y. (1998) 'Islamism and the Algerian Political Crisis: International Responses', *Cambridge Review of International Affairs*, Vol. 11, No. 2, p. 118.
[4] In total, around 2 million immigrants of Algerian origin reside in the EU.
[5] Roberts, H. (1995) 'Algeria's Ruinous Impasse and the Honourable Way Out', *International Affairs*, Vol. 71, No. 2, p. 247.
[6] Callies de Sallies, B. (1995) 'Algérie (1988-1995): De la crise à la guerre civile', *Les Cahiers de l'Orient*, Paris: Sari, No. 3, p. 46; Ghezali, S. (1996) 'Fausse éclaircie en Algérie', *Le Monde Diplomatique*, February, pp. 1-12; Spencer, C. (1996) 'Islamism and European Reactions: The Case of Algeria' in R. Gillespie (ed.) *Mediterranean Politics: Volume 2*, London: Pinter, p. 128.
[7] Riots spasmodically erupted at other times during the 1980s, but order was always quickly restored. The 1988 riots marked a much more serious breakdown in order. The

*UGTA* was the Algerian General Workers Union and the only significant union in the country. It was affiliated to the FLN, Algeria's only legal political party from independence until 1988. For a summary of the political situation in Algeria at this time, see Joffé, G. (1998) *Algeria in Crisis*, Briefing Paper No. 48, Middle East Programme, London: RIIA.
[8] Economist Intelligence Unit (1988) *Country Report: Algeria*, No. 3, p. 4.
[9] Algeria's population growth rate had reached 3 per cent by the end of the 1980s, and with a burgeoning young population, around 200,000 people were being added to the unemployment register each year.
[10] Officially, 150 people died in the rioting. Most unofficial sources suggest a figure of around 500. Economist Intelligence Unit (1995) *Algeria: EIU Country Profile 1994-5*, London: Economist Intelligence Unit, p. 5; '1978-1992: Des années d'effervescence en Algérie', *Monde Arabe: Maghreb-Machrek*, No. 154, October-December 1996, pp. 11-15.
[11] Front Islamique du Salut (1994) 'The Journey Through Time', *FIS Information Bureau Website*, http://www.fisalgeria.org/history.html.
[12] An overwhelming majority of the rioters were young people (15-25) for whom Islam promised a break with an old order that had failed them. See Verges, M. (1996) 'Les jeunes, le stade, le FIS: Vers une analyse de l'action protestaire', *Monde Arabe: Maghreb-Machrek*, No. 154, October-December, pp. 48-54.
[13] Question No. 1931/88 and Question No. 1932/88 by Mr Arbeloa Muru (S-E) Concerning the Popular Uprising and the New Political Situation in Algeria, *European Political Cooperation Documentation Bulletin*, 1989, Vol. 5, No. 2, Internet Edition, http://www.iue.it/EFPB/.
[14] *Agence Europe*, 22 October 1988, p. 6. The Community used some of its massive surplus stocks to provide essential food products to the Algerian people, including cereals, milk powder, butter, olive oil, sugar and vegetables.
[15] European Parliament (1988b) 'Resolution on repression in Algeria', *Official Journal of the European Communities*, OJC326, 17 November, p. 207; *Agence Europe*, 19 November 1988, p. 4.
[16] *Le Monde*, 12 October 1988, p. 4.
[17] 'Chronologies', *Monde Arabe: Maghreb/Machrek*, No. 124, April-May-June 1989, pp. 64-65.
[18] *Le Monde*, 15 October 1988, p. 2.
[19] Spencer, C. (1996) op. cit., p. 126. Islamic movements had always had a place in Algerian politics. However, the absence of multipartism prevented the Algerian Islamic movement from becoming an effective opposition. The reforms forced on Chadli opened the door for the formation of Islamic political parties.
[20] *Le Monde*, 17 October 1988, p. 1.
[21] *Middle East Economic Digest*, Vol. 32, No. 49, 9 December 1988, p. 13.
[22] Of Algeria's others exports, only manufactured goods (2%), foodstuffs, primarily wine (0.4%), and fresh citrus fruits (0.05%) were of any real significance.
[23] Oil, and particularly natural gas, were pivotal to Algeria's external trade balance, accounting for a massive 28.6 per cent of GDP in 1988. Economist Intelligence Unit (1989) *Algeria: EIU Country Report No 2*, London: Economist Intelligence Unit, p. 2.
[24] Chatelus, M, (1997) 'L'énergie en Méditerranée: espace régional ou marché mondial?', *Monde Arabe: Maghreb Machrek*, Special Issue, December, p. 21.
[25] Although the transnational pipeline was regarded as secure, by 1998 a small number of sabotage operations had been carried out on domestic pipelines within Algeria. The regime

made a point of making the gas and oil producing regions safe, a measure facilitated by the desert terrain on which the gas fields are located.

[26] *Sonatrach Internationale* is Algeria's state-owned oil and gas company.

[27] *Le Monde*, 11 January 1989, p. 1.

[28] In Spain's case, the credit agreement was signed by Algeria's Commerce Minister at the same time as discussions were being held with Spanish civil servants about the supply of gas to Enagas, Spain's state-owned gas supplier. In Italy's case, the linkage between its credit package and energy supplies was less obvious, though gas was on the agenda of the meeting at which the final touches were put to the agreement. More conspicuous was the link between the package and the construction of a new Fiat car assembly plant in Algiers in a joint venture between the Italian car-maker and a local manufacturer. See *Middle East Economic Digest*, Vol. 33, No. 11, 24 March 1989, p. 16 and Vol. 33, No. 20, 26 May 1989, p. 27.

[29] Spencer, C. (1993) *The Maghreb in the 1990s: Political and Economic Developments in Algeria, Morocco and Tunisia*, Adelphi Paper No. 274, London: IISS/Brasseys, p. 30.

[30] *Le Monde*, 11 March 1989, p. 2.

[31] Joffé, G. (1998) op. cit., p. 3.

[32] Roberts, H. (1992) 'The Algerian State and the Challenge of Democracy', *Government and Opposition*, Vol. 27, No. 4, p. 450.

[33] Rich, P. and Joseph, S. (1997) *Algeria: Democratic Transition or Political Stalemate?*, London: Saferworld, p. 6.

[34] Fontaine, J. (1992) 'Les élections législatives algériennes. Resultats du premier tour', *Monde Arabe: Maghreb/Machrek*, No. 135, Jan-Mar, p. 156.

[35] While there were reports of electoral irregularities involving the FIS, the Algerian Ministry of the Interior reported a turnout of around 60 per cent of the country's 13.1 million registered voters.

[36] *Le Monde*, 15 June 1990, p. 4.

[37] A review of official foreign ministry statements, press releases and media interviews around this time shows a pronounced tendency to play down the significance of events in Algeria. See Ministère des Affaires Etrangères, «http:///www.diplomatie.fr».

[38] Chadli had been trying to negotiate a power sharing deal with the FIS, a prospect which clearly alarmed the secular, francophone element of the army.

[39] Rich, P. and Joseph, S. (1997) op. cit., p.6.

[40] Ministère des Affaires Etrangères, 'Point de Presse', http:///www.diplomatie.fr, 28 January 1992.

[41] 'Statement on Algeria', No. 92/024, *European Political Cooperation Documentation Bulletin*, February 1992, p. 91.

[42] Clarke, M. (1989) 'The Foreign Policy System: A Framework for Analysis' in M. Clarke and B. White (eds.) *Understanding Foreign Policy: The Foreign Policy Systems Approach*, Aldershot and Brookfield (Vermont): Edward Elgar, p. 49.

[43] The idea of 'relational power' forms the backbone of Bachrach and Baratz's (1963) seminal article on 'non-decision making'. The crux of their argument, applied to community politics in the USA, is that those actors able to exercise effective power in intra-group relations can 'limit the scope of actual decision making to "safe issues"'. (p. 632). Bachrach, P. and Baratz, M.S. (1963) 'Decisions and Non-Decisions: An Analytical Framework', *American Political Science Review*, Vol. 57, No. 3, pp. 632-42.

[44] 'Statement on Algeria', No. 92/065, *European Political Cooperation Documentation Bulletin Online*, http://wwwarc1.iue.it/iue, 17 February 1992.

⁴⁵ The Commission adopted the same 'softly softly' approach as the member states. Commissioner Abel Matutes pledged continued support for Algeria's economic reform policies, although he issued a gentle warning that fundamental rights and freedoms had to be respected. See *Agence Europe*, 13 February 1992, p. 3.
⁴⁶ This contention was borne out by the electoral success of President Liamine Zeroual in 1995 and by regime politicians in 1997. Callies de Sallies, B. (1996) 'Algérie: accord de Rome et élection présidentielle', *Défense Nationale*, Vol. 75, No. 4, p. 122.
⁴⁷ Smith, B. (1998) 'Algeria: The Horror', *The New York Review of Books*, Vol. 45, No. 7, April 23, p. 27.
⁴⁸ It is not clear what direction a *FIS* government would have taken. Given the traditional strength of the army and the sizeable 'moderate' proportion of the population, it is unlikely that the *FIS* could simply have imposed a traditional Islamic government on Algerian society.
⁴⁹ Ghiles, F. 'Islamic Party Seeks Wide Powers in Algeria', *Financial Times*, 8 January 1992, p. 4.
⁵⁰ *Agence Europe*, 16 January 1992, p. 15.
⁵¹ The second tranche of the loan – 150 million ECUs – was withheld until 1996.
⁵² Economist Intelligence Unit (1992) *EIU Country Report No 4: Algeria*, London: Economist Intelligence Unit, p. 4.
⁵³ Haaland Matlary, J. (1997) *Energy Policy in the European Union*, Basingstoke: Macmillan, p. 55.
⁵⁴ *Agence Europe*, 27 March 1992, p. 10.
⁵⁵ Cesari, J. (1995) 'L'effet "Airbus"', *Les Cahiers de l'Orient*, Nos. 36-37, p. 177.
⁵⁶ Gobe, E. (1992) 'The Maghreb in Contemporary French Politics', *Journal of Arab Affairs*, Vol. 11, No. 2, p. 134.
⁵⁷ *Agence Europe*, 7 September 1991, p. 5.
⁵⁸ *Agence Europe*, 1 July 1992, p. 4.
⁵⁹ *Le Monde*, 1 July 1992, p. 5.
⁶⁰ 'Statement on the development of the internal situation in Algeria', Statement No. 93/406, *European Political Cooperation Documentation Bulletin Online*, http://wwwarc1.iue.it/iue.
⁶¹ Around 24,000 French citizens (out of a total of 76,000 foreign nationals) were either resident or working in Algeria in 1993. Mass evacuation was out of the question.
⁶² *Agence France Presse*, 21 June 1993, Internet Version, http://www.afp.com.
⁶³ Economist Intelligence Unit (1996) *Country Report: Algeria*, 4th Quarter, p. 11.
⁶⁴ *Jeune Afrique*, No. 1831, 7-13 February 1996, p. 55.
⁶⁵ 'Chronologies', *Monde Arabe: Maghreb/Machrek*, Special Issue, 1/1994, p. 247.
⁶⁶ Ibid. p. 248.
⁶⁷ Spencer, C. (1996) op. cit., p. 133.
⁶⁸ Webster, P. 'French Minister Who Eclipses Le Pen', *The Guardian*, 25 November 1993, p. 11.
⁶⁹ Jean-Pierre Phillibert (Rapporteur, Commission des lois constitutionelle), Debats Parlemenatires, Assemblée Nationale, *Journel Officiel*, Session of 16 June 1993, p. 1608.
⁷⁰ The *eradicateurs* were those in the Algerian military who believed that the only solution to the violence was systematically to wipe out the armed Islamic groups.
⁷¹ Zoubir, Y.H. and Bouandel, Y. (1999) op. cit., p. 7.

[72] Evidence began to emerge during 1994 that the French government had engaged in secret talks with the *FIS* via intermediaries. *Financial Times*, 28 December 1994, p. 2; Roberts, H. (1995) op. cit., p. 249.

[73] For useful analyses of the effect of the Islamists' campaign of violence on France, see Provost, L. (1996) 'Paris et Algers entre brouilles et complicités', *Le Monde Diplomatique*, September, pp. 4-5; Chenal, A. (1995) 'La France rattrapée par le drame algérien', *Politique Etrangère*, Vol. 60, No. 2, pp. 415-25.

[74] See, for example, Amnesty International (1994) *Annual Report*, http://www.amnesty.org.

[75] 'La Platforme de Rome', *Cahiers de l'Orient*, Nos. 36-7, 1995, pp. 9-11.

[76] Quoted in Khalaf, R. 'Algerian olive branch finds few takers: Government and extremists look set to continue the carnage as the west looks on', *Financial Times*, 19 January 1995, p. 4.

[77] Rich, P. and Joseph, S. (1997) op. cit., p. 17.

[78] Ibid., p. 18.

[79] Khalaf, R. 'Italy reassures Algiers over role in conflict', *Financial Times*, 3 February 1997, p. 4.

[80] Khalaf, R. 'Italy calls for peace initiative in Algeria', *Financial Times*, 29 January 1997, p. 4.

[81] Spencer, C. (1998a) 'Algeria' in B.A. Roberson (ed.) *The Middle East and Europe: The Power Deficit*, London: Routledge, p. 173.

[82] *Agence Europe*, 13 November 1997, p. 3.

[83] Interview, London, 15 Feburary 1999

[84] *Financial Times*, 14 January 1998, p. 5.

[85] 'Algeria calls for comprehensive cooperation with EU to fight terrorism', ArabicNews.com, 30 January 1998, «http://www.arabicnews.com/ansub/Daily/Day/980130/1998013019.html»,

[86] Haddam, A. (1998) 'A Letter to His Excellency Robin Cook, Foreign Minister of the United Kingdom', *FIS Information Bureau Website*, http://www.fisalgeria.org/communiques/TROIKA.html, 25 January.

[87] The Algerian government's decision to allow the UN mission was designed to placate its growing number of critics who were openly condemning its intransigence over human rights issues. At the same time, UN Secretary General Kofi Annan had come under pressure from human rights organisations such as Amnesty International and from the imprisoned *FIS* leader Abassi Madani to investigate the situation. For analysis of the UN initiative, see Spencer, C. (1998b) 'The End of International Enquiries? The UN Eminent Persons' Mission to Algeria', *Mediterranean Politics*, Vol. 33, No. 3, pp. 126-33.

[88] *Financial Times*, 21 July 1998, p. 3.

[89] United Nations (1998) *Report of the Panel Appointed by the Secretary-General of the United Nations to Gather Information on the Situation in Algeria*, New York. The Report was welcomed by the Algerian government, but condemned as a 'whitewash' by Amnesty International. Amnesty International (1998) 'UN panel report a whitewash on human rights', *News Release*, MDE 28/32/98, 16 September, http://www.amnesty.org/news/1998/52803298.htm.

[90] Youngs, R. (2001) *The European Union and the Promotion of Democracy*, Oxford: Oxford University Press, p. 107.

[91] Interview, Brussels, 15 October 1998.

[92] Interview, Brussels, 15 October 1998.

[93] Interview, Brussels, 14 October 1998.
[94] Interview, Brussels, 14 October 1998.
[95] Youngs, R. (2001) op. cit., p. 102.
[96] Ibid., p. 110-1.
[97] European Parliament, Committee on Foreign Affairs (1997) 'Ahmed Attaf accepts EP delegation', *Rapid Database*, http://www.europarl.eu.int/dg3/sdp/newsrp/en/n971127.htm#1 Brussels, 27 November.
[98] Interview, Brussels, 14 October 1998.
[99] It was a role that Algeria performed during the heyday of the non-aligned movement in the 1970s. Its defiant stance against colonialism and its confrontational style when dealing with the West gave it lasting authority. Algeria was, by all accounts, an effective and tough spokesman for the Arab group in the Barcelona process.
[100] Youngs, R. (2001) op. cit., p. 104.
[101] Djebbar, S. (1995) 'Evidence to the House of Lords Select Committee on the European Communities', *Relations Between the EC and the Maghreb*, London: HMSO, p. 98.
[102] 'L'Algérie n'appelera jamais au secours', *El Watan*, 2 December 1997, p. 5.
[103] Ritekie, D. (1996) 'L'Algérie renoue avec la croissance', *Jeune Afrique*, No. 1827, 11-17 January, p. 28. Ritekie was World Bank Director for the Middle East and North Africa.

# Chapter 8

# Conclusions

## Introduction

The negotiation of the Euro-Mediterranean Partnership in the mid-1990s represented a concerted attempt by the EU to devise a strategy towards a region of critical importance to its own future. At the turn of the 1990s the EU began to develop a stronger sense of purpose in its relationships with Mediterranean non-member countries. New policy objectives were elucidated and a package of measures was put together to support them. However, any positive assessment of the EU's plans for the region must be tempered by a rather more negative assessment of the EMP's actual record. A gap quickly appeared between rhetoric and reality as the Union's protective external trade regime and the chronic problem of Arab-Israeli relations seriously impeded the implementation of the Euro-Mediterranean initiative. More significantly, perhaps, the degree to which the EMP can actually change the asymmetric underlying structure of Euro-Med relations must be called into question.

This chapter moves towards a final analysis of the current genesis of EU Mediterranean policy, both in terms of the EMP initiative and its wider implications for the EU as a global actor. The first section considers what the development of the EMP tells us about the kind of strategic action that the EU produces. Section two assesses how far the EMP has bridged the divide between pillar I – the Union's foreign economic policy – and pillar II – the CFSP. This blurring between the two pillars was not deliberately and systematically pursued by the Union, but was driven by the nature of a strategy which demanded the harnessing of foreign economic policy instruments to political objectives. The third section revisits the 'civilian power' concept which attracted renewed attention at the start of the 1990s as a potential role for the Union in the post-Cold War world. On the face of it, the EMP incorporated many of the basic tenets of the civilian power concept. The final section employs Christopher Hill's seminal 'capabilities-expectations gap' thesis as an analytical tool to assess the extent to which the EMP has changed the EU's status as an international actor.[1]

## Strategic Action: The EU as Framework, EC as Agent

The word 'strategy' appears throughout the policy documents that set out the Union's proposals for a 'new' Mediterranean policy. The Commission clearly saw the need to sell its ideas to the member states and the partner countries as a long-term action plan, justifying the allocation of additional financial resources and trade concessions on the grounds that the Mediterranean region would become more secure. The EU would reap the dividends of substantial commercial, financial and diplomatic investments but these would be long-term benefits. This line of reasoning also served a legitimating function for the further Europeanisation of national Mediterranean policies. However, the Union's claim that the EMP was a strategy does not make it one, nor can we assess its effectiveness without reconsidering precisely what constitutes a 'strategy'.

The notion of EU strategic action assumes both an autonomous capacity to pursue policy strategies that are distinctly 'European' and some form of 'effective international agency'.[2] Taking the assumption that the EU can act strategically first, the EMP arose out of the political commitment of the member states to task the Union with reformulating Mediterranean policy. Perceptions converged around the view that European states had to carry a bigger share of the burden of post-Cold War security in the Mediterranean and eventually earmarked the EU as the most appropriate 'framework' to put in place the prescribed policy measures after brief experimentation with the CSCM, 5+5 dialogue and other sub-regional forums. Previous incarnations of Mediterranean policy had lacked a well-defined set of objectives. The label 'policy' was merely a convenient disguise for a disparate collection of agreements with Mediterranean non-member countries which were more a product of the 'logic of externalisation' than the result of any coherent, long-term planning.[3] By contrast, the purposes of the EMP were thoroughly examined and debated from the end of the 1980s onwards in the context of the wider debate about 'new' or 'soft' security. A considerable volume of analysis and research pointed to the need for policy change.

So as the outline of a strategy began to emerge, what were its principal objectives and how 'European' were they? The fundamental aims of the EMP project were to foster 'security and stability' in the Mediterranean by increasing the prosperity of the partner states and by enhancing cooperation at the governmental and societal levels. There was a strong sense of unity among the member states and EU institutions about the importance of Mediterranean security to European security. Northern member states were persuaded that the negative impact of instability in the Mediterranean region could spread throughout western Europe in the form of dramatically increased illegal immigration, damaging consequences for Europe's Islamic communities and threats to European economic interests in the partner countries. Meanwhile, the southern member states had manifestly vital economic and political interests in a stable Mediterranean region and increasingly took the view that the challenge could best be met by shifting national bilateral policies to the EU level. The Commission's proposals for the EMP therefore found a receptive audience, giving the project a strong European flavour from the outset.

The logic behind the EMP is worth reflecting upon here. In line with the 'securitisation' of the discourse surrounding the Union's relationships with its Mediterranean neighbours at the end of the 1980s, the Commission's proposals were based on a series of inter-connected arguments.[4] Together, they added up to a compelling case for the practical application of 'soft security' to EU Mediterranean policy. Their ideological grounding combined the classic functionalist approach to cooperative international relations with orthodox neo-liberal economic thinking. A clear link was identified between economic development, political and social stability and regional security. By extension, as the major trading partner of all the partner countries and the biggest provider of financial aid, the EU and its member states had special responsibilities to take the lead in building a new, socio-economically oriented framework for regional security.

Behind this 'logic of assistance', however, was a less progressive agenda, one centred on the domestic interests of the member states. The Barcelona Declaration contained references to combating terrorism and organised crime in both the first and third chapters. Crudely speaking, one of the priorities of the new Mediterranean policy for the member states was to provide safeguards against Islamic fundamentalism which in practice meant preserving the political status quo in many partner countries. The EU's 'non-decisions' on Algeria clearly exposed this rationale for the EMP. While the Union carefully avoided associating the EMP with a direct 'threat' from the south, fears of an Islamic 'domino effect' were widely expressed in European capitals. With the terrorist attacks on the World Trade Center of September 11 2001 came confirmation for many of the major security challenge of the new millennium.

An 'economic interest' argument is rather harder to sustain but cannot be overlooked in an explanation of the EMP. Despite the comparatively low volume of trade between the EU and the Mediterranean partner countries (when compared to the EU's trade with other states and regional groupings), there were sectors in which the Union had a fundamental interest in safeguarding its external economic interests. The hydrocarbon sector was excluded from the Euro-Mediterranean Agreements but occupied a prominent position in the follow-up programme of the Barcelona process. Moreover, the private sector in EU member states was always going to be the biggest beneficiary of liberalisation within the partner countries. The EMP contained both financial incentives and the promise of significant improvements in the partner countries' investment regimes, leaving European businesses in a powerful position to exploit their overwhelming comparative advantages in terms of capital, distribution infrastructures, production capacities and technology.[5] The point here is that the EU will be a net economic beneficiary of the EMP for a long time to come.[6]

The formulation of the EMP thus addressed several of the EU's key strategic interests. Some of its objectives could even be described as forward looking. However, the early stages of the implementation phase highlighted its shortcomings in delivering what it promised. First, the scope of the task that the EU set itself – economic 'transition' in the Mediterranean – was not backed by a commensurate level of financial assistance. Even allowing for the substantial increase in EU aid for the region provided by MEDA, the partner countries still lagged far behind the Central and Eastern European countries. In 1997, EU aid to the Mediterranean partners amounted to just over 3 ECU per capita, while the Central and Eastern European countries received around 11 ECU per capita.[7] The increase in the MEDA budget for 2000-06 (to 5.3 billion Euros) still only scratches the surface of the resource problem. The Union was faced by the familiar dilemma of demand for its limited financial assistance outstripping supply. This resource problem was highly political, pitting the northern 'Calvinist' liberalising tendency in the EU against the southern member states which stood firm on the need for something approximating parity in the division of EU funds between the east and south. The final financial agreements – like many EU package deals – left neither side satisfied.[8]

Second, the free-trade objective obliged the EU to open up its markets in the very sectors that were internally the most highly politicised: Mediterranean agricultural products and textiles.[9] For Michael Smith, politicisation has been the driving force behind the development of the core of EU foreign policy located in pillar I.[10] Yet what the EMP surely shows is that politicisation frequently restricts the ability of the EU to undertake strategic action, since the projected long-term benefits of such action are invariably set aside for short term political expediency. In EU Mediterranean policy, political expediency demanded the protection of domestic producers by member governments, calling into question the credibility of the Union's commitment to free trade. As Peter Petri argues, 'by themselves, free trade agreements with Europe will yield limited results, since no major market access concessions seem to be on the table'.[11] A recent World Bank report painted a bleak picture of the economic and social situation in the Middle East and North Africa, despite a slight improvement in GDP growth at the end of the 1990s.[12] But all the EU can offer is a transitional period of 12-15 years, modest financial aid and its technical expertise. The rest is left to market forces. The perception of the partner countries is that the EU remains stubbornly protectionist on many of the products that matter most to them.[13] As one diplomat put it: 'It is out of self-interest that Europe exploits the Mediterranean. The EU has to realise there is always a price to pay'.[14]

Third, the Union lacked the political power to keep the EMP on the rails when the breakdown of the Middle East Peace Process widened the diplomatic gulf between the Arab and Israeli participants. Face-saving diplomacy at successive meetings of Euro-Med Foreign Ministers in the late 1990s could not hide the fact that, by 2000, the wind had gone out of the Barcelona initiative's sails. The becalming of the Barcelona process raised questions about the wisdom of investing so much political capital in a multilateral forum with such a diverse membership. With sub-regional options available (Euro-Maghreb, Euro-Mashreq), expanding the partnership concept to the whole Mediterranean region may have been a serious strategic miscalculation.

Turning now to the agency argument, Michael Smith's contention that the EC is the primary agent for EU strategic action is clearly borne out by the content and institutional form of the Euro-Mediterranean Partnership.[15] Progress towards a free-trade area was heavily dependent on the results of negotiations with individual partner countries conducted according to the 'Community method', led by the Commission as chief negotiator. The MEDA aid package was also exclusively a Community instrument, administered by the Commission under the watchful eyes of the member states, the European Parliament and the EU's Court of Auditors. In more general terms, the functional, integrative dimension of the EMP built on the EU's own internal economic integration process. Cooperative programmes launched by the Barcelona process in sectors such as energy, the environment, industry, small businesses and telecommunications, were all based on the Community's organisational resources and experience in these policy areas.

However, the EMP also tells us much about the limitations of EC agency, some of which arise from the unique complexity of the EU policy process, others which result from the inter-governmental basis of the Barcelona process. The Commission took a leading role in proposing policy measures, negotiated the terms of the Euro-Mediterranean Agreements and administered the Community's budget for the Mediterranean. But the member states retained the final say over decisive issues and were heavily influenced by domestic political interests. The repeated blockages over agricultural trade concessions in the Council were the best illustration of the member states' capacity to restrict the scope for substantive policy change. The results of negotiations, more often than not, were trade deals that barely exceeded the status quo.[16]

Governmental prerogative dominated the early stages of the Barcelona process to an even greater extent. The direction, pace and progress of the follow-up process were also largely dictated by inter-governmental diplomacy. When governments refused to meet, there was little the EU could do about it. Funding for the various sectoral and expert networks might have been provided from the EC budget, but it was merely a tool for implementing measures adopted by governments. The Commission found itself in a potentially powerful role as coordinator of the Barcelona process, but it could not propose measures that would not receive the endorsement of the twenty-seven. The result was a cautious, low-key approach to the follow-up process, with ideas being tentatively mooted rather than vigorously pursued. As a senior official observed, the Commission was 'unlikely to be in a situation where it would want to go against the wishes of the states'.[17]

What kind of picture emerged as the EMP strategy began to take effect? The most obvious point is that the EU clearly reinforced its 'leadership' role in the region, extending its reach deeper into the economies, political systems and societies of the partner countries. In Central and Eastern Europe, the EU was 'catapulted into leadership' after 1989, and was forced to find rapid solutions to the challenge of bringing the former Soviet bloc countries into the fold.[18] In the Mediterranean, by contrast, the EU progressively built on an already dominant economic position to the point where formal agreements with it became an essential element of third countries' foreign economic policies. There are no signs that the partners' dependence on exports to the EU – between 60 and 70 per cent of their total exports – will contract in the near future. In short, by the early 2000s the EU had made itself indispensable to the partner countries, if not politically, then certainly economically.

The EMP also accelerated the unidirectional process of extending selected parts of the EU's order to the Mediterranean partner countries. Again, the principal conduits for this process were pillar I policy instruments. Signatories of the Euro-Mediterranean Agreements would be obliged to bring their customs, tariff and taxation regimes into line with those of the EU. Stricter enforcement of the Union's rules of origin, alignment of public procurement procedures and the adoption of EU product standards meant that governments would be forced to adapt their administrative and regulatory systems to the EU model, requirements that in most cases had significant financial implications.[19] If the Commission, and organisations such as the OECD, IMF and World Bank were to be believed, the spin-off for the partners would be a steady increase in trade amongst themselves, integration into the global economic order and higher economic growth. Most partner governments bought this argument, having no realistic alternatives.

Nonetheless, there are good reasons to question both the manner in which the Union is imposing its order on the Mediterranean partners, and the appropriateness of the programme of harmonisation for states with comparatively underdeveloped economies, bureaucracies and political systems. The EMP falls short of the all-embracing governance framework currently being extended to the accession candidates. Upon their accession, the CEECs, Cyprus and Malta in theory stand to benefit from substantial compensation for the negative socio-economic effects of compliance with and integration into the EU order. The Mediterranean non-member countries, by contrast, continue to rely heavily on outside financial and technical assistance both to carry out the prescribed reforms and alleviate the negative effects of austerity. Much depends on the ability of the partners to attract significantly higher levels of inward investment and on the development of an as yet nascent private sector. The EMP may well help establish the conditions for a flourishing private sector, but the onus is on self-reliance and the unpredictable behaviour of private capital.

If there are doubts about the capacity of the EMP to deliver economic change, they are compounded by misgivings about its capacity to enhance the region's security. Analysts of EU foreign policy, as well as practitioners, remain sceptical about its capacity for strategic action in the continued absence of a Common Foreign and Security Policy that equips the Union with a 'hard security' capability. The argument is that its strategies will always be somehow incomplete without the option of military action. Proactive CFSP actions, such as the EU's funding of the Palestinian elections, are still the exception rather than the rule. Pillar I might be the locus for external policy-making, but without the 'hard security' capability to back it up, the Union cannot become a self-reliant foreign policy actor. There were few indications in the early 2000s that developments in European Security and Defence Policy had significantly improved the Union's ability to act in this area. Confidence-building measures and dialogue on politico-security issues are undeniably useful starting points, but are unlikely to be of much utility if the gloomiest predictions of mass immigration, terrorism, regime collapse and weapons proliferation are realised.

## Bridging the Divide: The Pillarisation Problem

The problem of consistency between pillars I and II (and, increasingly, pillar III) remains largely unresolved. Wrangling between the member states, Commission and European Parliament over competencies has become a stock feature of the EU's foreign policy-making process. Such disputes are symptomatic of the continuing sensitivity of national governments to what might be termed supranational creep in the foreign policy sphere. The EMP did not entirely escape the competency problem, as exemplified by the sidelining of the Commission in the negotiation of the Barcelona Declaration, by stalemate in the Council over British objections to the use of qualified majority voting on the suspension of MEDA aid, and by the different institutional formulae used for EU representation in the two Barcelona coordination committees. However, the pillarisation issue had only a peripheral effect on the actual functioning of the EMP. Although the three chapters of the Barcelona Declaration resembled the EU's own three pillar structure, no clear link was established between the two. The Barcelona process was explicitly designed to have its own dynamic, outside the direct control of the EU.

When sporadic intermeshing of pillars I and II did occur in the EMP, it was driven by the nature of the initiative, by ad hoc procedural creativity, and, as one official put it, 'for the sake of convenience'.[20] No formal decision was initially taken to actively and systematically bridge the divide between the EC pillar and the CFSP, despite calls from the European Parliament to generate CFSP Joint Actions for security measures adopted in the Barcelona process. The 2000 Common Strategy for the Mediterranean Region went some way to addressing the issue of cross-pillar consistency, but was imprecise about how better internal policy coordination would be achieved.[21] However, coherence remains essential, since all three chapters were directed at the broader goal of enhancing regional security. When internal divisions over competencies surfaced within the Union, the partner countries clearly regarded it as a sign of weakness.

As the common institutional link between the three chapters, the Commission was in a good position to put a pillar I label on work in the follow-up process. Its key asset in this respect was its power to propose measures funded by the Community budget, which it was quick to exploit in the first chapter. The proposal for military involvement in a disaster relief mechanism funded by EC money illustrated how practical considerations could override the kind of governmental sensitivity that would ordinarily subject such a proposal to lengthy, dogmatic debates in the Council. Paradoxically, the Commission's task was made easier by the weakness of the CFSP, since measures could only be funded from the CFSP budget if formal Joint Actions were agreed, a possibility apparently ruled out before the Barcelona process began.

That said, the significance of this rare use of the EC budget to fund politico-security measures should not be overstated. The approval of the member states owed more to practicality and downright common sense than to any deliberate transfer of power to the Commission. The measures on the table, such as financing for a network of defence institutes, were part of a low key confidence-building programme and therefore lacked the kind of overtly political content that might have drawn objections from the less communitarian member states.[22] That the Barcelona Declaration was a political rather than a legal document also contributed to the de-sensitisation of this type of measure. When it came to the more politically sensitive measures, in particular the Stability Charter, national governments determined the boundaries of the possible.

One of the more interesting outcomes of the EMP, and of the EU's activities in the Mediterranean in general, was an increased propensity to deploy economic policy instruments to pursue distinctively political objectives. The most obvious case was the Middle East Peace Process where the EU occasionally adopted a decidedly more combative stance in its quest for political relevance. As well as becoming paymaster of the Palestinian Authority, it showed a growing willingness to rattle its commercial sabre over the Israeli government's policies in the Occupied Territories. For a brief period, the signs were that the Union's economic weight was beginning to pay dividends in terms both of its profile in the region and its status as an 'ally' of the Palestinians.

In a less high profile way, the EMP also saw the introduction of stronger political conditionality attached to the MEDA budget and to the Euro-Mediterranean Agreements. Both instruments included clauses for suspension, based on a Commission proposal, in the event of human rights abuses, provisions which promised to subject the partner governments to closer scrutiny of their behaviour at home. The power of the European Parliament (and national parliaments) to withhold assent to the agreements and to refuse to authorise the MEDA budget line added to the potential for these economic instruments to be used as political weapons. Although Turkey was the only partner country to have its MEDA funding blocked, for reasons related as much to its relationship with Greece as to human rights concerns, the Union's willingness to flex its muscles was nevertheless evident early on in the EMP.

This type of ad hoc linkage between economic policy instruments and political objectives will continue to be the norm. It reflects the general trend in EU foreign policy for finding pragmatic solutions when existing procedures fail to generate effective collective action, as is routinely the case. The practice of nominating Special Envoys, for instance, initially a product of the Union's inability to agree on how to deal with the crisis in the former Yugoslavia, has become a firmly established feature of the Union's diplomatic repertoire. Given the fragility of the Barcelona process, the Union can ill-afford to jeopardise the already dwindling output of measures by engaging protracted debates about the proper legal bases for action. Such flexibility may be essential to the future credibility of EU foreign policy in the region.

## Revisiting the Civilian Power Concept

Both literally and normatively, the 'civilian power' concept is deeply embedded in the Euro-Mediterranean Partnership.[23] By definition, 'soft security' demands a shift of emphasis away from traditional power politics towards a more idealistic, visionary approach to international relations. Along with the 'economics first' approach, a whole chapter of the Barcelona process was devoted to 'civilian' issues spanning culture, religion and the idea of encouraging the development and participation of 'civil society'. On paper, the inclusion of a human face to the EMP was in keeping with the Union's use of what Hill calls 'moral suasion' as a policy instrument.[24] The implication was that the EU's approach to democracy, human rights and governmental-societal relations should be the standard for members of the Euro-Mediterranean Partnership.

But the civilian power concept also implies passivity on traditional politico-security issues, something that does not square with the agenda of the EMP. The first chapter of the Barcelona Declaration makes direct references to, *inter alia,* sovereignty, weapons proliferation and even the need to refrain from developing military capacities beyond legitimate defence requirements. Reading between the lines, the first chapter anticipates future political crises in the region, whether domestic or international. France's push for a Stability Charter, despite the attempt to sell it as a 'political statement', was evidence of an active effort on the EU's part to have in place politico-security safeguards if the 'soft security' strategy fails.

The real relevance of civilian power Europe in the EMP context was to be found in the perceptions and expectations of the partner countries. With most Mediterranean states having been dragged into the superpowers' battle for dominance, the European Union always (symbolically) represented a less threatening presence in the international system. In the power vacuum left by the end of Cold War, Mediterranean non-member countries were centripetally attracted to the EU by the 'magnetic force of economics'.[25] They joined a growing queue of third countries knocking on the EU's door for membership, upgraded Association Agreements and increased economic support. Among the Mediterranean partners, Cyprus and Malta stand on the threshold of accession, Turkey sits in the waiting room and Morocco has had formal and informal applications for membership rejected. All the partners expect the EU to meet its obligations as a benevolent dispenser of resources from north to south and as the keyholder of access to the lucrative single European market. In that sense, the civilian power concept has a tangible product to offer.

The EMP also showed the extent to which there was demand for the EU as a civilian political power. For the Arab Mediterranean group in particular, the Union's presence was sought after as an effective counterweight to the USA in the Middle East Peace Process. Indeed, Arab governments reproached the Union for being insufficiently forceful with the Binyamin Netanyahu's government, and for appointing a diplomat – Miguel Moratinos – rather than a politician as its Special Envoy to the Peace Process. More generally, the EU is widely regarded a model for peaceful international relations between states with a history of bloody conflict. The creation of the Arab Maghreb Union and (shelved) proposals for a regional organisation to capitalise on peace in the Middle East both foresaw political integration along the lines of the European integration experience.

However, mistrust persisted about the EU's motives for devoting what was seen as excessive attention to the political and security dimension of the Barcelona process. To illustrate the point, at the same time that the Union was talking about peace, prosperity and stability in the region, its southern member states were discussing, among other things, the creation of EuroMarFor.[26] Not surprisingly, these initiatives were regarded with deep suspicion by the Maghreb states.[27] As one diplomat argued:

> The security issue is a very real and deep one, and we do understand the concerns in Europe, some of which are genuine. But some are the result of scaremongering, some are a result of stereotypes and prejudices which we don't like. As far as we are concerned, there hasn't been, at any time, any need for Europe to have any military concerns.[28]

The Union had to be ultra-cautious on following up the democratisation and human rights elements of the EMP. It was perhaps no coincidence that uptake of the MEDA Democracy budget, which was set up to promote the activities of non-governmental organisations in the partner countries, was slow. There was a fine line between nudging the partners in its preferred direction and outright political interference.

The question remains: can an EU Mediterranean strategy be effective without an independent hard security dimension? Given time, and the benefit of several years of closer cooperation between the northern and southern shores, the idea of a regional soft security community appears to be a realistic prospect. In this respect, a militarily empowered EU implementing its own defence policy in the Mediterranean might prove to be counter-productive. As Karen Smith argues:

> The end of the civilian power image would entail giving up far too much for far too little. An EU intervention capability could be seen by outsiders as a step towards the creation of a superpower that uses military instruments to pursue its own interests.[29]

Alternatively, the increasing international trend towards using military means for selective humanitarian interventions may well see pressure grow on the EU to equip itself with a genuine politico-security capability.[30] The crisis in Kosovo during 1999 once again exposed the EU's powerlessness to intervene even where it had a strong interest in doing so. Growing instability in the Middle East, the demonstrable threat posed by modern terrorism and weapons proliferation all point to the enduring utility of military intervention as an instrument of last resort. Civilian power Europe, however laudable, may be redundant.

## Closing the Capabilities-Expectations Gap?

In important respects, the EMP narrowed the capabilities-expectations gap in EU Mediterranean policy. On the capabilities side, the EMP delivered two main improvements. First, the Union displayed a significant (and arguably surprising) degree of internal cohesiveness over the formulation of its Mediterranean strategy. The Commission's proposals passed through the Council largely unscathed, a measure of the convergence among the member states about the need for policy change. Critically, the southern member states secured the endorsement of the northern group to the MEDA budget. In this sense, moves to strengthen the Union's machinery for identifying common interests and agreeing the basis for foreign policy actions seemed to have paid off.

Second, the EMP equipped the Union with an array of instruments that expanded the policy choices available to it. The coupling of the Euro-Mediterranean Agreements to MEDA and the Barcelona process brought increased coherence to EU Mediterranean policy. Arguably the most significant development was the multilateralization of policy which offered a clear pathway, albeit one conditional upon conflict resolution, to regional integration. If the Union is to exercise decisive influence over future development in the Mediterranean and benefit from the extension of its own sphere of influence in the region, then the Barcelona process should be regarded as a step in the right direction.

Such is the economic and political diversity of the partner countries that it is difficult to generalise about their expectations of the EMP and the European Union. There are clearly realistic expectations about what the EU can achieve as a political actor, and the limitations of the CFSP are widely acknowledged. In this respect, the Barcelona process has so far failed to live up to their expectations, with the EU more concerned to keep all the participants satisfied than to use the process as a means to influence Israel's policy on the Palestinian territories.

On the economic front, the highest possible level of financial assistance and the maximum level of market access are priorities for all. Here, the Mediterranean partners join a long line of developing countries looking to deepen their links to an altruistic EU, which is still regarded as a 'bridge' between rich and poor. Yet there have been warning signs that the EU may be 'losing interest' in development policy, appearing preoccupied with its own budgetary problems and the massive transfer of resources that will accompany eastern enlargement. Few of the partner countries can hope to accede to the Union, and failure to achieve the kind of economic growth required to provide employment for rapidly expanding populations is likely to leave governments helpless if the most apocalyptic forecasts of social explosions are borne out.

The Euro-Mediterranean Agreements have failed to meet the partners' expectations, however optimistic they may have been. Having experienced three decades of largely unfulfilled promises on access to the EU's agricultural markets, they reasonably expected a considerable improvement in the terms of trade in this sector. Once again, however, negotiators came up against the inherent conservatism of the CAP and the protectionist instincts of the member states. As Likke Friis concludes in a study of EU-CEEC relations, the EU is 'highly efficient in defending its own 'domestic interest" in external negotiations, but more inefficient in playing a truly constructive role for its surroundings'.[31] The comparative importance of agricultural trade to the EU and the partner countries throws the EU's miserliness in this sector into even sharper relief. As is the case with financial resources, however, there appears to be little prospect of substantial improvement in the prevailing terms of trade.

The EMP balance sheet shows a boost for the Union's capacity to control its relationships with the Mediterranean partner countries, but a persistent, substantive failure to meet their expectations. The bottom line is that the EU may be spreading itself too thinly in the external relations sphere, creating expectations that it simply cannot meet either economically or politically. Progressive force in the international order or not, the EU's first priority is to serve European interests, a fact inevitably reflected in the structure of its relationships with third countries.

The EMP is undeniably a sign of progress in European integration, and of a European Union that is gradually acquiring the capacity to order the world around it in a more systematic and coherent way. But the acid test of successful strategic action is surely the attainment of long-term objectives and a genuinely transformative impact. Effective strategies involve the identification of objectives, the agreement of targets, the allocation and distribution of resources in pursuit of those objectives and targets, and the development of feedback mechanisms to enable adjustments to be made. The EMP only goes part of the way to fulfilling these criteria. In the final analysis, partnership is unlikely to be enough.

## Notes

[1] Hill, C. (1993) 'The Capability-Expectations Gap, or Conceptualising Europe's International Role', *Journal of Common Market Studies*, Vol. 31, No. 3, pp. 305-28; Hill, C. (1998) 'Closing the capabilities-expectations gap?' in J. Peterson and H. Sjursen (eds) *A Common Foreign Policy for Europe: Competing Visions of the CFSP*, London: Routledge, pp. 18-38.

[2] Smith, M. (1998) 'Does the flag follow trade? "Politicisation" and the emergence of a European foreign policy' in J. Peterson and H. Sjursen (eds.) *A Common Foreign Policy for Europe: Competing Visions of the CFSP*, London: Routledge, p. 94.

[3] Schmitter, P. (1969) 'Three Neofunctional Hypotheses about International Integration', *International Organization*, Vol. 23, pp. 161-7.

[4] See Huysmans, J. (2000) 'The European Union and the securitization of migration' *Journal of Common Market Studies*, Vol. 38, No. 5, pp. 751-778; Pugh, M. (2000) *Europe's Boat People: Maritime Cooperation in the Mediterranean*, Chaillot Paper 41, Institute for Security Studies of the WEU, Paris; Buzan, B., Wæver, O., de Wilde, J. (1998) *Security: A New Framework for Analysis*, London: Lynne Rienner Publishers.

[5] Most interviewees from the partner countries drew attention to the negative short-term domestic economic effects of implementing free-trade agreements.

[6] For a discussion of the impact of free-trade agreements on the partner countries, see Marks, J. (1998b) 'The European Challenge to North African Economies: The Downside to the Euro-Med Partnership Initiative', *Journal of North African Studies*, Vol. 3, No. 2, pp. 47-58. Marks argues that the downside to the free-trade initiative has been understated in the clamour for economic reform.

[7] A simple division of aid by population confirms these figures. By comparison, the 1994-1999 Financial Perspective agreed at the 1992 Edinburgh European Council projected

structural fund support of 400 ECUs per capita to Greece and Portugal in 1999. See Senior Nello, S. and Smith, K. (1997) 'The Consequence of Eastern Enlargement of the European Union in Stages', *EUI Working Paper*, No. 97/51, Florence: Robert Schuman Centre, European University Institute, p. 25. By extension, the CEECs should require at least as high a figure if they are to 'catch up' with even the poorer EU Member States.

[8] Galloway, D. (1999) 'Keynote Article: Agenda 2000 – Packaging the Deal' in G. Edwards and G. Wiessala (eds) *The European Union: Annual Review 1998/1999 of the Journal of Common Market Studies*, Oxford: Blackwell, pp. 9-35.

[9] In the textile sector, the EU was forced to open up its markets by the dismantling of the MFA and measures agreed in the GATT. In the agriculture sector, protectionism remained its watchword.

[10] Smith, M. (1998) op. cit., p. 93.

[11] Petri, P. (1997) *Trade Strategies for the Southern Mediterranean*, OECD Technical Papers No. 127, Paris: OECD, p. 54.

[12] World Bank (2001) *Annual Report 2001*, Internet Edition, http://www.worldbank.org/annualreport/2001/wbar2001.htm.

[13] The most common complaints from representatives of the partner countries interviewed were, firstly, that the level of financial assistance would not provide adequate compensation for the 'shock' of free-trade. Secondly, while most governments claimed to be prepared for new competition from the EU, most also expressed concern that their exporters would continue to be discriminated against in favour of European producers.

[14] Interview, 4 November 1997.

[15] Smith, M. (1998) op. cit., p. 82.

[16] To reiterate, the Commission's mandates to negotiate the Euro-Mediterranean agreements forced it to closely adhere to existing trade flows and to avoid making new concessions on 'sensitive' products.

[17] Interview, Brussels, 13 December 1996.

[18] Pelkmans, J. and Murphy, A. (1991) 'Catapulted into leadership: The Community's trade and aid policies *vis-à-vis* Eastern Europe', *Journal of European Integration*, Vol. 24, Nos. 2-3, p. 28.

[19] European Commission (1998) *The Euro-Mediterranean Partnership and the Single Market*, COM (98) 320, 22 September, Brussels.

[20] Interview, Brussels, 16 December 1996.

[21] Spencer, C. (2001) 'The EU and Common Strategies: The Revealing Case of the Mediterranean', *European Foreign Affairs Review*, Vol. 6, No. 1, p. 47.

[22] Interview, Brussels, 13 December 1996.

[23] For a discussion of this distinction between the literal and normative applications of the civilian power concept, see Hill, C. (1990) 'European Foreign Policy: Power Bloc, Civilian Model or Flop?' in R. Rummel (ed.) *The Evolution of an International Actor: Western Europe's New Assertiveness*, Boulder and Oxford: Westview, pp. 31-55.

[24] Ibid., p. 33.

[25] Rosencrance, R. (1998) 'The European Union: A New Type of International Actor' in J. Zielonka, op. cit., p. 18.

[26] Italy, France, Spain and Portugal established Eurofor, a rapid reaction landforce, and its maritime counterpart Euromarfor, during the WEU's 1995 Summit in Lisbon. See Parsdorfer, C. (1998) 'La politique méditerranéenne de l'UE', *Développement et Coopération*, No. 3, May-June, pp. 12-14.

[27] For a critical North African perspective on the new forces, see 'La Libye et la Tunisie denoncent la creation de l'EUROFOR', *La Vie Economique*, 15-21 November 1996, pp. 7-9.

[28] Interview, Brussels, 25 March 1997.
[29] Smith, K. (1998) 'The Instruments of European Foreign Policy' in J. Zielonka (ed.) *Paradoxes of European Foreign Policy*, The Hague: Kluwer Law International, p. 79.
[30] Hoffmann, S. (1998) *World Disorders: Troubled Peace in the Post-Cold War Era*, Lanham (MA): Rowman and Littlefield, esp. pp. 152-176.
[31] Friis, L. (1997) *When Europe Negotiates: From Europe Agreements to Eastern Enlargement*, Copenhagen: Institute of Political Science.

# Bibliography

Algieri, F. (1996) 'In Need of a Comprehensive Approach: The European Union and Possible External Security Challenges' in F. Algieri, J. Janning and D. Rumberg (eds) *Managing Security in Europe*, Guterslöh: Bertelsmann, pp. 189-207.
Aliboni, R. (1992a) 'Southern European Security: Perceptions and Problems' in R. Aliboni (ed.) *Southern European Security in the 1990s*, London: Pinter, pp. 1-14.
Aliboni, R. (1992c) 'The Mediterranean Dimension' in W. Wallace (ed.) *The Dynamics of European Integration*, London: Pinter, 2nd Edition, pp. 155-67.
Allen, D. (1996) 'The European Rescue of National Foreign Policy' in C. Hill (ed.) *The Actors In Europe's Foreign Policy*, London and New York: Routledge, pp. 288-304.
Allen, D. (1998) 'Who Speaks for Europe? The Search for an Effective and Coherent External Policy' in J. Peterson and H. Sjursen (eds) *A Common Foreign Policy for Europe: Competing Visions of the CFSP*, London: Routledge, pp. 41-58.
Anderson, S. (1992) 'Western Europe and the Gulf War' in R. Rummel (ed.) *Toward Political Union: Planning a CFSP in the EC*, Boulder and Oxford: Westview, pp. 147-60.
Armstrong, K. and Bulmer, S. (1998) *The Governance of the Single European Market*, Manchester: Manchester University Press.
Ayari, C. (1992) *Enjeux Méditerranéens: Pour une coopération euro-arabe*, Paris: CNRS.
Babarinde, O. (1998) 'The European Union's Relations with the South: A Commitment to Development?' in C. Rhodes (ed.) *The European Union in the World Community*, Boulder and London: Lynne Rienner, pp. 127-46.
Bahaijoub, A. (1993) 'Morocco's argument to join the EC' in G. Joffé (ed.) *North Africa: Nation, State and Region*, London: Routledge, pp. 235-46.
Baldwin, D.A. (1993) 'Neoliberalism, Neorealism and World Politics' in D.A. Baldwin (ed.) *Neorealism and Neoliberalism: The Contemporary Debate*, New York: Columbia University Press, pp. 3-25.
Barbé, E. (1995) 'European Political Cooperation: The upgrading of Spanish foreign policy' in R. Gillespie, F. Rodrigo and J. Story (eds) *Democratic Spain: Reshaping External Relations in a Changing World*, London and New York: Routledge, pp. 106-22.
Barbé, E. (1996) 'Spain: The Uses of Foreign Policy Cooperation' in C. Hill (ed.) *The Actors in Europe's Foreign Policy*, London and New York: Routledge, pp. 108-29.
Barbé, E. (1998) 'Balancing Europe's Eastern and Southern Dimensions' in J. Zielonka (ed.) *Paradoxes of European Foreign Policy*, The Hague: Kluwer Law International, p 117-29.
Barbé, E. and Izquierdo, F. (1997) 'Present and Future of Joint Actions for the Mediterranean Region' in M. Holland (ed.) *Common Foreign and Security Policy: The Record and Reforms*, London and Washington: Pinter, pp. 120-35.
Bensidoun, I. and Chevallier, A. (1996) *Europe-Méditerranée: Le pari de l'ouverture*, Paris: Economica.
Biad, A. (2000) 'The Debate on CBMs in the Southern Mediterranean' in H.G. Brauch, A. Marquina and A. Biad (eds) *Euro-Mediterranean Partnership for the $21^{st}$ Century*, Basingstoke: Macmillan.
Bideleux, R. (1996) 'Bringing the East Back In' in R. Bideleux and R. Taylor (eds) *European Integration and Disintegration*, London: Routledge, pp. 225-52.

Booth, K. (1991) 'Introduction. The Interregnum: World Politics in Transition' in K. Booth (ed.) *New Thinking About Strategy and International Security*, London: HarperCollins, pp. 1-23.
Bourrinet, J. (1979) *Le Dialogue Euro-Arabe*, Paris: L'Harmattan.
Bourrinet, J. (1994) 'Aspects économiques: trois défis majeurs pour la coopération' in J. Bourrinet (ed.) *La Méditerranée: Espace de Coopération*, Centre d'Etudes et de Recherches Internationales et Communautaires, Université d'Aix-Marseilles III, Paris: Economica, pp. 201-17.
Brauch, H.G. (2000) 'From Confidence to Partnership Building Measures in Europe and the Mediterranean: Conceptual and Political Efforts Revisited' in H.G. Brauch, A. Marquina and A. Biad (eds) *Euro-Mediterranean Partnership for the $21^{st}$ Century*, Basingstoke: Macmillan.
Bulmer, S. (1991) 'Analysing EPC: The Case for Two-tier Analysis' in M. Holland (ed.) *The Future of European Political Cooperation: Essays on Theory and Practice*, Basingstoke: Macmillan, pp. 70-91.
Buzan, B (1991a) *People, States and Fear: An Agenda for International Security Studies in the Post Cold War Era*, Boulder (CO): Lynne Rienner.
Buzan, B. (1991b) 'Is International Security Possible?' in K. Booth (ed.) *New Thinking About Strategy and International Security*, London: HarperCollins, pp. 31-55.
Buzan, B. (1994) 'The Interdependence of Security and Economic Issues in the "New World Order"' in R. Stubbs and G.R.D. Underhill (eds) Political Economy and the Changing Global Order, London: Macmillan, pp. 89-102.
Buzan, B., Wæver, O. and de Wilde, J. (1998) *Security: A New Framework for Analysis*, London: Lynne Rienner Publishers.
Calleya, S. (1997) *Navigating Regional Dynamics in the Post-Cold War World: Patterns of Relations in the Mediterranean Area*, Aldershot: Dartmouth.
Calleya, S. (2000) 'Regional Dynamics in the Mediterranean' in S. Calleya (ed.), *Regionalism in the Post-Cold War World*, Aldershot: Dartmouth.
Callies de Sallies, B. (1995) 'Algérie (1988-1995): De la crise à la guerre civile', *Les Cahiers de l'Orient*, Paris: Sari, No. 3, pp. 45-59.
Chatelus, M. (1996) 'Economic cooperation among southern Mediterranean countries' in R. Aliboni, G. Joffé and T. Niblock (eds) *Security Challenges in the Mediterranean*, London: Frank Cass, pp. 83-113.
Chourou, B. (2001) 'The (Ir)relevance of Security Issues in Euro-Mediterranean Relations' in F. Tanner (ed.) *The European Union as a Security Actor in the Mediterranean: ESPD Soft Power and Peacemaking in Euro-Mediterranean Relations*, Zurich: Center for Security Studies and Conflict Research, pp. 57-74.
Clarke, M. (1989) 'The Foreign Policy System: A Framework for Analysis' in M. Clarke and B. White (eds) *Understanding Foreign Policy: The Foreign Policy Systems Approach*, Aldershot and Brookfield (Vermont): Edward Elgar, pp. 26-59.
Coffey, P. (1976) *The External Economic Relations of the EEC*, London: Macmillan.
Corbett, R., Jacobs, F. and Shackleton, M. (1995) *The European Parliament*, $3^{rd}$ edition, London: Cartermill.
Croft, S., Redmond, J., Wyn Rees, G. and Webber, M. (1999) *The Enlargement of Europe*, Manchester: Manchester University Press.
Crouzatier, J. (1988) *Géopolitique de la Méditerranée*, Paris: Publisud.
Delors, J. (1990) 'Europe's Ambition', *Foreign Policy*, No. 180, Autumn, pp. 14-27.
De Marco, G. (1997) Speech to Annual Ambassadors' Conference, Valletta, August 1992, Ministry of Foreign Affairs of Malta, *Malta's Foreign Policy in the Nineties*, Valletta: Ministry of Foreign Affairs of Malta.

Domestici-Met, M and Dubois, L. (1990) 'Le Rôle de l'Europe: La Communauté Européenne' in J. Bourrinet (ed.) *La Méditerranée: Espace de Coopération?*, Paris: Economica.
Duchêne, F. (1972) 'Europe's Role in World Peace' in R. Mayne (ed.) *Europe Tomorrow: Sixteen Europeans Look Ahead*, London: Fontana, pp. 32-49.
Easton, D. (1965) *A Framework for Political Analysis*, Englewood Cliffs: Prentice-Hall.
Echeverría Jesús, C. (1993) 'La Reforma de la Politica Mediterranea de la Comunidad Europea', in A. Marquina (ed.), *El Flanco Sur de la Otan*, Madrid: Editorial Complutense.
Flaesch-Mougin, C. (1990) 'Competing Frameworks: The Dialogue and its Legal Bases' in G. Edwards and E. Regelsberger (eds) *Europe's Global Links: The European Community and Inter-regional Cooperation*, London: Pinter.
Fridhi, N. and Quatremer, J. (1996) *Le Nouvel Espace Economique Euro-Méditerranéen*, Brussels: Club de Bruxelles.
Friis, L. (1997) *When Europe Negotiates: From Europe Agreements to Eastern Enlargement*, Copenhagen: Institute of Political Science.
Gallino, D. (1991) 'Security challenges as perceived in the Mediterranean NATO countries' in M. Jopp, R. Rummel and P. Schmidt (eds) *Integration and Security in Western Europe: Inside the European Pillar*, Boulder and Oxford: Westview, pp. 95-114.
Gambles, I. (1989) 'Prospects for West European Security Cooperation', *Adelphi Papers*, No. 244, London: IISS.
Ginsberg, R. (1989) *Foreign Policy Actions of the European Community: The Politics of Scale*, London: Admantine Press.
Ginsberg, R. (2001) *The European Union in International Politics: Baptism of Fire*, Oxford and Lanham: Rowman and Littlefield.
Grasa, R. (1995) 'El Mediterráneo desde una perspectiva globalizadora de la seguridad: Una mirada a a dimensión cooperativa de la conflictividad', *Papers: Revista de Sociologica*, No. 46, Bellaterra: Universidad Autònoma de Barcelona, pp. 25-42.
Grilli, E.R. (1993) *The European Community and the Developing Countries*, Cambridge: Cambridge University Press.
Groux, J. and Manin, P. (1985) *The European Communities in the International Order*, Luxembourg: Office for Official Publications of the European Communities.
Guy Peters, B. (1996) 'Agenda-setting in the European Union' in J. J. Richardson (ed.) *European Union: Power and Policy-making*, London: Routledge, pp. 61-76.
Haaland Matlary, J. (1997) *Energy Policy in the European Union*, Basingstoke: Macmillan.
Haddaoui, R. (1993) 'Le nouveau visage de l'émigration marocaine' in The Philip Morris Institute, *Vers un Politique Européenne de l'Immigration*, Brussels: The Philip Morris Institute.
Hayes-Renshaw, F. and Wallace, H. (1997) *The Council of Ministers*, Basingstoke: Macmillan.
Henig, S. (1976) 'Mediterranean Policy in the Context of the External Relations of the European Community, 1958-73' in A. Shlaim and G.E. Yannopoulos (eds) *The EEC and the Mediterranean Countries*, Cambridge: Cambridge University Press, pp. 305-24.
Heywood, P. (1995) *The Government and Politics of Spain*, Basingstoke: Macmillan.
Hill, C. (1990) 'European Foreign Policy: Power Bloc, Civilian Model or Flop?' in R. Rummel (ed.) *The Evolution of an International Actor: Western Europe's New Assertiveness*, Boulder and Oxford: Westview, pp. 31-55.
Hill, C. (1992) 'The Foreign Policy of the European Community: Dream or Reality?' in R.C. Macridis (ed.) *Foreign Policy in World Politics*, 8th edition, London: Prentice Hall, pp. 108-42.

Hill, C. (1997) 'The Actors Involved: National Perspectives' in E. Regelsberger, P. de Schoutheete de Tervarent and W. Wessels, *Foreign Policy of the European Union: From EPC to CFSP and Beyond*, Boulder (CO): Lynne Rienner, pp. 85-97.

Hill, C. (1998a) 'Closing the Capabilities-Expectations Gap?' in J. Peterson and H. Sjursen (eds) *A Common Foreign Policy for Europe: Competing Visions of the CFSP*, London: Routledge, pp. 18-38.

Hill, C. (1998b) 'Convergence, Divergence and Dialectics' in J. Zielonka (ed.) *Paradoxes of European Foreign Policy*, The Hague: Kluwer Law International, pp. 35-53.

Hill, C. and Wallace W. (1996) 'Introduction: Actors and actions' in C. Hill (ed.) *The Actors in Europe's Foreign Policy*, London: Routledge, pp. 1-16.

Hocking, B. and Smith, M. (1997) *Beyond Foreign Economic Policy: The United States, the Single European Market and the Changing World* Economy, London: Pinter.

Hoffmann, S. (1995) *The European Sisyphus: Essays on Europe, 1964-1994*, Boulder and Oxford: Westview Press.

Hoffmann, S. (1998) *World Disorders: Troubled Peace in the Post-Cold War Era*, Lanham: Rowman and Littlefield.

Huleileh, S., Bashkin, G. and Al-Qaq, Z. (1999) *Guidelines for Final Status Economic Negotiations Between Israel and Palestine*, Jerusalem: Israel/Palestine Centre for Research and Information.

Ifestos, P. (1987) *European Political Cooperation: Towards a Framework of Supranational Diplomacy*, Aldershot: Avebury.

International Institute for Strategic Studies (1988) *Prospects for Security in the Mediterranean, Parts I-II-III*, Adelphi Papers, Nos. 229-230-231, London: IISS.

Joffé, G. (1998) *Algeria in Crisis*, Briefing Paper No. 48, Middle East Programme, London: RIIA.

Joffé, G. (1994) 'The European Union and the Maghreb' in Gillespie, R. (ed.), *Mediterranean Politics: Volume 1*, London: Pinter.

Jorgensen, K.E. (1993) 'EC External Relations as a Theoretical Challenge: Theories, Concepts and Trends' in F.R. Pfetsch ed. *International Relations and Pan Europe: Theoretical Approaches and Empirical Findings*, Munster: Campus Verlag, pp. 211-34.

Kaufmann, J. (1988) *Conference Diplomacy: An Introductory Analysis*, Dordrecht: Martinus Nijhoff.

Keohane, R.O. and Hoffmann, S. (1989) 'Institutional Change in Europe in the 1980s' in R.O. Keohane and S. Hoffmann (eds) *The New European Community: Decision-Making and Institutional Change*, Boulder and Oxford: Westview, pp. 1-39.

Keohane, R.O. and Hoffmann, S. (1993) 'Conclusion: Structure, Strategy and International Roles' in R.O. Keohane, J.S. Nye and S. Hoffmann (eds) *After the Cold War: International Institutions and State Strategies in Europe, 1989-1991*, Cambridge (MA): Harvard University Press, pp. 381-404.

Khader, B. (1996) *Le Partenariat Euro-Méditerranéen*, Louvain-la-Neuve: CERMAC.

Khader, B. (1997) *Le Partenariat Euro-Méditerranéen Apres la Conférence de Barcelone*, Paris: L'Harmattan.

Kintis, A.G. (1997) 'The EU's Foreign Policy and the War in the Former Yugoslavia' in M. Holland (ed.) *Common Foreign and Security Policy: The Record and Reforms*, London and Washington: Pinter, pp. 148-173.

Kissinger, H. (1994) *Diplomacy*, New York and London: Simon and Schuster.

Krasner, S.D. (1983) *International Regimes*, Ithaca (NY): Cornell University Press.

Krenzler, H. and Schneider, H.C. (1997) 'The Question of Consistency' in E. Reglesberger, P. de Schoutheete de Tervarent and W. Wessels (eds) *Foreign Policy of the European Union: From EPC to CFSP and Beyond*, Boulder and London: Lynne Rienner, pp. 120-34.

Lahav, G. (1993) 'Immigration, Hypernationalism and European Security' in J. Philip Rogers (ed.) *The Future of European Security*, Basingstoke: Macmillan, pp. 74-81.
Lasok, D. (1994) *Law and Institutions of the European Union*, 6th Edition, London: Butterworth and Co.
Lasswell, H.D. (1950) *Politics: Who Gets What, When, How?*, New York: Peter Smith.
Lodge, J. (1989) 'European Political Co-operation: Towards the 1990s' in J. Lodge (ed.) *The European Community and the Challenge of the Future*, London: Pinter.
Lopez García, B. (1992) 'Les mouvements de population en Méditerranée' in M. Dumas (ed.) *Méditerranée Occidentale: Sécurité et Coopération*, Paris: Fondation pour les études de défense nationale, pp. 45-56.
Lowi, T. (1967) 'Making Democracy Safe for the World: National Politics and Foreign Policy' in J. Rosenau (ed.) *Domestic Sources of Foreign Policy*, New York: The Free Press, pp. 295-331.
March, J. and Olsen, J.P. (1989) *Rediscovering Institutions*, New York: Free Press.
Marks, J. (1989) 'The Concept of Morocco in Europe' in G. Joffé (ed.) *Morocco and Europe*, Occasional Paper 7, London: School of Oriental and African Studies, pp. 13-23.
Marquina, A. (1991) 'Spain' in M. Jopp, R. Rummel and P. Schmidt (eds) *Integration and Security in Western Europe: Inside the European Pillar*, Boulder, Co. and Oxford: Westview, pp. 197-207.
Marquina, A. (1993) 'Security and cooperation in the Western Mediterranean: The Spanish Policy' in A. Marquina (ed.) *El Flanco Sur de la OTAN*, Madrid: Editorial Complutense, pp. 61-70.
Matthews, J.D. (1977) *Association System of the European Community*, New York: Praeger.
McDonagh, B. (1998) *Original Sin in a Brave New World: An Account of the Negotiation of the Treaty of Amsterdam*, Dublin: Institute of European Affairs.
Meunier, S. and Nicolaides, K. (2000) 'EU Trade Policy: The exclusive versus shared competence debate' in M. Green Cowles and M. Smith (eds) *The State of the European Union: Volume 5*, Oxford: Oxford University Press, pp. 325-46.
Miall, H. (1991) 'New Visions, New Voices, Old Power Structures' in K. Booth (ed.) *New Thinking About Strategy and International Security*, London: HarperCollins, pp. 293-312.
Monar, J. (1993) 'The Foreign Affairs System of the Maastricht Treaty: A Combined Assessment of the CFSP and EC External Relations Elements' in J. Monar, W. Ungerer and W. Wessels (eds) *The Maastricht Treaty on European Union: Legal Complexity and Political Dynamics*, Brussels: European Interuniversity Press.
Moravcsik, A. (1998) *The Choice for Europe: Social Purpose and State Power from Messina to Maastricht*, London: UCL Press.
Morgan, R. (1973) *High Politics, Low Politics: Towards a Foreign Policy for Western Europe*, London: Sage.
Mortimer, E.J. (1991) 'New Fault Lines: Is a North-South Confrontation Inveitable in Security Terms?' in International Institute for Strategic Studies, *New Dimensions in International Security*, Adelphi Paper 296, London: IISS, pp. 80-81.
Nigoul, C. (1991) 'Quelques remarques sur les facteurs économiques et sociaux de l'insécurité en méditerranée' in H. El Malki (ed.) *La Méditerranée en question: Conflits et interdépendances*, Casablanca: Fondation du Roi Abdul-Aziz and Paris: Éditions du CNRS.
Northedge, F.S. (ed.) (1969) *The Foreign Policy of the Powers*, London: Faber and Faber.
Nuttall, S. (2000) *European Foreign Policy*, Oxford: Oxford University Press.
Nye, J. (1990) *Bound to Lead: The Changing Nature of American Power*, New York: Basic Books, pp. 173-201.

Odlander, J. (1993) 'Order, What Order? The European Community in a Sea of Change' in R. Morgan, J. Lorentzen, A. Leander and S. Guzzini (eds) *New Diplomacy in the Post Cold War World*, London: Macmillan, pp. 272-81.
Peterson, J. (1996) *Europe and America: The Prospects for Partnership*, London: Routledge.
Peterson, J. and Bomberg, E. (1999) *Decision-Making in the European Union*, Basingstoke: Macmillan.
Piening, C. (1997) *Global Europe: The European Union in World Affairs*, Boulder and London: Lynne Rienner.
Pierson, P. (1998) 'The Path to European Integration: A Historical-Institutionalist Analysis' in W. Sandholtz and A. Stone Sweet (eds) *European Integration and Supranational Governance*, Oxford: Oxford University Press, pp. 27-58.
Pijpers, A. (1991) 'European Political Cooperation and the Realist Paradigm' in M. Holland (ed.) *The Future of European Political Cooperation: Essays on Theory and Practice*, Basingstoke: Macmillan, pp. 8-26.
Pollack, M. (1998) 'The Engines of Integration? Supranational Autonomy and Influence in the European Union' in W. Sandholtz and A. Stone Sweet (eds) *European Integration and Supranational Governance*, Oxford: Oxford University Press, pp. 217-49.
Pomfret, R. (1992) 'The European Community's Relations with the Mediterranean Countries' in J. Redmond (ed.) *The External Relations of the European Community*, Basingstoke: Macmillan, pp. 77-92.
Pugh, M. (2000) *Europe's Boat People: Maritime Cooperation in the Mediterranean*, Chaillot Paper 41, Institute for Security Studies of the WEU, Paris.
Ravenel, B. (1990) *Mediterranée, le Nord contre le Sud?*, Paris, L'Harmattan.
Redmond, J. (1994) 'Introduction' in J. Redmond (ed.) *Prospective Europeans: New Members for European Union*, Hemel Hempstead: Harvester Wheatsheaf, pp. 3-17.
Regelsberger, E. (1991) 'The Twelve's Dialogue with Third Countries - Progress Towards a *Communauté d'Action*' in M. Holland (ed.) *The Future of European Political Cooperation: Essays on Theory and Practice*, Basingstoke: Macmillan, pp. 3-26.
Rhein, E. (1992) 'The Community's External Reach' in R. Rummel (ed.) *Toward Political Union: Planning a Common Foreign and Security Policy in the EC*, Boulder and Oxford: Westview, pp. 29-39.
Rich, P. and Joseph, S. (1997) *Algeria: Democratic Transition or Political Stalemate?*, London: Saferworld.
Roberson, B.A. (1998) 'Introduction' in B.A.Roberson (ed.) *The Middle East and Europe: The Power Deficit*, London: Routledge.
Rosecrance, R. (1998) 'The European Union: A New Type of International Actor' in J. Zielonka (ed.) *Paradoxes of European Foreign Policy*, The Hague: Kluwer Law International, pp. 15-24.
Rosenthal, G.G. (1975) *The Men Behind the Decisions: Cases in European Policy-Making*, Lexington, USA: DC Heath and Company.
Rosenthal, G.G. (1982) *The Mediterranean Basin: Its Political Economy and Changing International Relations*, London: Butterworth Scientific.
Ruggie, J-G. (1993) (ed.) *Multilateralism Matters: The Theory and Praxis of an Institutional Form*, New York: Columbia University Press.
Rühle, M. and Williams, N. (1996) 'The Greater Union's New Security Agenda: NATO and the EU' in F. Algieri, J. Janning and D. Rumberg (eds) *Managing Security in Europe: The European Union and the Challenge of Enlargement*, Gütersloh: Bertelsmann Foundation, pp. 89-109.
Rummel, R. (1997) 'The CFSP's Conflict Prevention Policy' in M. Holland (ed.) *Common Foreign and Security Policy: The Record and Reforms*, London: Pinter, pp. 105-9

Rummel, R. and Wiedemann, J. (1998) 'Identifying institutional paradoxes of CFSP' in J. Zielonka (ed.) *Paradoxes of European Foreign Policy*, The Hague: Kluwer Law International, pp. 53-66.
Saleh, A. (1983) *The Euro-Arab Dialogue: A Study in Associative Diplomacy*, London: Pinter.
Sandholtz, W. and Stone Sweet, A. (eds) *European Integration and Supranational Governance*, Oxford: Oxford University Press.
Scharpf, F.W. (1997) *Games Real Actors Play: Actor-Centred Institutionalism in Policy Research*, Boulder (CO): Westview.
Scharpf, F. (1999) *Governing in Europe: Effective and Democratic?*, Oxford: Oxford University Press.
Sedelmeier, U. and Wallace, H. (1996) 'Policies towards Central and Eastern Europe' in H. Wallace and W. Wallace (eds) *Policy-Making in the European Union*, Oxford: Oxford University Press, pp. 353-87.
Shlaim, A. (1976) 'The Community and the Mediterranean Basin', in K.J. Twitchett (ed.) *Europe and the World: The External Relations of the Common Market*, London: Europa Publications, pp. 77-120.
Sid Ahmed, A. (2000) 'Economic convergence and "catching up" in the Mediterranean: Diagnosis, Prospect and Limitations of the Barcelona process and elements for a strategy' in Brauch, G., Marquina, A. and Biad, A. (eds) *Euro-Mediterranean Partnership for the 21$^{st}$ Century*, Basingstoke: Macmillan.
Siotis, J. (1981) 'The Politics of Greek Accession' in G. Minet, J. Siotis and P. Tsakaloyannis (eds) *The Mediterranean Challenge: VI*, Brighton: Sussex European Research Centre, pp. 85-120.
Sjostedt, G. (1977) *The External Role of the European Community*, Farnborough: Saxon House.
Smith, H. (1995) *European Union Foreign Policy and Central America*, London: Macmillan.
Smith, H. (1998) 'The EU in Latin and Central America' in J. Peterson and H. Sjursen (eds) *A Common Foreign Policy for Europe? Competing Visions of the CFSP*, London: Routledge, pp. 152-68.
Smith, H. (2002) *European Union Foreign Policy: What it is and What it Does*, London: Pluto.
Smith, K. (1998) 'The Instruments of European Foreign Policy' in J. Zielonka (ed.) *Paradoxes of European Foreign Policy*, The Hague: Kluwer Law International, pp. 67-85.
Smith, K. (1999) *The Making of EU Foreign Policy: The Case of Eastern Europe*, Basingstoke: Macmillan
Smith, M. (1996a) 'The EU as an International Actor' in J.J. Richardson (ed.) *European Union: Power and Policy-Making*, London: Routledge, pp. 247-62.
Smith, M. (1998) 'Does the Flag Follow Trade? "Politicisation" and the Emergence of a European Foreign Policy' in J. Peterson and H. Sjursen (eds) *A Common Foreign Policy for Europe: Competing Visions of the CFSP*, London: Routledge, pp. 77-94.
Smith, M.E. (1998a) 'Rules, Transgovernmentalism and the Expansion of European Political Cooperation' in W. Sandholtz and A. Stone Sweet (eds) *European Integration and Supranational Governance*, Oxford: Oxford University Press, pp. 305-33.
Smith, M.E. (1998b) 'What's Wrong with the CFSP? The Politics of Institutional Reform' in P-H. Laurent and M. Maresceau (eds) *The State of the European Union: Volume 4*, Boulder and London: Lynne Rienner, pp. 149-75.

Smith, S. (1994) 'Foreign Policy Theory and the New Europe' in W. Carlsnaes and S. Smith (eds) *European Foreign Policy: The EC and Changing Perspectives in Europe*, London: Sage, pp. 1-20.

Soetendorp, B. (1999) *Foreign Policy in the European Union: Theory, History and Practice*, London and New York: Longman.

Spencer, C. (1993) *The Maghreb in the 1990s: Political and Economic Developments in Algeria, Morocco and Tunisia*, Adelphi Paper No. 274, London: Brasseys/IISS.

Spencer, C. (1996) 'Islamism and European Reactions: The Case of Algeria' in R. Gillespie (ed.) *Mediterranean Politics: Volume 2*, London: Pinter.

Spencer, C. (1998) 'Algeria' in B.A. Roberson (ed.) *The Middle East and Europe: The Power Deficit*, London: Routledge.

Stavridis, S. (1997) 'The Common Foreign and Security Policy: Why Institutional Arrangements Are Not Enough' in S. Stavridis, E. Mossialos, R. Morgan and H. Machin (eds) *New Challenges to the European Union: Policies and Policy-Making*, Aldershot: Dartmouth, pp. 85-121.

Sutton, M. (1989) 'Economic aspects of Morocco's relations with Europe' in G. Joffé (ed.) *Morocco and Europe*, Occasional Paper 7, London: School of Oriental and African Studies, pp. 25-32.

Tonra, B. (2000) 'Denmark and Ireland' in I. Manners and R. G. Whitman (eds) *The Foreign Policies of European Union Member States*, Manchester: Manchester University Press, pp. 224-42.

Tooze, R. (1994) 'Foreign Economic Policy in the New Europe: A Theoretical Audit of a Questionable Category' in W. Carlsnaes and S. Smith (eds) *European Foreign Policy: The EC and Changing Perspectives in Europe*, London: Sage, pp. 61-83.

Tovias, A. (1990) *Foreign Economic Relations of the European Community: The Impact of Spain and Portugal*, London: Lynne Rienner Publishers.

Tovias, A. (1999) Regionalism and the Mediterranean in G. Joffe (ed.) *Perspectives on Development: The Euro-Mediterranean Partnership*, London: Frank Cass.

Wallace, H. (1983a) 'Negotiation, Conflict and Compromise: The Elusive Pursuit of Common Policies' in H. Wallace, W. Wallace and C. Webb *Policy Making in the European Community*, 2$^{nd}$ edition, Chichester: John Wiley and Sons, pp. 43-80.

Wallace, W. (1983b) 'Less than a Federation, More than a Regime: The Community as a Political System' in H. Wallace, W. Wallace and C. Webb (eds) *Policy Making in the European Community*, 2$^{nd}$ Edition, Chichester: John Wiley and Sons, pp. 403-436.

Wallace, H. (1996a) 'Politics and Policy in the EU: The Challenge of Governance' in H. Wallace and W. Wallace (eds) *Policy Making in the European Union*, Oxford: Oxford University Press, pp. 3-36.

Wallace, W. (1996b) 'Government without Statehood: The Unstable Equilibrium' in H. Wallace and W. Wallace (eds) *Policy-Making in the European Union*, Oxford: Oxford University Press.

Waltz, K. (1986) 'Anarchic Orders and Balances of Power' in R.O. Keohane (ed.) *Neorealism and its Critics*, New York: Columbia Press, pp. 98-130.

Webb, C. (1983) 'Theoretical Perspectives and Problems' in H. Wallace, W. Wallace and C. Webb (eds) *Policy Making in the European Community*, 2$^{nd}$ Edition, Chichester: John Wiley and Sons, pp. 1-41.

Weiler, J.H.H. (1983) 'The External Legal Relations of Non-unitary Actors: Mixity and the Federal Principle' in D. O'Keefe and H.G. Schermers (eds) *Mixed Agreements*, London: Kluwer, pp. 35-83.

Weiler, J.H.H. and Wessels, W. (1988) 'EPC and the Challenge of Theory' in A. Pijpers, E. Regelsberger and W. Wessels (eds) *European Political Cooperation in 1980s: A*

*Common Foreign Policy for Western Europe?*, Dordrecht: Martinus Nijhoff, pp. 229-57.
Wessels, W. (2001) 'The Amsterdam Treaty in Theoretical Perspective: Which Dynamics at Work?' in W. Wessels and J. Monar (eds) *The European Union after the Treaty of Amsterdam*, London and New York: Continuum, pp. 70-86.
White, B. (1989) 'Analysing Foreign Policy: Problems and Approaches' in M. Clarke and B. White (eds) *Understanding Foreign Policy: The Foreign Policy Systems Approach*, Aldershot: Edward Elgar, pp. 1-26.
White, B. (2001) *Understanding European Foreign Policy*, Basingstoke: Palgrave.
Whitman, R. (1998) *From Civilian Power to Superpower? The International Identity of the European Union*, Basingstoke: Macmillan.
Wistrich, E. (1992) *After 1992: The United States of Europe*, London: Routledge.
Xenakis, D. and Chryssochoou, D. N. (2001) *The Emerging Euro-Mediterranean System*, Manchester: Manchester University Press.
Youngs, R. (2001) *The European Union and the Promotion of Democracy: Europe's Mediterranean and East Asian Policies*, Oxford: Oxford University Press.
Zielonka, J. (1998) *Explaining Euro-paralysis: Why Europe is Unable to Act in International Politics*, Basingstoke: Macmillan.

### Journal Articles

Aghrout, A. (2001) 'The Euro-Maghreb Free Trade Area: Challenges and Opportunities', *The European Union Review*, Vol. 5, No. 3, pp. 15-32.
Aliboni, R. (1990) 'The Mediterranean Scenario: Economy and Security in the Regions South of the European Community, *The International Spectator*, Vol. 25, No. 2, pp. 138-54.
Aliboni, R. (1992b) 'Italian Security Policy in a Changing International Environment, *Jerusalem Journal of International Relations*, Vol. 14, No. 2, pp. 90-102.
Allen, D. and Smith, M. (1990) 'Western Europe's Presence in the Contemporary International Arena', *Review of International Studies*, Vol. 16, No. 1, pp. 19-37.
Awwad, E. (1997) 'Paix menacée au Proche-Orient', *Défense Nationale*, No. 53, January.
Bachrach, P. and Baratz, M.S. (1963) 'Decisions and Non-Decisions: An Analytical Framework', *American Political Science Review*, Vol. 57, No. 3, pp. 632-42.
Barbé, E. (1996) 'The Barcelona Conference: Launching Pad of a Process', *Mediterranean Politics*, Vol. 1, No. 1, pp. 25-42.
Basfao, K. and Henry, J-R. (1991) 'Le Maghreb et l'Europe: Que faire de la Méditerranée?', *Vingtième Siècle Revue d'Histoire*, Vol. 32, Oct-Dec, pp. 44-5.
Beck, M. (1997) 'Can Financial Aid Promote Regional Peace Agreements? The Case of the Arab-Israeli Conflict', *Mediterranean Politics*, Vol. 2, No. 2, pp. 49-70.
Ben Yahia, H. (1993) 'Security and Stability in the Mediterranean: Regional and International Changes', *Mediterranean Quarterly*, Vol. 4, No. 1, pp. 1-10.
Bull, H. (1982) 'Civilian Power Europe: A Contradiction in Terms?', *Journal of Common Market Studies*, Vol. 21, No.1, pp. 149-70.
Bulmer, S. (1994) 'The Governance of the European Union: A New Institutionalist Approach', *Journal of Public Policy*, Vol. 13, No. 4, pp. 351-80.
Bulmer, S. (1998) 'New Institutionalism and the Governance of the Single European Market', *Journal of European Public Policy*, Vol. 5, No. 3, pp. 365-86.
Callies de Sallies, B. (1996) 'Algérie: accord de Rome et élection présidentielle', *Défense Nationale*, Vol. 75, No. 4, pp. 109-23.

Cesari, J. (1995) 'L'effet "Airbus", *Les Cahiers de l'Orient*, Nos. 36-37, pp. 177-8.
Chatelus, M. (1997) 'L'énergie en Méditerranée: espace régional ou marché mondial?', *Monde Arabe: Maghreb Machrek*, Special issue, Dec, pp. 19-30.
Chatelus, M. and Petit, P. (1997) 'Le partenariat euro-méditerranéen: Un projét régional en quête de cohérence', *Monde Arabe: Maghreb Machrek*, Special Issue, December, pp. 3-7.
Chenal, A. (1995) 'La France rattrapée par le drame algérien', *Politique Etrangère*, Vol. 60, No. 2, pp. 415-425.
Cova, C. (1985) 'La politique communautaire en faveur de la zone méditerranéenne', *Revue du Marché Commune*, No. 291, pp. 525-6.
Cram, L. (1994) 'The European Commission as a Multi-Organisation: Social Policy and IT Policy in the EU', *Journal of European Public Policy*, Vol. 2, No. 1, pp. 195-217.
Cremasco, M. (1990) 'The Mediterranean Area in Perspective', *The International Spectator*, Vol. 25, No. 2.
Daguzan, J. (1992) 'Coopération régionale et sécurité collective en Méditerranée', *Revue d'Economie Régionale et Urbaine*, No. 4, pp. 569-80.
De Vasconcelos, A. (1993) 'Disintegration and Integration in the Mediterranean', *The International Spectator*, Vol. 28, No. 3, pp. 67-78.
Devuyst, Y. (1999) 'The Community Method After Amsterdam', *Journal of Common Market Studies*, Vol. 37, No. 1, pp. 109-20.
Escallier, R. (1991) 'La transition démographique', *Etat du Maghreb*, Paris: La Découverte.
Feld, W.J. (1965) 'The Association Agreements of the European Communities: A Comparative Analysis', *International Organization*, Vol. 19, pp. 223-247.
Fontaine, J. (1992) 'Les élections législatives algériennes', *Monde Arabe: Maghreb/Machrek*, No. 135, Jan-Mar.
Friis, L. and Murphy, A. (1999) 'The European Union and Central and Eastern Europe: Governance and Boundaries', *Journal of Common Market Studies*, Vol. 37, No. 2, pp. 211-32.
Galloway, D. (1999) 'Keynote Article: Agenda 2000 – Packaging the Deal' in G. Edwards and G. Wiessala (eds) *The European Union: Annual Review 1998/1999 of the Journal of Common Market Studies*, Oxford: Blackwell, pp. 9-35.
Garrett, G. and Tsebelis, G. (1996) 'An Institutionalist Critique of Intergovernmentalism', *International Organization*, Vol. 50, No. 2, pp. 269-99.
Ghebali, V. (1993) 'Towards a CSCE in the Mediterranean: The CSCM' in M.R. Lucas (ed.) *The CSCE in the 1990s: Constructing European Security and Cooperation*, Baden-Baden: Nomos, pp. 335-43.
Ghezali, S. (1996) 'Fausse éclaircie en Algérie', *Le Monde Diplomatique*, February, pp. 1-12.
Ginsberg, R. (1999) 'Conceptualising the European Union as an International Actor: Narrowing the Theoretical Capabilities-Expectations Gap', *Journal of Common Market Studies*, Vol. 37, No. 2, pp. 429-54.
Gobe, E. (1992) 'The Maghreb in Contemporary French Politics', *Journal of Arab Affairs*, Vol. 11, No. 2, pp. 129-40.
Grieco, J. (1988) 'Anarchy and the Limits of Cooperation: A Realist Critique of the Newest Liberal Institutionalism', *International Organization*, Vol. 42, No. 3, pp. 9-31.
Grosser, A. (1963) 'General De Gaulle and the Foreign Policy of the Fifth Republic', *International Affairs*, Vol. 39, No. 2, pp. 553-66.
Guazzone, L. (1990) 'The Mediterranean Basin', *The International Spectator*, Vol. 25, No. 4.
Guy Peters, B. (1994) 'Agenda Setting in the European Community', *Journal of European Public Policy*, Vol. 1, No. 1, pp. 9-26.

Hadar, L.T. (1991) 'The United States, Europe and the Middle East', *World Policy Journal*, Vol. 8, No. 3, pp. 421-47.
Heisbourg, F. (2000) 'Europe's Strategic Ambitions: The Limits of Ambiguity', *Survival*, Vol. 2, No. 2, pp. 5-15.
Hill, C. (1993) 'The Capability-Expectations Gap, or Conceptualising Europe's International Role', *Journal of Common Market Studies*, Vol. 31, No. 3, pp. 103-29.
Hill, C. (2001) 'The EU's Capacity for Conflict Prevention', *European Foreign Affairs Review*, Vol. 6, No. 3, pp. 315-33.
Hix, S. (1994) 'The Study of the European Community: The Challenge to Comparative Politics', *West European Politics*, Vol. 17, pp. 1-30.
Hugon, P. (1993) 'L'Europe et le tiers monde: entre la mondialisation et la régionalisation', *Revue Tiers Monde*, Vol. 34, No. 136, pp. 725-48.
Huysmans, J. (2000) 'The European Union and the Securitization of Migration' *Journal of Common Market Studies*, Vol. 38, No. 5, pp. 751-78.
Joffé, G. (2000) 'Foreign investment and the rule of law' in A. de Vasconcelos and G. Joffé (eds) *Mediterranean Politics, Special Issue on the Barcelona Process: Building a Euro-Mediterranean Regional Community*, Vol. 5, No. 1, p. 34, pp. 33-52.
Juppé, A. (1995) 'Quel horizon pour la politique étrangère de la France?', *Politique Étrangère*, Vol. 60, No. 1, pp. 245-59.
Kebabdjian, G. (1995) 'Le libre-échange Euro-Maghrebin: Une évaluation macro-économique', *Révue Tiers Monde*, Vol. 36, No. 144, pp. 747-70.
Kramer, H. (1993) 'The European Community's Response to the "New Eastern Europe"', *Journal of Common Market Studies*, Vol. 31, No. 2, pp. 213-44.
Krasner, S. (1984) 'Approaches to the State', *Comparative Politics*, Vol. 16, No. 2, pp. 223-46.
Laipson, E. (1990) 'Thinking about the Mediterranean', *Mediterranean Quarterly*, Vol. 1, No. 1, pp. 50-66.
Lambert, J. (1971-2) 'The Cheshire Cat and the Pond: EEC and the Mediterranean area', *Journal of Common Market Studies*, vol. 10, no. 1, pp. 37-46.
Levi, M. (1972) 'La C.E.E. et les pays de la Méditerranée', *Politique Etrangère*, Vol. 37, No. 6, pp. 801-822.
Lowi, T. (1964) 'American Business, Public Policy, Case Studies and Political Theory', *World Politics*, Vol. 16, No. 4, pp. 677-715.
Lowi, T. (1971) 'Four Systems of Policy, Politics and Choice', *Public Administration Review*, Vol. 32, No. 4, pp. 298-310.
Marks, J. (1995) 'Looking for a New Deal from the EU', *Middle East Economic Digest*, Vol. 39, No. 20, 19 May, pp. 2-3.
Marks, J. (1998a) 'High Hopes and Low Motives: The New Euro-Mediterranean Partnership Initiative', *Mediterranean Politics*, Vol. 1, No. 1, pp. 1-24.
Marks, J. (1998b) 'The European Challenge to North African Economies: The Downside to the Euro-Med Partnership Initiative', *Journal of North African Studies*, Vol. 3, No. 2, pp. 47-58.
Mearsheimer, J. (1990) 'Back to the Future: Instability in Europe After the Cold War', *International Security*, Vol. 15, No. 1, pp. 5-56.
Mezdour, S. (1993) 'Les desequilibres economiques en economie ouverte (cas du Maghreb)', *Revue Algerienne des Sciences Juridiques, Economiques et Politiques*, Vol. 31, No. 3, pp. 511-29.
Moravcsik, A. (1991) 'Negotiating the Single European Act: National Interests and Conventional Statecraft in the European Community', *International Organization*, Vol. 45, No. 1, pp. 19-56.

Moravcsik, A. (1993) 'Preferences and Power in the International Community: A Liberal Intergovernmentalist Approach', *Journal of Common Market Studies*, Vol. 31, No. 4, pp. 473-524.
Moravcsik, A. (1997) 'Taking Preferences Seriously: A Liberal Theory of International Politics', *International Organization*, Vol. 51, Autumn, pp. 513-53.
Moravcsik, A. (1999) 'A New Statecraft? Supranational Entrepreneurs and International Cooperation', *International* Organization, Vol. 52, No. 3, pp. 267-306.
Mortimer, R. (1991) 'Islam and Multiparty Politics in Algeria', *Middle East Journal*, Vol. 45, No. 4, pp. 575-93.
Müller-Brandeck-Bocquet, G. (2002) 'The New CFSP and ESDP Decision-Making System of the European Union', *European Foreign Affairs Review*, Vol. 7, No. 3, pp. 257-82.
Nicolaides, K. and Meunier, S. (1999) 'Who Speaks for Europe? The Delegation of Trade Authority in the European Union', *Journal of Common Market Studies*, Vol. 37, No. 3, pp. 477-501.
Nienhaus, V. (1999) 'Promoting Development through a Euro-Mediterranean Free Trade Zone?', *European Foreign Affairs Review*, Vol. 4, No. 4, pp. 501-18.
Nugent, N. (1995) 'The Leadership Capacity of the European Commission', *Journal of European Public Policy*, Vol. 2, No. 4, pp. 603-2.
O'Sullivan, E. (1995) 'Cementing Peace with Prosperity', *Middle East Economic Digest: Middle East Business Weekly*, Vol. 37, No. 38.
Parsdorfer, C. (1998) 'La politique méditerranéenne de l'UE', *Développement et Coopération*, No. 3, May-June, pp. 12-14.
Pelkmans, J. and Murphy, A. (1991) 'Catapulted into leadership: The Community's trade and aid policies *vis-à-vis* Eastern Europe', *Journal of European Integration*, Vol. 24, Nos. 2-3, pp. 125-51.
Pigasse, J. (1995) '15+12: Donnant-donnant', *Jeune Afrique*, Vol. 36, No. 1822, 7-13 December, pp. 12-14.
Pollack, M. (1994) 'Creeping Competence: The Expanding Agenda of the European Community', *Journal of Public Policy*, Vol. 14, No. 2, pp. 95-145.
Pollack, M. (1997) 'Delegation, Agency and Agenda-Setting in the European Union', *International Organization*, Vol. 51, No.1, pp. 99-134.
Provost, L. (1996) 'Paris et Algers entre brouilles et complicités', *Le Monde Diplomatique*, September, pp. 4-5.
Puchala, D.J. (1999) 'Institutionalism, Intergovernmentalism and European Integration', *Journal of Common Market Studies*, Vol. 37, No. 2, pp. 317-31.
Putnam, R. (1988) 'Diplomacy and Domestic Politics: The Logic of Two-level Games', *International Organization*, Vol. 42, No. 3, pp. 427-460.
Ravenhill, J. (1990) 'The North-South Balance of Power', *International Affairs*, Vol. 66, No. 4, pp. 39-51.
Reglesberger, E. and Wessels, W. (1996) 'The CFSP Institutions and Procedures: A Third Way for the Second Pillar', *European Foreign Affairs Review*, Vol. 1, No. 2, pp. 29-54.
Renier, Y. (1988) 'L'Europe et le sud de la Méditerranée', *Le Courrier*, No. 108, Brussels: Economic and Social Committee of the European Communities, March/April, pp. 53-57.
Ritekie, D. (1996) 'L'Algérie renoue avec la croissance', *Jeune Afrique*, No. 1827, 11-17 January, p. 28.
Roberts, H. (1992) 'The Algerian State and the Challenge of Democracy', *Government and Opposition*, Vol. 27, No. 4, pp. 433-54.
Roberts, H. (1995) 'Algeria's Ruinous Impasse and the Honourable Way Out', *International Affairs*, Vol. 71, No. 2, pp. 247-67.
Scharpf, F. (1988) 'The Joint-Decision Trap: Lessons from German Federalism and European Integration', *Public Administration*, Vol. 66, No. 3, pp. 239-78.

Schmitter, P. (1969) 'Three Neo-Functional Hypotheses About International Integration', *International Organization*, Vol. 33, No. 2, pp. 161-66.

Sid Ahmed, A. (1993) 'Les relations économiques entre l'Europe et le Maghreb', *Revue Tiers Monde*, Vol. 34, No. 136, Oct-Dec, pp. 759-80.

Smith, B. (1998) 'Algeria: The Horror', *The New York Review of Books*, Vol. 45, No. 7, April 23, pp. 27-31.

Smith, M. (1996b) 'The European Union and a Changing Europe: Establishing the Boundaries of Order', *Journal of Common Market Studies*, Vol. 43, No. 1, pp. 5-28.

Smith, M. E. (2001) 'Diplomacy by Decree: The Legalization of EU Foreign Policy', *Journal of Common Market Studies*, Vol. 39, No. 1, pp. 81-106.

Smyrl, M. (1998) 'When (and How) Do the Commission's Preferences Matter?', *Journal of Common Market Studies*, Vol. 36, No. 1, pp. 79-100.

Spencer, C. (1997) 'Building confidence in the Mediterranean', *Mediterranean Politics*, Vol. 2, No.2, pp. 23-48.

Spencer, C. (1998) 'The End of International Enquiries? The UN Eminent Persons' Mission to Algeria', *Mediterranean Politics*, Vol. 33, No. 3, pp. 126-33.

Spencer, C. (2001) 'The EU and Common Strategies: The Revealing Case of the Mediterranean', *European Foreign Affairs Review*, Vol. 6, No. 1, pp. 31-51.

Stavridis, S. (2001) '"Militarising the EU: The Concept of Civilian Power Europe Revisited', *The International Spectator*, Vol. 36, No. 4, p. 43-50.

Stevens, C. (1990) 'The Impact of Europe 1992 on the Maghreb and Sub-Saharan Africa', *Journal of Common Market Studies*, Vol. 24, No. 2, pp. 217-41.

Stone Sweet, A. and Sandholtz, W. (1997) 'European Integration and Supranational Governance', *Journal of European Public Policy*, Vol. 4, No. 3, pp. 297-317.

Tovias, A. (1997) 'The Economic Impact of the Euro-Mediterranean Free Trade Area Initiative in Mediterranean Non-Member Countries', *Mediterranean Politics*, Vol. 2, No.1, pp. 31-52.

Verges, M. (1996) 'Les jeunes, le stade, le FIS: Vers une analyse de l'action protestaire', *Monde Arabe: Maghreb-Machrek*, No. 154, October-December, pp. 48-54.

Waltz, K. (1993) 'The Emerging Structure of International Politics', *International Security*, Vol. 18, No. 2, pp. 44-79.

Wessels, W. (1997) 'An Ever Closer Fusion? A Dynamic Macro-political View on Integration Processes', *Journal of Common Market Studies*, Vol. 35, No. 2, pp. 267-300.

Young, A. (2000) 'The Adaptation of European Foreign Economic Policy: From Rome to Seattle', *Journal of Common Market Studies*, Vol. 38, No. 1, pp. 93-116.

Zoubir, Y.H. and Bouandel, Y. (1998) Islamism and the Algerian Political Crisis: International Responses', *Cambridge Review of International Affairs*, Vol. 11, No. 2, pp. 117-33.

## Official Documents

Aliboni, R., Said Aly, A. and de Vasconcelos, A. (1997) *Euromesco Working Group on Political and Security Cooperation/Working Group on Arms Control, Confidence Building and Conflict Prevention - Joint Report*, Lisbon, April.

Centre d'Etudes Prospectives et d'Informations Internationales (1988) 'La dette des pays méditerranées', *Problèmes économiques*, No. 2062, Paris: La Documentation Française.

Council Regulation (EC) *Financial and Technical Measures to Accompany (MEDA) the reform of economic and social structures in the framework of the Euro-Mediterranean Partnership*, No. 1488/96, Official Journal OJ L 189, Brussels, 30 July 1996.

Council Secretariat (1996) 'Euro-Mediterranean Conference, Barcelona, 27-28 November 1995: Thematic Discussions', *Transmission Note*, Euro-Med 3/96, Brussels, 13 February.
De Charette, H. (1995) 'Interview with the Minister of Foreign Affairs in "Al-Ahram Weekly"', *Official Documentation: Ministry of Foreign Affairs*, Paris: Ministry of Foreign Affairs, 26 July.
Djebbar, S. (1995) 'Evidence to the House of Lords', *Eleventh Report from the House of Lords: Relations Between the EU and the Maghreb Countries*, 11 November, London: HMSO.
Dimeglio, W. (1995) *Pour un Partenariat Industriel avec le Maghreb et les PECO: Rapport au Premier Ministre*, Paris: La Documentation Française.
Economic and Social Committee (1989) 'Opinion on the Mediterranean Policy of the European Community', Economic and Social Committee, *Official Journal* C221, 28 August.
Economic and Social Committee (1992) 'Opinion on the Mediterranean Policy of the European Community', *Official Journal* C40, 17 February.
European Commission (1979) *Report on the Global Mediterranean Policy and Enlargement of the Community*, SEC 79/103, April.
European Commission (1989a) *Redirecting the Community's Mediterranean Policy*, SEC (89) 1961, 23 November.
European Commission (1989c) *Redirecting the Community's Mediterranean Policy*, SEC (89) 1961 Final.
European Commission (1990a) *Towards a New Mediterranean Policy*, SEC (90) 812, 1 June.
European Commission (1991a) *Proposal for a Council Regulation (EEC) concerning financial cooperation in respect of all the Mediterranean non-member countries*, COM (91) 48 Final, 19 February.
European Commission (1991b) *Additional financial aid to for countries in the Middle East and Mediterranean affected by the Gulf War*, COM (91) 61 Final, 28 February
European Commission (1992) *The Future of Relations Between the Community and the Maghreb*, SEC (92) 401, 30 April.
European Commission (1993a) *Future Relations between the Community and the Middle East*, COM (93) 375, 8 September.
European Commission (1993b) 'EC Support to the Middle East Peace Process', *Communication from the Commission to the Council and the European Parliament*, COM (93) 458, 29 September.
European Commission (1994) *Strengthening the Mediterranean Policy of the European Union: Establishing a Euro-Mediterranean Partnership*, COM (94) 427 Final, 19 October.
European Commission (1995a) *Euro-Mediterranean Conference*, Doc No. 19/95, Brussels.
European Commission (1995b) *Barcelona Declaration and Work Programme*, Brussels.
European Commission (1995c) *Proposal for a Council and Commission Decision on the conclusion of a Euro-Mediterranean Agreement establishing an Association between the European Communities and the Member states on the one part, and the Kingdom of Morocco, on the other part*, COM (95) 740 Final.
European Commission (1995d) *Strengthening the Mediterranean Policy of the European Union: Proposals for a Euro-Mediterranean Partnership*, COM (95) 72, 8 March.
European Commission (1995e) *Proposal for a Council Regulation on Financial and Technical Measures to Support the Reform of Economic and Social Structures in Mediterranean Non-member Countries and Territories*, COM (95) 204.

European Commission (1996) *Joint Report from the Presidency and Commission: Mediterranean Policy – Follow Up to Barcelona*, 3 December.
European Commission (1998a) *The Role of the European Union in the Peace Process and its Future Assistance to the Middle East*, COM (97) 715 Final.
European Commission (1998b) 'EU - Israel: Implementation of the interim agreement in the framework of a strengthened regional cooperation', *Press Release* IP/98/426, Strasbourg, 13 May.
European Commission (1998d) *The Euro-Mediterranean Partnership and the Single Market*, COM (98) 320, 22 September.
European Commission (2000a) *Reinvigorating the Barcelona Process*, COM (2000) 497 Final.
European Commission (2000b) *The Barcelona Process: Five Years On 1995-2000*, Luxembourg: Office for Official Publications of the European Communities.
European Commission (2002a) *The Barcelona Process: 2001 Review*, Brussels.
European Council (1993) 'Conclusions of the European Council meeting in Brussels', *European Political Cooperation: Documentation Bulletin*, Brussels, p. 590.
European Council and Council of the Union (1995) *Draft Mandate for the 1996 Intergovernmental Conference*, Brussels, 16 January.
European Council (2000) *Common Strategy of the European Council of 19 June 2000 on the Mediterranean Region*, 2000/458/CFSP, Official Journal of the European Communities L183, 22 July, Brussels.
European Parliament (1988a) (Committee on External Economic Relations), *Report on Economic and Trade Relations Between the EEC and the Mediterranean Countries Following Enlargement of the Community*, A2-325/88, December.
European Parliament (1988b) 'Resolution on repression in Algeria', *Official Journal of the European Communities*, OJC326, 17 November.
European Parliament (1991) (Committee on External Economic Relations) *Report on a Revamped Mediterranean Policy*, Brussels, 3 May.
European Parliament (1995a) *EC-Turkey Relations – Human Rights in Turkey*, Doc. No. PE195.288, Brussels, December.
European Parliament (1995b) *Report on the Mediterranean Policy of the European Union with a View to the Barcelona Conference*, A4-232/95, Brussels, 3 October.
European Parliament (1996a) *Briefing on the Common Foreign and Security Policy*, JF/bo/103/96, Luxembourg, March.
European Parliament (1996b) *Report on the Conclusion of a Euro-Mediterranean Agreement*, A4-0173/96, Brussels.
European Parliament (1996c) *Report on the Proposal for a Council Regulation on Financial and Technical Cooperation Measures to Accompany the Reform of Economic and Social Structures in the Framework of the Euro-Mediterranean Partnership (MEDA)*, A4-0198/96, Brussels.
European Parliament (1996d) *Report on the Middle East Peace Process*, Doc. No. A4-0351/96, 4 November.
European Parliament (1997) *Report on the Joint Report by the Presidency of the Council and the Commission on Mediterranean Policy - follow up to the Barcelona Conference*, A4-0027/97, Brussels.
European Parliament (1998) (Delegations for Cooperation with the Maghreb, Machrek and Gulf Countries) *Hearing on the Euro-Mediterranean Partnership*, March.
General Affairs Council (1998) *2111th Council Meeting*, Luxembourg, 29 June.
Haddaoui, K. (1995) 'Evidence to the House of Lords', *Eleventh Report from the House of Lords: Relations Between the EU and the Maghreb Countries*, 11 November, London: HMSO.

Hoekman, B. and Djankov, S. (1996) *Catching Up With Eastern Europe? The European Union's Mediterranean Free Trade Initiative*, World Bank Research Working Paper 1562, Washington: World Bank.

Israeli Mission to the European Communities (1997) *Note d'Information*, 25 February, Brussels.

Köhler, M. (1994) *Towards a Comprehensive Policy Framework for Relations Between the European Union and the Mediterranean Basin*, Working Paper W-10, Directorate General for Research (DGIV), European Parliament, Brussels, November.

Langer, B. (1993) 93/451, Question No H-1095/93 on the Israel/Palestine Peace Process, *European Political Cooperation: Documentation Bulletin*, Brussels, p. 538.

NATO (1992) *The Transformation of an Alliance: The Decisions of NATO's Heads of State and Government*, Brussels: NATO Office of Information and Press.

OECD (1997) (Development Assistance Committee) *Development Cooperation*, Paris: OECD, p. A67-8.

Petri, P. (1997a) *Trade Strategies for the Southern Mediterranean*, OECD Development Centre, Technical Papers No. 127, Paris: OECD.

Petri, P. (1997b) *The Case of Missing Foreign Investment in the Southern Mediterranean*, OECD Technical Papers, No. 128, Paris: OECD.

Reflection Group (1995) *Report for the 1996 IGC*, Brussels: Office for Official Publications of the European Communities.

Roque, A. (1997) Position paper presented at Civil Forum Euromed, Malta 1997 in *Le Dialogue Interculturel en Méditerranée,* Valletta: Foundation for International Studies, Unversity of Malta.

Salt, J. (1991) *Current and Future International Migration Trends Affecting Europe*, Strasbourg: Council of Europe.

United Nations (1998) *Report of the Panel Appointed by the Secretary-General of the United Nations to Gather Information on the Situation in Algeria*, New York.

### Working Papers

Fouet, S. (1998) *The Middle-East Peace Process: de jure – de facto realities. What is the Role of Europe?*, Presentation to Summer School on The Mediterranean and the New International Order, University of Catania, 5-12 July.

Guy Peters, B. (1998) 'The New Institutionalism and Administrative Reform: Examining Alternative Models', *Estudios Working Papers 1998/113*, Madrid: Instituto Juan March de Estudios e Investigaciones.

Khader, B. (1997) *L'Europe, le proche-orient et la Palestine, 1957-1999: Synthèse et enseignements*, Paper presented to Seminar, 'The EU's Common Foreign and Security Policy and World Responsibilities', Institut d'Etudes Européennes, Brussels, 3-5 October.

Pargeter, A. (2001) *Italy and the Western Mediterranean*, Working Paper 26/01, ESRC "One Europe or Several?" Programme, Brighton: Sussex European Institute.

Senior Nello, S. and Smith, K. (1997) 'The Consequence of Eastern Enlargement of the European Union in Stages', *EUI Working Paper*, No. 97/51, Florence: Robert Schuman Centre, European University Institute.

Xenakis, D. (1998) 'The Barcelona Process: Some Lessons From Helsinki', *Jean Monnet Working Papers in Comparative and International Politics*, No. JMWP 17.98, Catania: University of Catania.

Young, A. (1998) *Interpretation and 'Soft Integration' in the Adaptation of the European Community's Foreign Economic Policy*, Sussex European Institute Working Paper No. 29, Brighton: University of Sussex.

Youngs, R. (2002) *The European Union and Democracy in the Arab-Muslim World*, Working Paper No. 2, Brussels: Centre for European Policy Studies.

**Internet References**

Aliboni, R. (1997) 'Policy analysis and public policy in the Euro-Med context: Euromesco as a confidence-building measure', Presentation, *Euro-Med Information and Training Programme for Diplomats*, Malta, 15-17 March, Valletta: Mediterranean Academy for Diplomatic Studies, http://www.diplomacy.edu/euromed/training/documents/aliboni.htm.

Amnesty International (1994) *Annual Report*, http://www.amnesty.org.

Committee of Independent Experts (1999) *First Report on Allegations Regarding Fraud, Mismanagement and Nepotism in the European Commission*, Brussels, 15 March, http://www.europarl.eu.int/experts/en/3.htm.

Council of Ministers (1996a) *Declaration by the Presidency on Behalf of the European Union on the Middle East Peace Process*, PESC/96/83, October 1, Rapid Database, http://europa.eu.int/rapid/cgi.

Council of Ministers (1996b) *1958th Council Meeting: General Affairs*, Luxembourg: 28-29 October, http://europa.eu.int/rapid.

Dumas, R. (1991) 'Interview à Europe 1', *Déclarations de politique étrangère depuis 1990*, Paris: Ministère des Affaires Etrangères, 14 November, http://www.diplomatie.fr/cgi/nph-bwcgis/BASIS/epic/www/doc/SF.

Egyptian State Information Service (1998) *Letter from Cairo*, No. 202, June 11-13, Internet Edition, http://www.uk.sis.gov.eg/public/letter/html/frame202.htm.

EUROMESCO (2002) *Working Group I - First Year Report: Security and Common Ground in the Euro-Med Partnership*, Paper 17, June, http://www.euromesco.org/euromesco/publi_artigo.asp?cod_artigo=78885#1.

European Commission (1989b) *Commission Proposes Renewed Mediterranean Policy*, Press Release, P/89/71, Rapid Database, http ://europa.eu.int/rapid/cgi.

European Commission (1990b) *Relations Between the European Community and the Arab Maghreb Union*, Memo/90/58, Rapid Database, http://europa.eu.int/rapid/cgi.

European Commission (1997) *Second Euro-Mediterranean Ministerial Conference*, Malta, 15-16 April, http://www.euromed.net.

European Commission (1998c) *Euro-Mediterranean Partnership: Conclusions of the Second Conference of the Ministers of Culture*, http://europa.eu.int/comm/external_relations/euromed/conf/sect/culture2.htm.

European Commission (2002b) *Euro-Mediterranean Partnership Regional Strategy Paper 2002-2006 and Regional Indicative Programme 2002-2004*, http://europa.eu.int/comm/external_relations/euromed/rsp/, p. 10.

European Council (1992) *Conclusions of the Presidency*, Rapid Database, http://europa.eu.int/rapid/cgi/.

European Parliament, Committee on Foreign Affairs (1997) 'Ahmed Attaf accepts EP delegation', *Rapid Database*, http://www.europarl.eu.int/dg3/sdp/newsrp/en/n971127.htm#1 Brussels, 27 November.

Friis, L. (1998) 'The End of the Beginning' of Eastern Enlargement – Luxembourg Summit and Agenda-setting', *European Integration Online Papers (EioP)*, Vol. 2, No. 7,

http://eiop.or.at/eiop/texte/1998-007a.htm.
Front Islamique du Salut (1994) 'The Journey Through Time', *FIS Information Bureau Website*, http://www.fisalgeria.org/history.html.
Gillespie, R. (1997) 'Northern European Perceptions of the Barcelona Process', *Revista CIDOB d 'Afers Internacionals*, No. 37, Internet Version, http://www.cidob.es/Castellano/Publicaciones/ Afers/37.html.
Haddam, A. (1998) 'A Letter To His Excellency, Robin Cook, Foreign Minister of the United Kingdom', *FIS Information Bureau Website*, http://www.fisalgeria.org/communiques/TROIKA.html, 25 January.
Hamdani, S. (1996) 'The Barcelona Declaration: A Partnership Looking for Implementation and Improvement', *Workshop*, http://www.diplomacy.edu/wshop/abarcel/papers/Hamdani.htm.
Hollis, R. (1995) *After Madrid: The EU and the Peace Process*, Palestinian Academic Society for the Study of International Affairs, Seminar, March, http://www.passia.org.
House of Lords Select Committee on the European Union (2001) *Ninth Report: The Common Mediterranean Strategy*, http://www.parliament.the-stationery-office.co.uk/pa/ld200001/ldselect/ldeucom/ldeucom.htm.
Joffé, G. (2001) 'European multilateralism and soft power projection in the Mediterranean' in F. Tanner (ed.) *The European Union as a Security Actor in the Mediterranean: ESPD, Soft Power and Peacemaking in Euro-Mediterranean Relations*, Zürcher Beiträge zur Sicherheitspolitik und Konfliktforschung, No. 61, Zürich, http://www.fsk.ethz.ch/documents/Beitraege/zu_61/ zu_61_chapter2.pdf.
Kadry Said, M. (1999) *Confidence Building Measures: A Pratical Approach*, EuroMeSCo's Working Group on the Euro-Mediterranean Charter for Peace and Stability, October, http://194.235.129.80/euromesco/publi_artigo.asp?cod_artigo=38747.
Karkutli, N. and Bützler, D. (1999) *MEDA Democracy Evaluation, Final Report: Evaluation of the MEDA Democracy Programme 1996 – 1998*, http://www.euromed.net/meda/evaluation/mdp/final-report-meda-96-98-16.htm.
Khader, B. (1996) 'Euro-Mediterranean Partnership (EMP): The Unaccomplished Tasks', *Institute for Prospective Technological Studies*, Report 25, Seville, http:// www.jrc.es/iptsreport/vol25/english/MED1E256.htm.
Marín, M. (1997) *The European Union's Mediterranean Policy*, Address to the Nobel Institute, Oslo, May 23, http://europa.eu.int/rapid.
Matutes, A. (1989) 'Commissioner Matutes reviews issues for the Community in the Mediterranean', *Speech to Pio Manzu Conference*, Rimini, Press Release IP/89/776, Rapid Database, http ://europa.eu.int/rapid/cgi.
Minasi, N. (1998) 'The Euro-Mediterranean Free Trade Area and its Impact on the Economies Involved', *Jean Monnet Working Papers in Comparative and International Politics*, JMWP 16.98, Catania: University of Catania, http://www.fscpo.unict.it/vademec/jmwp16.htm.
Peters, J. (1997) *Europe and the Middle East Peace Process: Emerging from the sidelines*, Centre for Euro-Mediterranean Studies, University of Reading, http://www.rdg.ac.uk/EIS/GSEIS/EMC/pubs.html, May, pp. 5-6.
Solana, J. (2001) 'Europe: Security in the Twenty-First Century', The Olaf Palme Memorial Lecture, *CFSP High Representative Website*, http://ue.eu.int/solana/default.asp?lang=en, 20 June.
Stavridis, S. (2002) 'The First Two Parliamentary Fora of the Euro-Mediterranean Partnership: An Assessment', *Jean Monnet Working Papers in Comparative and International Politics*, No. 40, May, University of Catania, http://www.fscpo.unict.it/EuroMed/jmwp40.htm.

The Tami Steinmetz Center for Peace Research, Tel Aviv University (1997) *Israeli-Palestinian People to People Peace Index*, http://spirit.tau.ac.il/code/instit.html.
United Nations General Assembly (1990) *Strengthening of Security and Cooperation in the Mediterranean Region*, Resolution A/RES/45/79, 12 December, http://heimedac.unige.ch/V/T/1310.html.
Vedrine, H. (1998) 'Réunion Informelle des Ministres des Affaires Etrangères de l'Union européenne', *Point de Presse du Ministre des Affaires Etrangères*, Edinburgh 14 March, http:// www.diplomatie.fr/cgi/nph-bwcgis/BASIS.
World Bank (2001) *Annual Report 2001*, Internet Edition, http://www.worldbank.org/annualreport/2001/wbar2001.htm.

# Index

agriculture 28-9, 49, 51
   and the Euro-Mediterranean
      Agreements 56-61, 107, 179
   Mediterranean products 29, 30,
      32-7, 39, 55, 101
Algeria 7, 44, 46, 53, 75, 102, 105,
   147-9, 151, 171
   elections 153-4
   EU mission (1998) 158-9
   and the Euro-Mediterranean
      Partnership 147, 160-4
   Front Islamique du Salut 157
   gas exports 97, 147, 150-51, 153-5,
      160, 164-5
   Groupe Islamique Armé 155-7
   and the IMF 149, 154, 157
   Islamic movements 149, 151-3,
      155, 162, 164
   trade with EU 150
Aliboni, Roberto 88
Amnesty International 157
Arab-Israeli War (1973) 31
Arab-Israeli relations 70, 75, 77-8,
   81, 87, 140, 169, 172
Arab League 75, 134, 143
Arab Maghreb Union 50, 53, 97, 177
Arafat, Yasser 113, 126, 128, 130,
   134, 137, 140, 144
Association Agreements 27, 28, 29,
   30, 32, 38, 43, 96, 177
Attaf, Ahmed 158, 159, 161
Austria 158

Bachrach, Peter 165
Badini, Antonio 76, 90
Balladur, Edouard 72, 74, 105, 156
Barak, Ehud 145
Baratz, Morton S. 165
Barbé, Esther 72, 128
Barcelona process 100-101, 109,
   178; *see also* Euro-
      Mediterranean Partnership
Barcelona Conference 71-6, 89, 112-13

Barcelona Declaration 72, 75-6, 78,
   82-84, 98, 106, 110, 112, 125,
   135, 161, 171, 176-7
   and the Common Foreign and
      Security Policy 175
   Economic and Financial Chapter
      81-4, 102
   Euro-Med Committee 81, 113
   and the European Commission 108
   and human rights 111, 161
   and the Middle East Peace
      Process 75, 123, 135, 133-7
   origins of 69-72
   Palermo meeting 136, 144
   Political and Security Chapter 73-5,
      177
   Senior Officials Committee 75,
      79, 81, 100, 112-13, 134
   Social, Cultural and Human
      Affairs Chapter 84-6
   Stability Charter 176
   Work Programme 74, 77-84
Belgium 75, 103, 158
Bildt, Carl 129
Bouandel, Youcef 147
Boudiaf, Mohamed 155
Bouteflika, Abdelaziz 161, 162
van den Broek, Hans 108
Bush, George W. 12
Buzan, Barry 48

Cardoso e Cunha, Carlos 155
Chadli, Benjedid 148-9, 151-2, 154,
   165
Charette, Hervé de 128, 129
Chirac, Jacques 78, 128
Christopher, Warren 129
Çiller, Tansu 111
'civilian power' 2, 11, 12, 48, 176-8, 181
Clarke, Michael 152
Cold War 26, 37, 44, 47, 103, 171
Common Agricultural Policy 33, 38,
   57, 60, 107, 179

Common European Security and Defence
    Policy (EU) 1, 6, 14, 20, 174
Common Foreign and Security Policy
    (EU) 3, 5-7, 9-10, 14, 17, 20, 174
    and Algeria 162
    decision making 6
    and the Euro-Mediterranean
        Partnership 76, 78-9, 169, 175, 179
    High Representative 6, 136
    and the Middle East 127-89, 136,
        140
    and Palestinian elections 174
    'pillars' 136, 141
    Policy Planning and Early
        Warning Unit (EU) 6, 13
    St Malo Declaration 20
Common Strategy for the
    Mediterranean (EU) 77, 136, 175
Conference on Security and
    Cooperation in Europe 53, 71
Conference on Security and
    Cooperation in the Mediterranean
    53, 70-1, 170
confidence and security building
    79-80, 174
Cook, Robin 131, 158, 159
Cooperation Agreements 28-9, 37
COREPER 59, 113
Council of Ministers (EU) 28, 36, 99, 106
    and the Barcelona process 72, 112
    and the Euro-Mediterranean
        Association Agreements 56,
        59, 98, 108
    and the European Commission
        56-7, 59
    General Affairs Council 72
    and MEDA 105, 109
    Presidency 91, 95, 98, 103, 112-13, 129
    Secretariat 113-15
    Troika 76, 112-13, 129
    Working Groups 112, 121
Court of Auditors (EU) 145, 173
cut flowers 58, 61, 104
Cyprus 36, 46, 55, 62, 80, 96, 174, 177

debt crisis 44-5, 51, 62, 83
Delors, Jacques 13, 71, 124, 155
Denmark 103
Dini, Lamberto 158
Dumas, Roland 124, 152

East Jerusalem 134
Economic and Social Committee (EU)
    49, 57
Egypt 34, 46, 55, 105, 131
    agricultural exports 57, 59
    and the Barcelona process 75
enlargement (EU) 26, 32; see
    also European Union
    Mediterranean 32, 35-8
Euro-Arab Dialogue 31, 40
EuroMarFor 178
Euro-Mediterranean Association
    Agreements 25, 43, 55-62, 71,
    74, 86, 96-106, 110, 112, 117,
    121, 123, 174, 176, 179
    Algeria 148, 160-61, 163
    Palestinian territories 137, 139
Euro-Med Civil Forum 87
Euro-Mediterranean Parliamentary
    Forum 85, 110
Euro-Mediterranean Partnership 1, 11,
    15-16, 43, 69-70, 72-3, 76, 95, 177
    179 see also Barcelona process
    and Algeria 147, 160-63, 166
    and Arab-Israeli relations 72, 87,
        169, 177
    budget 65, 74, 81-2, 86, 105-106,
        109, 111, 171-2, 176
    civil society 110
    and EU member states 98, 101-6
    and Foreign Direct Investment
        83
    free trade area 71, 81-3, 172
    link with Middle East Peace
        Process 77, 125, 133-7, 141,
        172
    and Non-Governmental
        Organisations 84-5, 97
    origins 52-3, 55-6, 96, 109
    and strategic action 169-72
    theory 96-103
EuroMeSCo 80, 91
European Commission 10, 33-4, 36,
    49-51, 54-5, 70, 84, 95, 106,
    174-5
    and Algeria 149, 151, 160, 166
    and the Barcelona process 108
    and the Common Foreign and
        Security Policy 54
    DG1B 57, 59, 70, 86, 107-8, 111, 113

and the Euro-Mediterranean
  Partnership 98-9, 106-9, 116,
  169-70, 179
and Israel 100, 138-9, 145-6
and MEDA 105, 108-9, 120
and the Middle East 57, 125-6, 137
negotiation of Euro-Mediterranean
  Association Agreements 56-7,
  101, 106-7, 138
and the Palestinian territories 138-9
relationship with the Council of
  Ministers 51, 56-7, 59
relationship with the European
  Parliament 111
and strategic action 170
and trade negotiations 37
European Community 1, 15, 26, 28, 30
'Community method' 5, 10
European Council
  Brussels (1993) 127-8
  Cannes (1995) 74, 100-101, 105
  Corfu (1994) 70
  Edinburgh (1992) 105, 107, 180
  Essen (1994) 70
  Lisbon (1992) 54
  Luxembourg (1991) 155
  Strasbourg (1989) 49
European Court of Justice 40, 106
European Development Fund 100,
  105, 119
European Investment Bank 50, 126
Europeanization 4
European Parliament 49, 95, 173, 175-6
  and Algeria 149, 160
  and the Euro-Mediterranean
    Partnership 109-12
  and the Euro-Mediterranean
    Parliamentary Forum 110
  and MEDA 111, 120
  negotiation of Euro-
    Mediterranean Association
    Agreements 110, 120-21
  and Turkey 110-11
European Political Cooperation 5,
  30-31, 127, 152-3
European Union 51-2, 97-9
  aid to Algeria 154-5
  and Algeria 158, 151-4, 162-3
  as a 'civilian power' 2, 11-12,
    176-8

Common Commercial Policy 4, 9,
  26, 32
defence policy 5-6
development policy 28-31
eastern enlargement 44, 49, 61,
  88, 171, 173, 174, 181
enlargement 96-7, 105, 108, 117
foreign policy 5-6, 10-13, 54, 175
and human rights 162
and Israel 110, 135, 138-9, 142-4
and the Middle East 52-4
and the Middle East Peace
  Process 74, 124-7, 132-3, 137,
  142, 179
and the Palestinian Authority 110
and the Palestinian Territories
  110, 127, 131-3, 137, 139
'pillars' 175
and the Regional Economic
  Development Working Group
  124, 127, 133
strategic action 12-14, 87, 98,
  114, 169, 170, 172
trade policy 73, 96, 103-4
and Turkey 110-11

Fassino, Pierre 158
Federal Republic of Germany 29, 32
FEMISE 82
Fernandez Ordoñez, Francisco 69, 71
foreign economic policy 1, 2, 15, 18, 53
France 26-8, 49, 104, 158, 161
  agriculture policy 58
  and Algeria 102, 147-52, 155-6,
    161-2, 167
  and the Barcelona process 70-71,
    74-5, 101, 113
  Council Presidency 74, 112
  and the Euro-Mediterranean
    Partnership 103, 107, 112
  and Islam 47, 70-1, 152, 155
  Loi Pasqua 157
  and the Maghreb 27, 31, 52-3,
    118, 147-8
  and MEDA 105
  and the 'Mediterranean lobby' 49,
    53, 58
  Muslims in 157
  and the Palestinian Authority 128-9
  Socialist Party 149

Stability Pact (Central and
  Eastern Europe) 74, 177
Stability Charter (Mediterranean) 78
Friis, Likke 24, 96, 98, 179
Front de liberation nationale 151-2,
  164; *see also* Algeria
Front Islamique du Salut 148,
  151-4, 165-6; *see also* Algeria
  and the Algerian elections 152-4
  and the European Union 158-9
  and France 167

Gadhaffi, Muammar 75
GATT 35, 40
  Uruguay Round 45-6, 51, 61, 181
  Germany 47, 57-8, 103-5
  and the Barcelona process 113, 129
  and the Euro-Mediterranean
    Agreements 58, 104
  and MEDA 105, 107
de Gaulle, Charles 31
Ginsberg, Roy 9, 23, 34, 139
Global Mediterranean Policy 25,
  30-37, 52
Gonzalez, Felipe 53, 71, 88, 129
Greece 26-8, 33, 35, 37-8, 101, 181
  Council Presidency 70
  and the Euro-Mediterranean
    Partnership 80
  and Turkey 80, 113, 176
Green, Pauline (MEP) 111
Groupe Islamique Armé 155-7; *see
  also* Algeria
Gulf War 43, 52, 65

Haaland Matlary, Janne 155
Hachani, Abdelkader 153
Hadar, Leon 124
Haddam, Anwar 159
Hebron 128, 130
Heisbourg, François 13
Henig, Stanley 27
Hill, Christopher 2, 7, 8, 169
  'capabilities-expectations gap' 11,
    177-9
Hoffmann, Stanley 9, 10, 11

International Monetary Fund 51, 97,
  100, 149, 154, 163, 174
Ireland 113, 114

Islam 47-8, 73, 170-1
Israel 36, 46, 53, 123
  and the Barcelona process
    134-6
  and the European Union 40,
    100-101, 124, 128-31, 135,
    137-8, 176
  and the Middle East Peace Process
    55
  and the Palestinian Territories 77,
    81, 89, 176
  relations with Arab states 70
  settlements policy 134, 143
Italy 26, 38, 49, 52, 57, 89, 158, 161
  agricultural exports 33, 38-9, 58
  and Algerian gas 150, 165
  and the Barcelona process 70, 71, 76
  Council Presidency 76, 89, 113
  and EU Mediterranean policy 29,
    33, 39, 49
  and the Euro-Mediterranean
    Partnership 107, 112
Izquierdo, Fernando 128

Jordan 46, 75, 104, 131
Joseph, Paul 158
Juppé, Alain 156

Kebir, Rabah 156
Keohane, Robert 9, 10, 12
Khader, Bichara 76
Kinkel, Klaus 147, 158
Kissinger, Henry 8, 123
Kohl, Helmut 119
Kosovo 178

Lebanon 46, 69, 91, 127, 129
Levy, David 113, 129, 130, 134, 138,
  145
liberal intergovernmentalism 9-10,
  101-102, 104, 118
Libya 46, 53, 75, 89, 92
Liikanen, Erkki 108
Lomé Convention 31, 34, 105
Lowi, Theodore 95, 98, 100, 115, 118
Luxembourg 52, 78, 103, 113, 114
  and Algeria 158

McDonagh, Bobby 6
Maghreb 27, 29, 32-3, 37, 44, 50, 54

## Index

and the Barcelona process 73, 172, 178
and the European Union 29-30, 50, 70, 103
Malek, Rheda 156
Malta 27, 33, 36, 46, 55, 62, 96, 134
 and the Euro-Mediterranean Partnership 70, 78, 174, 178
mandate 130-32
de Marco, Guido 70
Marín, Manuel 73, 75, 83, 88, 105, 107, 112, 134, 138, 139
Marquina, Antonio 88
Mashreq 47, 128, 172
Matutes, Abel 44, 47, 49, 53, 64, 88, 155, 166
MEDA 1, 81-2, 85, 96-101, 103, 105, 160, 163, 179; *see also* Euro Mediterranean Partnership
 Democracy 111, 178
 negotiations 105-111, 115, 120
de Michelis, Gianni 49, 70, 71
Middle East 43, 54, 83, 97, 172, 176, 178
Middle East Peace Process 7, 55, 61, 69-70, 74, 76, 80, 90, 123-46, 176
 Arms Control and Regional Security Working Group 125
 and the Barcelona process 79, 112-14, 133-7, 172
 and the Euro-Mediterranean Partnership 133-6, 172
 final status talks 132
 Madrid Conference (1991) 124-5, 141
 Oslo Declaration 125, 129, 134-5, 139
 Paris Interim Protocol on Economic Relations 145
 Regional Economic Development Working Group 124, 133
 Washington Agreements 124-5
 Washington Donors' Conference 132
 Wye River Memorandum 132
van Mierlo, Hans 134
Mitterrand, François 149, 151, 152
Moïsi, Dominique 158
Moratinos, Miguel 123, 129, 133, 137, 142, 177

Moravcsik, Andrew 9, 101, 102, 103, 104, 118
Morocco 26, 28, 29, 40, 46, 47, 51, 54, 70, 83
 Association Agreement 29, 32-4
 and the Euro-Mediterranean Partnership 55
 and the European Union 29, 32, 37, 44
 negotiation of Euro-Mediterranean Association Agreement 56, 58-9, 71, 101, 104, 110, 120
 and Spain 104
Mubarak, Hosni 59
Muslims 47, 52

NATO 4, 12, 14, 19, 71, 79
neo-realism 9-9
Netanyahu, Binyamin 177
 Government 129-32, 137, 138, 139, 142, 144
Netherlands, The 29, 52, 103, 113
 Council Presidency 113
 and the Euro-Mediterranean Association Agreements 58, 104
 and the Middle East Peace Process 125
Norway 126

Organisation for Economic Cooperation and Development 174
Organisation for Security and Cooperation in Europe 48, 69

Palestinian Authority 87, 123, 128, 131
 and the Barcelona process 69, 71, 136
 Interim Agreement with EU 110
 relationship with EU 132, 138-9, 176
Palestinian Liberation Organisation 55, 126
Palestinian Territories 53, 140, 144-5, 179
 Gaza and the West Bank 138
 and Israel 81
Pasqua, Charles 152, 156
Patten, Christopher 3
Peters, Joel 125
Peterson, John 7
Petri, Peter 172

Piening, Christopher 52
Pierson, Paul 96
Pijpers, Alfred 8
Policy Planning and Early Warning Unit (EU) 6, 13
'politicisation' 15, 62, 100, 172
Poos, Jacques 145, 158
Portugal 26, 35, 36-8, 51, 57, 104, 180
   and the Euro-Mediterranean Association Agreements 59
Prats, Xavier 83
Pujol, Jordi 88

Queyranne, Jean-Jacques 149

Rabin, Yitzhak 126
realism 8, 14
Redirected Mediterranean Policy 43, 49-52
Redmond, John 27
Regnault, Henri 46
Rhein, Eberhard 30, 34, 86, 133
Rich, Sarah 158
Roberts, Hugh 148, 151
Rosenthal, Glenda 29
Ross, George 144
Russia 75, 124

St Malo Declaration 20
Sant'Egidio Community 157-8
Scandinavian member states (EU) 57, 161
Scharpf, Fritz 97, 117
security 48
   Mediterranean 44, 47-9, 97, 102, 170
Single European Act 24, 39
Single European Market 46-7
Sjursen, Helene 7
Smith, Barbara 153
Smith, Karen 178
Smith, Michael 15, 172
Soares, Mario 159
Solana, Javier 1, 3, 59
Sonatrach 150-51, 155, 165
Spain 33, 35-8, 49, 53-4, 57, 71
   and Algeria 101, 149-50, 161-5
   and the Barcelona process 70-71, 74-5, 84, 113
   and the Euro-Mediterranean Agreements 59, 104
   and the Euro-Mediterranean Partnership 103, 112
   and MEDA 105
   and the 'Mediterranean lobby' 49, 57, 70-71
   and the Middle East Peace Process 74-5, 129
   relationship with Arab states 71
Special Envoys (EU) 129, 136, 140, 176-7
Spencer, Claire 80, 153, 156
Spring, Dick 129
Stavridis, Stelios 11
strategic action 1, 12-14, 87, 98, 114, 169, 170, 172
Syria 46, 69, 75, 91, 110, 127, 136

Tovias, Alfred 32
Treaty of Amsterdam (EU) 6, 13, 19, 90
Treaty of Nice 6
Treaty of Rome 26, 28
Treaty on European Union 5, 17, 54, 86
Tunisia 26, 28-9, 34, 36, 46-7, 83
   Association Agreement 34
   and the Euro-Mediterranean Partnership 54-5
   negotiation of Euro-Mediterranean Association Agreement 56, 58, 70-71, 110
Turkey, 33, 36, 46-7, 55, 62
   and the Euro-Mediterranean Partnership 176-7
   and the European Parliament 110-11
   and Greece 80, 113, 176
   relationship with the European Union 27, 37, 110-11

UNESCO 84
UNIMED 82
United Kingdom 32, 47, 57, 98, 103, 107, 131, 158
   and Algeria 158-9
   and the Middle East Peace Process 131, 136
Union Générale de Travailleurs Algériens 148, 164
United Nations 48, 159, 167
USA 12, 29, 107, 124, 132, 140, 144, 147
   and the Barcelona process 75
   Clinton Administration 132

and Israel 129, 139
and Mediterranean security 53, 79, 74
and the Middle East Peace
  Process 123, 125, 129, 131,
  133, 144, 177
relationship with the European
  Union 124, 129, 133

de Vasconcelos, Alvaro 49
Védrine, Hubert 131

Waigel, Theo 105, 119
Wallace, Helen 15
Wessels, Wolfgang 22

Western European Union 5, 14, 19
White, Brian 13
World Bank 97, 107, 157, 163, 172, 174
World Trade Organisation 60, 82, 100, 118

Yahia, Habib Ben 26
Yaoundé Convention 28, 34
Youngs, Richard 82, 85
Yugoslavia 176

Zeroual, Liamine 158, 160, 166
Zielonka, Jan 12
Zoubir, Yahia 147